GONE BUT NOT FORGOTTEN

By PATRICIA FOX-SHEINWOLD

BELL PUBLISHING COMPANY
New York

BY THE AUTHOR

BOOKS

Too Young To Die

Husbands And Other Men I've Played With:
  Successful Bridge Partnerships

The Jolly Time Party Book

Crossword Puzzle Dictionary

ESSAYS

Seeing The Blind As They See Us

Slugging It Out In The Ring

The Day Of The One Night Stands

Where You Thought You'd Never Be:
  In A Gay Marriage

My Last Date With A Teen-Ager

Too Much TM

Copyright © MCMLXXXII, MCMLXXXI by Ottenheimer Publishers, Inc.
Library of Congress Catalog Card Number: 81-67680
All rights reserved.
This edition is published by Bell Publishing Company,
a division of Crown Publishers, Inc.
Published under arrangement with Ottenheimer Publishers, Inc.
Printed in the United States of America.

DEDICATION

*friend is a six-letter word,
for Evelyn*

ACKNOWLEDGMENTS

Special thanks to Douglas McClelland.

The author wishes to thank the following individuals for their generous assistance: John R. Adler, Charles Bourgeois, Richard Deacon, Jane Dulo, Teresa Helfer, Richard Katz, Constance Keene, Brooks Kerr, Barbara Lea, Jim Lowe, Carol Sloane, Richard Sudhalter and Jane Courtland Welton.

The author expresses thanks and appreciation for the courtesy of the following individuals and companies who provided the photographs, some never published, that are included in this book: Edmund Anderson, Irena Chalecka, Walt Disney Studio, Frank Driggs, Larry Edmunds Bookshop (Git Luboviski), Joe Franklin, William Ransom Hogan Jazz Archives (Alma Williams), Major Holly, Sally Horwich, Eleanor Keaton, Doug McClelland, *Movie Star News*, and United Press International (Angelo Perez).

The author has included many photographs from her personal collection.

CONTENTS

FOREWORD

The New Immortals

We are accustomed to thinking of immortality in art in terms of established masterworks that are a great many years, if not centuries, old. Greek dramatists and sculptors, Byzantine architects, Renaissance painters, English poets and playwrights, American authors . . . artists of every description, nationality and era have bequeathed to us an inheritance that is staggeringly rich and varied. And it is permanent. . . at least until earthquakes, vandals, or atomic bombs wipe some or all of it away.

Until now, though, our artistic inheritance was necessarily confined to forms as "Grecian goldsmiths make, of hammered gold and gold enameling" as the Irish poet Yeats put it. Nothing animate could survive, and the only records of performing artists and the technicians who staged them, were descriptions or depictions and, more recently, photographs. But an unheralded change has occurred.

It is a truism that those who live in a particular period are unable to judge how subsequent ones will regard even the works of which they are most fond and value most highly. However, it seems a safe bet (not that any of us will be around to collect) that the individuals Patricia Fox-Sheinwold documents so ably in this book will, and already have, achieve immortality because of the medium they worked in: films. . . and another medium in which their films appear, television. TV, which moviedom feared so highly, will serve to expose old films and thereby perpetuate them.

Assuming, that is, that the negative film libraries are kept in good repair and can reproduce prints. Sadly, this is a big assumption because motion picture films are being permitted to deteriorate. But, if our period has any compassion for those to come, the films will be preserved, and if they are, motion picture actors have joined the gods on Mount Olympus and will live literally forever. I would be most surprised if the inhabitants of the year 3000 (why look ahead further than that?) would never have heard of John Wayne, Mae West, Humphrey Bogart, Charlie Chaplin, Alfred Hitchcock, Walt Disney, etc. Because of the then-equivalent of cable TV, they will not be forgotten as will, I fear, many if not most contemporary luminaries from other fields of art.

It's rather bewildering to think of these Hollywood humans appearing again and again over the centuries in exactly the same forms we have watched them or their creations, never aging or fading from the screen, reaching audiences of far greater magnitude than they can command even now. They will be dead, but not their living images.

While some of them, like Chaplin and perhaps Hitchcock, Disney and Fields, may have been geniuses, Ms. Sheinwold's cast achieved immortality partly or largely because of the needs of the movies to have stars and commercial properties. They would have achieved what's been called "horizontal" penetration . . . popular for the moment . . . except that the very commercialism of Hollywood working in a durable medium has given them "vertical" penetration as only great artists have had before.

"Go and catch a falling star. . ." Not on your Life! Get out of the contract! Find me a new attraction! For the star shining securely in Hollywood, heaven was (and is) the studio's dream. The on-camera personality of the performer, the ability to bring the audience to the movie house . . . the same applied to star producers . . . became the standard of artistic success in films. And that standard is what the future will have to grapple with.

Good? Bad? We are in no position to judge. But we do know with certainty that motion pictures, less than 100 years old, have changed the face of civilization without, for the most part, the intention to do so. Whatever else can be said about them, these actors . . . from the infancy of the movies . . . will endure. And that, in a world that appears to change so fast that historical memory itself seems threatened, is a monumental feat and deserves a tribute.

ARTHUR HERZOG

INTRODUCTION

The Movies

Before there were movies, a picture in motion had to be developed. This dates back to the 1870s. Next came the first movie film. Although some researchers dispute this, most agree that it was made by Thomas Edison on a film provided by George Eastman in 1889. This was done in the first movie studio. Built in New Jersey for the Edison Company in 1893, it was called the Kinetographic Theatre.

An actor was needed, and the Edison Company hired comedian Fred Ott, whose act was a sneezing routine. And so in 1893, Ott sneezed his way into film history. In order to show the film, a contraption called the Edison Kinetoscope was built: the viewer looked through an eyepiece at the top, similar to a microscope. But it wasn't until 1894 when Woodville Latham perfected a machine that could project these pictures on a screen that we got movies (on a screen) as we know them today.

The actors moved in very limited areas, camera technique was unknown, and music came from recordings not necessarily suited to the action. In the early 1900's, Edwin S. Porter made two films which became the fundamental format for all movies. **The Life of an American** was the first documentary. In it he used "cut-backs:" shots interspersed with the ongoing action. In 1903, Porter made his epoch, **The Great Train Robbery**, which contained plot and action and could be seen for ten cents a ticket.

In 1907, an out of work actor, David Wark Griffith, wandered into the Edison Studio and was hired by Porter to work in a one-reeler, **The Eagle's Nest**.

D.W. Griffith, fortunately for the world, forsook acting and became a director. He broke the mold of movies and birthed a new art. **For Love of Gold** (1909), he departed from the old "one-scene one-shot" method ' by changing the camera's position. Hence, he conceived "long-shot, mid-shot, close-shot", all of which remains the classic approach to movies. Then he added "a method of assembly and composition of these lengths of film" all taken at varying distances, and the foundation of modern technique was established. Working hand-in-hand with cameraman G.W. "Billy" Bitzer, the "fade-out" shot was accidentally discovered, but not accidentally added to their camera vocabulary. Then one day, Mary Pickford, a fifteen-year old girl, walked into their studio. After her initial debut on film, Griffith promoted her to leading parts, and the beginning of "stars" was created. The silent era of film was on its way.

Until 1927, movies, good or bad, were nothing more than pantomime. With the advent of sound, "talkies" forced dialogue and pantomime into a combination known to be incompatible. Hence, most talking pictures did not work. Constant dialogue worked on the stage but not on the screen. Action was needed, mugging was out, and a good speaking voice was essential. And finally, the personality had to shine through. Star worship was familiar to those involved in the entertainment world, and so the public demanded its heroes on the screen. Some of the silent film idols survived, others faded into oblivion. But in their passing they had created the "star system," and during the Golden Era of Hollywood, the 30's and 40's, the system would produce more stars than in the galaxy over Hollywood.

By the mid-Twenties the public's interest began to wane. Except for the big films, audiences stayed away very much like the way they would stay away when television first came along.

Edison's work on sound had been carried on by the technicians and engineers at the Bell Telephone Company, and now they offered Vitaphone to the sagging studios. One by one the device was turned down until The Warner Brothers (Harry, Jack, Albert and Sam) contracted for the exclusive use of their patent. On August 6, 1926 at the Manhattan Opera House in New York City the voice of Will H. Hayes said on the first Vitaphone program, "Sound would usher in a new era in pictures and music."

In October of 1927 Warner Brothers released **The Jazz Singer**, starring Al Jolson. It was a silent picture except for three Jolson songs and a bit of dialogue. Audience reaction was overwhelming. The "talkies" were born.

The 32-year old silent motion picture era ended. Edwin S. Porter died in 1941 at the age of seventy-one. D.W. Griffith suffered greatly when sound took over, and only time has shown us his true genius. He died in 1948 at the age of sixty-eight. Al Jolson died in 1950 at the age of sixty-four, still wondering why he took a straight salary instead of stock in the company offered by Warner Brothers.

The historical meeting of some of the founders of the Academy of Motion Pictures Arts and Sciences in its temporary offices at the Hollywood Roosevelt Hotel. May 1927. Standing, l-r: Cedric Gibbons, J. A. Ball, Carey Wilson, George Cohen, Edwin Loeb, Fred Beetson, Frank Lloyd, Roy Pomeroy, John Stahl, Harry Rapf. Seated: Louis B. Mayer, Conrad Nagel, Mary Pickford, Douglas Fairbanks, Frank Woods, M. C. Levee, Joseph Schenck, Fred Niblo.

During the era of the studio star system, Paramount Pictures issued its roster of contract players. Circa 1947.

1. WILLIAM BENDIX	9. GEORGE REEVES	17. DOROTHY BARRETT	25. VIRGINIA FIELD	33. GARY COOPER	41. LUCILLE BARKLEY
2. HOWARD DA SILVA	10. WILLIAM DEMAREST	18. JUNE HARRIS	26. BURT LANCASTER	34. DOROTHY LAMOUR	42. NANETTE PARKS
3. MACDONALD CAREY	11. RICHARD WEBB	19. PATRIC KNOWLES	27. LIZABETH SCOTT	35. JOAN CAULFIELD	43. WANDA HENDRIX
4. BARRY FITZGERALD	12. JOHNNY COY	20. MAVIS MURRAY	28. BOB HOPE	36. WILLIAM HOLDEN	44. MONA FREEMAN
5. CECIL KELLAWAY	13. RAE PATTERSON	21. JOHN LUND	29. OLGA SAN JUAN	37. SONNY TUFTS	45. STANLEY CLEMENTS
6. MARILYN GRAY	14. ROGER DANN	22. MIKHAIL RASUMNY	30. MARY HATCHER	38. SALLY RAWLINSON	46. ANDRA VERNE
7. STERLING HAYDEN	15. BILLY DeWOLFE	23. FRANK FAYLEN	31. BING CROSBY	39. ALAN LADD	47. GAIL RUSSELL
8. CATHERINE CRAIG	16. RENEE RANDALL	24. ARLEEN WHELAN	32. JANET THOMAS	40. VERONICA LAKE	48. PAT WHITE

COMEDIANS
SATIRISTS
HUMORISTS

'Twas the saying of an ancient sage,
that humour was the only test of gravity;
and gravity, of humour . . .
                    Shaftesbury

W.C. Fields in **Never Give a Sucker An Even Break.**
1941. Ironically, he loved many of the things he
claimed to hate.

W. C. FIELDS

Born: January 29, 1879
Germantown, Pennsylvania

The birth date and facts concerning the early life of William Claude Dukenfield, (he dropped the "Duken," accepted the enforced "s", and retained his initials) are as confusing and varied as any puzzle dreamed up by Parker Brothers' computers.

However, most biographers prefer the version that W.C. lived a Dickensesque existence: at the age of eleven he ran away from home, after a fight with his father. The father supposedly hit him on the head with a shovel, and W.C. retaliated by hitting him with a wooden crate. Then he split for the wilds of Philadelphia. From there on, so the story goes, he slept in doorways, on top of pool-tables, and in packing crates; keeping himself alive by stealing, chiseling, and cheating.

The second version* says that his father accidentally stepped on a rake, which hit W.C. on the forehead. Angered by this, he ran to the home of nearby relatives for a few days. W.C.'s sister, Adel, said in an interview, "He was about nineteen when he left home for the first and last time."**

No one agrees on the exact date of his birth, but what does it matter? The world agrees that he was indeed born. The one point on which all biographers concur is that when he left home, he left with two things...the ability to read and to write. Fields, himself, would probably revel in the biographical controversy, and if alive, would do absolutely nothing to straighten it out. In speaking about the world, he wryly said, "It's a funny world. A man's lucky to get out of it alive." While he was here, he displayed a character, a personality that was highly complex, full of contradiction and connivancy. He departed, leaving a character that has been imitated and analyzed more often than any other.

His British cockney father, James, hawked fruit and vegetables from a horse-drawn cart, and according to Fields, "punctuated his sentences with slaps across the face." These were unusually painful as parts of his fingers were missing. W.C.'s distaste for vocal music stemmed from his father's drunken attempts at singing. Later in life, one of W.C.'s live-in ladies used to sing behind the locked door of her bathroom. Despite his threats of setting her on fire, she persisted. He liked her guts.

His mother, Kate Felton, bore four more children and maintained the shabby but comfortable Philadelphia establishment. Her gift to her son was constant running commentaries about visitors or current events. In the form of "asides," she would hurl invectives about the guests interspersed with comedy. Fields' mumbling "asides" are attributed to his mother.

The Fields mystique always included his juggling. One version has him sitting under a pear tree from whence a seckel dropped, causing him to gather a few more and throw them in the air. W.C. said it was an apple tree. Another version has him, age seven, at a fair viewing jugglers. Another credits a juggling act, The Burns Brothers, as his source of wonderment. Whatever. Again, the world agrees that he became one of the greatest jugglers of all time, practicing as much as sixteen consecutive hours. Juggling became his entrance into show business. Lack of funds turned out to be an asset rather than a hindrance. Instead of performing with the usual trappings, Fields had to make do with free props. One of his greatest feats made use of a hat with a cigar on top of it. The hat rested on one foot. With just one flip, the hat landed on his head and the cigar dropped into his mouth!

His early work saw his rise from two-bit jobs in and around Philadelphia, to American vaudeville circuits such as Keith's and the Orpheum and to performances abroad until he joined "the Ziegfeld Follies" in 1915. Billed as "The Eccentric Juggler", "The Tramp Juggler," and "America's Greatest Burlesque Juggler", he constantly worked on his act and slowly added humor. One of the butts of his humor, especially when he missed, was his wife, Harriet Hughes, whom he married in 1900. He added her to the act and billed her as "the Silent Tramp's Assist-

*__W.C. Fields, By Himself__, Commentary by Ronald J. Fields (New York: Warners Paperback Library).

**Ibid., p. 23.

ant". Hattie, as he called her, stayed on until their only child, W.C., Jr., was born in 1904. From then on their relationship consisted of voluminous correspondence which ranged on his part from deep concern for his wife and son, to eventual bitter resentment for her constant wrangling over money. Apparently after Hattie stopped working, her idleness and laziness caused hypochondria, and her attitude towards her traveling husband impinged on Junior's feelings for his father. Fields supported her all of his life, put his son through college, and cared for his parents equally well. The wrangling over money continued even after his death when his will was successfully contested.

Mrs. Harriet Fields (left) widow of W.C. and her son Claude, conferring with Mrs. Una Davis, wife of the Fields' lawyer. Three years after W.C.'s death and the legal claims to his fortune were still unsettled. Los Angeles, 1949.

In 1915, at the age of 36, W.C. signed with Flo Ziegfeld. He was already an established star whose salary would now grow from a few hundred a week to several thousand a week. He moved into the first of many rented mansions replete with servants he never trusted. His brushes with the domestics were to cause a lot of infighting, but at least they wouldn't rob him en masse. He lived in the first mansion with his mistress of seven years, Bessie Poole, and he fathered another son, whom he acknowledged to be his. He also acquired a valet. An ex-stagehand, William Blanche was a midget whom Fields used to bounce about, making his anger viable. Later Blanche appeared in Fields' famous golf skit as the caddy.

In the Follies (from 1915 through 1921, he never missed an edition), Fields worked with other great zanies such as Fanny Brice, Eddie Cantor, Bert Williams, Will Rogers, and Ed Wynn. Wynn caught a bit of Fields' dislike for being upstaged when one night he hid under W.C.'s pool-table and drew unexpected laughs for his "schtick" done on instruction from Ziegfeld. "Follies Flo" reportedly hated comics, as they distracted the audience from his beauties. Anyway, Fields swatted Wynn on the head with his cue stick, which drew even greater laughter from the audience. W.C.'s hatred of upstaging and scene stealing carried over into movies with Baby Le Roy. Told to "push him a little," Fields bounced him seventeen feet. Yet the other side of Fields, a side not generally known, showed itself when he deliberately wrote Le Roy into his next film after Le Roy's contract had expired, thus insuring that Baby would be re-hired.

Hattie and W.C. were never divorced, but that did not keep women out of his life. He had a sort of Victorian attitude towards women, which charmed them, and a patter that could lure them into his life and domicile. His wariness of sex, according to him, stemmed from an incident in his youth. He went to see a "nudy" film but fell asleep. When he awakened, the film, now in the third reel, was not a "nudy" but one on venereal disease accompanied by a **Swan Lake** score. "From then on," said he, "every time I heard that music, I wanted to run for a Wasserman." The last woman in his life was Carlotta Monti, who cared for him through

Carlotta Monti, long time mistress of Fields, displays photo of herself as a young actress as she stands next to W.C.'s 16-cylinder Cadillac awarded to her (1954) after an eight-year court battle. The 1938 vintage limousine was offered at auction for $75,000. Hollywood, 1980.

W.C. always said he hated Philadelphia and had disdain for anything or anyone connected with the U.S. government. His grandson, W.C. Fields III, shown here, lived in Philadelphia, liked the city, and works for the FBI with the bank robbery unit. He is holding a statue of his grandfather and fortunately, it can't talk! Philadelphia, 1975.

his illness and bouts of severe alcoholism. She, along with other intended recipients in his will, was not provided for after the will was contested.

He was considered generous by his friends. He was known to provide for his family. And yet his most famous title was "The Miserly Millionaire." This title and trait developed after he was robbed. As a young traveling man, he asked to be paid in gold coins. These he hid on his person, only to be relieved of them by a thief. From then on, he would deposit the money in any bank, in any town where he happened to be working. Each account was under a pseudonym, and as the years passed, he forgot the names and the places. As in his movies, his deviousness was so cunning that he outsmarted himself. There is reportedly almost a million dollars lying around unclaimed in various bank accounts.

His distrust of his servants extended to everyone. He called the United States government "Uncle Whiskers," and said that, "like everyone else, it was out to get more than it decently was entitled to." Hence, he did his own tax forms and according to agent/manager Bill Grady, Fields even got a refund from the IRS when he claimed a donation to a charity in the Solomon Islands. He would never sign his real name unless it was on a "gilt-edged iron-clad contract." Of lawyers he said, "Secret agents for the Treasury Department," who would turn him in for back taxes.

Actor Dick Gautier displays his art work in his home. Paying tribute to four of the great comedians, his oil paintings (l-r) are: Charles Chaplin, Buster Keaton, Ed Wynn, and W.C. Fields. 1975.

The presenter, W.C. Fields; the grasping hand, Mack Sennett; the occasion, the Academy Awards, 1937.

Ah...but this is the Fields we love! The man who belted anything established; who butted anyone who was self-assured. His prejudices created his comedy. According to writer Robert Lewis Taylor, "Most persons, as a scholar has noted, harbor a secret affection for anybody with a low opinion of humanity. Fields' defiance of civilization, over a period of sixty-seven years, became an institution in which the public took pride."*

Put another way, Fields never got over the traumas of his childhood and proclaimed his feelings on film and on paper. He insulted middle-class morality, mocked the virtuous institution called "family life", and despised civil authority and anything that reeked of fair play.

The character that Fields had been working on for years finally jelled in the musical comedy, **Poppy,** which opened in New York City in 1923. The role of Eustace McGargyle, created for the play, was one of the classic roles of the American stage. Fields never strayed too far away from that character. The *New York Tribune* reviewer for the show said, "We suspect him [Fields] to be the funniest man in town since Will Rogers went away." The show ran for over a year. In 1925 it was made into a silent film, retitled **Sally of the Sawdust.** In 1936, Paramount Pictures remade **Sally** and called it **Poppy.**

Fields' first movie, **Pool Shark,** was made in 1915. **The Golf Specialist,** made in 1930, was his first sound film. Although W.C. made forty-two films throughout his life, only thirty have survived. The four Fields masterpieces were made when he was in his sixties: **You Can't Cheat An Honest Man,** (1939); **The Bank Dick,** (1940); **My Little Chickadee**, (1940); **Never Give a Sucker An Even Break,** (1941). He made four more films after these, appearing as "a guest." He was by then showing the strain of his continuing illness which was attributed to a lifetime of two quarts of gin a day.

W.C. reigned as "The Monarch of Booze." He could mix a martini in his sleep and would start the day with a double before breakfast. Devoted to Shakespeare, he said, "If Falstaff had stuck to martinis, he'd be with us today." At one time he tried to conceal the gin in pineapple juice, suspiciously considered another addiction, but it was soon revealed and resulted in an enforced drying out at a sanitarium. There Fields quipped, "Seems they found some urine in my alcohol."

His one outwardly acknowledged personal sensitivity was his nose. On camera, he'd allow pokes at his potato-like proboscis. Off camera, he was extremely touchy. His close friends John Barrymore and Gene Fowler would mock his nose, but Fields would depart with words such as, "You are poking fun at an unfortunate with an affliction."*

Fields always hated holidays. In a final irony, his drinking caught up with him one Christmas day. He died of cirrhosis of the liver caused by chronic alcoholism.

There are several versions of his last words. The one Fields would probably like is, "I'm leaving some money for a college for white children only." Then he winked. And died.

W.C. FIELDS
Died: December 25, 1946,
Los Angeles, California

*Gene Fowler, **Minutes of the Last Meeting** (New York: Viking).

W.C. asked to write his own epitaph: **"Here lies W.C. Fields. On the whole, I'd rather be here than in Philadelphia."** Shown here the year he died, 1946.

*W.C. Fields, His Follies and Fortunes** (New York: Signet Classics).

6

W.C. Fields and Baby Le Roy. **It's a Gift.** 1934.

Fields and Freddie Bartholomew in **David Copperfield.** 1935. Playing Mr. Micawber, after Charles Laughton turned down the role, Fields appears in only four major scenes, total screen time about half an hour. Yet, playing it "straight," Fields was essential to the continuity of the story and did justice to the part.

Fields in his first sound film, a short for **RKO**, before joining Mack Sennett. The film was an extension of his vaudeville act in the Ziegfeld Follies replete with Fieldsian humor complemented by an over-sized golf bag, a driver with a rubber shaft that wrapped itself around his neck, and a caddy who almost upstaged him. **The Golf Specialist.** 1930.

Fields and Tammany Young in **Six of a Kind** (1934), where as the sheriff, W.C.F. manages to work in a game of billiards. His first film, **Pool Sharks** (1915), showed him repeating his famous pool game routine, which had its origin in vaudeville.

(l-r) Martha Raye, W.C. Fields, and Shirley Ross in **The Big Broadcast**. 1938.

Fields opened on Broadway in the musical **Poppy,** in 1923 and scored a tremendous success. This led to the making of the screen version retitled, **Sally of the Sawdust,** directed by D.W. Griffith in 1925. This photo is from the re-make of **Sally,** called by its original title **Poppy.** 1936.
(Man with Fields unidentified)

You Can't Cheat An Honest Man, original story by Charles Bogle (W.C. nom de plume). This was the first of his four masterpieces. Shown here with Constance Moore. 1939.

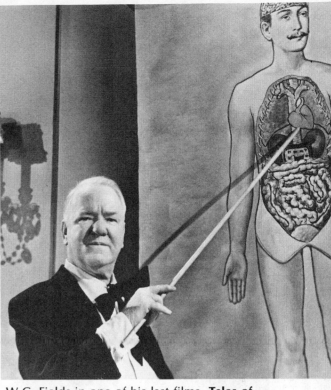

The third masterpiece, **My Little Chickadee,** co-authored with Mae West. To her face he called her "My Little Fuzzywishwash." Behind her back, he called her "My Little Brood Mare." 1940.

W.C. Fields in one of his last films, **Tales of Manhattan.** In order to reduce running time, his 20-minute sequence of an anatomy lesson was cut. 1942.

Fields in **The Bank Dick,** which he wrote under the name of Mahatma Kane Jeeves. The film shocked some. Others noted that Fields correctly reflected society and its acceptance of corruption without a murmur. He showed that newfound wealth does not automatically assure happiness. He played the town drunk and the embezzler. And if it works, and you get away with it—he was about thirty years ahead of Watergate. 1940.

Rod Steiger, in a typical Fields outfit, on the set recreating Fields' classic **Poppy,** which Fields made in 1936. His makeup took two hours to apply and a half hour to remove. Steiger is on the left, Fields on the right. 1975.

Charlie Chaplin meek and mild
Took a sausage from a child.
When the child began to cry
Charlie slapped him in the eye.

So sang British children to the melody of "Gentle Jesus." And around the world children of other countries sang about Charlie, Chali, Charlot, Carlo . . . everyone knew Charles Spencer Chaplin. Shown here, 1966.

CHARLES CHAPLIN

Born: April 16, 1889 London, England

Born in the poverty-stricken section of Walworth, Charles Spencer Chaplin was a penniless, hungry street urchin who, by the time he was thirty, would amass a great fortune and attain world-wide fame. Never before in history had a civilian, as opposed to generals and heads of state, become a "household" name; a name known to everyone regardless of origin, occupation, or age. Intense ambition, putting everything else second, does not tell the whole story.

Charles Chaplin, Senior, was a music hall singer who deserted his wife when Charlie, Jr. was a baby, and who died of alcoholism at the age of thirty-seven.

Hannah, his mother, was a singer/dancer, who used the stage name of Lily Harley. She suffered from intermittent vocal problems. On one occasion when Charlie was only five and her voice gave out, she thrust him onto the stage to finish her act. He imitated her cracking voice and was rewarded with thunderous applause from the audience who tossed coins at him. This tragicomic scene was Charlie's entrance into show business. Mimicking her was natural for him. He credits his mother with "powers of observation, and mimicry that were remarkable. She taught me whatever I knew."

Hannah had other problems of more severe consequence. Prone to mental breakdowns, she was constantly in and out of mental institutions, leaving Charlie to fend for himself. This he did by singing and dancing on street corners for pennies. At age seven, he was spotted on the street and hired to tour with a group of clog-dancers called The Eight Lancaster Lads. A year and a half later, he was back in London where he returned to school for two years, ending his formal education.

Charlie was not completely alone. His half-brother Sydney lived with them and had taken the family name. They lived in a combination of poorhouse-orphanages when Hannah's meager wages as a seamstress failed and she was hospitalized. Sydney escaped to Africa; Charlie, to the London streets where he managed to stay alive. When Sydney returned, he went into the music halls trying to persuade Charlie to do the same, to give up his dream of being a great actor. Charlie, aged 16, had toured England in **Sherlock Holmes** and in the first production of **Peter Pan.** His first real break had come through his association with H.A. Saintsbury, a gifted playwright and director. Saintsbury taught him how to act, how to listen when other actors spoke, how to believe in what he was doing on stage, and above all, not to "mug" or "milk" lines for laughter.

Two years later, Charlie joined Sydney in the Fred Karno Company. And Karno taught him the fine points of comedy. "Wistful! Make him wistful!" Karno insisted. Charlie learned that "wistful" meant putting a pillow under a fellow's head after you've knocked him out cold! Another lesson he learned was that when he was appearing on stage in a serious fashion he had to stay serious. When his cane fell with a clatter, he bowed to retrieve it but his hat fell off and so did the stuffing inside of it. The audience howled. Remembering Saintsbury (don't milk or mug), he did not burlesque his performance. The more serious he became, the louder the audience laughed. The Chaplin formula was developing.

Off stage, Charlie's lover image was also being formulated. He had his first serious romance with a sixteen-year old actress, Hetty Kelly. When he returned from a European tour, he was stunned and saddened to find that she had died. Now at age nineteen, he had lost the two women in his life. Hannah, still institionalized, had kept her son close to her. His feelings for her and for Hetty were very deep. Throughout his life, these two types of women, the young and the helpless, would greatly influence him. Some he would marry, and some he chose to star in his films.

Charlie successfully toured with the Karno Company for six years until 1913. The company made two tours in America, and on the second tour Charlie was signed by

Mack Sennett, founder of the Keystone Comedies. Although his salary of $150 a week made him feel like a millionaire, in Hollywood he was just another comic grinding out one-reelers for Sennett whose style of fast, furious improvisations was vastly different from the slow-moving, more subtle Karno style.

But the Chaplin style, talent, and skill would change all that. Charlie could toss a cigarette butt over his shoulder, turn faultlessly as it fell, and then give the butt a short kick in mid-air sending it into a perfect arc. His early acrobatic training endowed him with superb balance and ideal control.

After many months of trying out different costumes and characters, he hit his famous "tramp" outfit in **Kid Auto Races at Venice,** a two-reeler. Other factors were also important to the timing of the emergence of Chaplin. The film industry had advanced technologically; there was mass film distribution the world over; the cost of admission was only a nickel per flick; and with a plethora of just "funny" men, viewers were waiting for an actor of Chaplin's stature to emerge.

In two brief years, 1914-1915, his fame rocketed. On a visit to New York City in 1915, he was so popular that police had to escort him off the train even before it reached its final destination in Grand Central Station. Now in the Eighties, it is estimated that over 300 million people have been reached by Chaplin's work.

Charlie entertaining crowds at Liberty Bond Drive. Criticized for his civilian status, rejected by the army because of his slight stature, he compensated by working tirelessly for the cause. 1918.

After thirty-five movies with Sennett, he moved to Essanay for fifteen films, and then to Mutual Studios for twelve films where he earned $10,000 a week. By 1918, when he signed with First-National, he received $1,000,000 for eight films over which he had total artistic control. He built his own studio in Los Angeles where every Chaplin film was produced until 1952. Great artists from other fields such as dancers Nijinsky and Anna Pavlova and Australian soprano Dame Nellie Melba would come to visit and to watch him work. In 1919, with D.W. Griffith, Mary Pickford, and Douglas Fairbanks, Sr., he formed the film company United Artists.

(l-r) Charlie Chaplin, Mary Pickford, Douglas Fairbanks, Sr., three of the original founders of United Artists founded in 1919. Shown here in 1924.

Rumors flew about his long-running romance with Edna Purviance, his leading lady from 1915 to 1923, but it was Mildred Harris, an MGM extra, whom the twenty-nine year old Charlie married in 1918. Reminiscent of Hetty Kelly, teenage, virginal young things attracted him. He was able to play Professor Higgins to his personal pygmalionized Eliza Doolittles.

Lita Grey Chaplin, Charlie's second wife, displays her book about their life together. She is shown outside of their son's home. Charles, Jr. was found unconscious by his grandmother, Mrs. Lillian Grey and died a few minutes later. Hollywood, 1968.

This first marriage and the second one, in 1924 to nubile Lillita Grey (née Lolita Mc-Murry) followed his pattern. Both were frought with scandal and bad press. Each had overtones of "shotgun" rapidity fired by "on guard" mothers of the brides.

Chaplin's first child by Mildred died three days after birth. Two were born of the second marriage by Lita: Sydney, who had a moderately successful life in the theater, ending up as a wealthy businessman; and Charlie Jr., who died in 1968 after a tumuluous life.

Charles Chaplin, Jr. and "The Kid," Jackie Coogan, look over a script as a possible joint screen effort. 1958.

In between the two marriages, Chaplin had lots of women. He announced his engagement to actress Pola Negri in 1922. His palatial Beverly Hills mansion was built at this time, but Pola turned her affection towards idol Rudolph Valentino. Typically, Hollywood gossiped that Chaplin's true love was Marion Davies, mistress of tycoon William Randolph Hearst. But what was emerging throughout this cupidity, which cost him a fortune, was that the "Little Fellow," who had been adored by the public, was losing ground with his audiences.

Among his films made during these years were some of his materpieces: **The Kid** (1921) and **The Gold Rush** (1925). His first six-reeler had been **Tillie's Punctured Romance** (1914), but **The Kid** was the first feature-length film written and directed by Chaplin. **Shoulder Arms,** made in 1918 with brother Sydney, was his gift to WWI troops, as he had been rejected by the army when he tried to enlist.

Charlie's matrimonial miseries took a left turn (as did his politics) in the person of Paulette Goddard, a chorus girl, mid-twenties in age. He chose her as the *gamin* for **Modern Times** (1936). She was sophisticated, intelligent, and a distinct improvement over the first two wives. She played a return engagement in **The Great Dictator** (1940). They separated shortly afterward and this time without any scandal or acrimony.

Chaplin with third wife and protégée Paulette Goddard. They met in 1932 when she was a chorus girl, lived together for awhile, married in the mid-Thirties, and divorced in 1940. Circa 1938.

The Forties became the low point in his life both publicly and politically as his private life erupted once more. In June '41 he met actress Joan Barry, put her on salary for $75.00 a week, groomed her for a film, became her lover, and according to her, was the father of her two aborted children. By October '42, he had grown tired of her and even had her jailed once when he caught her sneaking into his home because she suspected another woman. She was correct. The woman was eighteen-year old Oona O'Neill, daughter of the famous playwright. Outraged Joan, now pregnant again, sued him on two counts: one, violating the Mann Act (prohibiting the interstate transportation of women for immoral purposes) of which he was acquitted; and two, claiming that he was the father of her daughter. Oona proved her devotion and faith in Charlie by marrying him in June of 1943 despite her family's violent objections. Meanwhile back in the courtroom, Charlie was exonerated on the paternity charge but made to pay child support. And the latter ruling by the jury is where his personal life adjuncts his public image on the screen and off of it.

With his back to camera, Justice of the Peace, Clinton P. Moore marries Charlie and Oona O'Neill. Looking on are Catherine Hunter, Chaplin's secretary and newspaper columnist, Barry Crocker.

Charlie and Oona after ceremony in Carpenteria, California. June 17, 1943.

In the early Forties, America was once again on the verge of war. During WWI and after it, America was only too happy to laugh at and with Charlie. But now the United States was full of old-fashioned patriotism and extremely puritanical. Its heroes and idols were to fit the mold. Charlie was advocating the second front in Eastern Europe, speaking out against deportation of the alledged Communist, composer Hans Eisler, and rallying for Henry Wallace. All of this heaped upon his scandalous private life, problems with Internal Revenue, and even a plagiarism suit running concurrently with **Modern Times** and **The Great Dictator** produced cries of "propaganda."

Although the "talkies" had arrived in 1927, Charlie did not find his voice until later. **City Lights** and **Modern Times** did not contain a final speech as did **The Great Dictator.** Chaplin (in public) spoke out, "I had to do it. They had their laughs and it was fun, wasn't it? Now I want them to listen . . . I wanted to see the return of decency and kindness. I'm no Communist . . . just a human being who wants to see in this country a real democracy and freedom from this infernal regimentation which is crawling over the rest of the world."

The Great Dictator was a frank, hard-hitting, bold attack on Fascism. Only the most carping of critics suggested that the final speech was mushy and prolix. The film garnered four Academy Award nominations and all lost.

"Why aren't you an American citizen?" people now asked. Chaplin in part replied, "I have no political persuasions whatsoever . . . I belong to no political party, and I have

After his acquittal of violating the Mann Act (U.S. 1856-1922), Chaplin was then involved in a paternity suit. Here Joan Barry, holding her daughter, Carol Ann, whirls around to face Chaplin during the trial. Joseph Scott, Miss Barry's attorney, asked and was granted permission by the court to place Chaplin, Joan, and baby "in proximity" to each other for comparison before the jury. Los Angeles, 1944.

never voted in my life . . . I don't believe in making any division of people, I think that is dangerous. My patriotism has never been to one country, one class, but to the whole world." Chaplin paid taxes in the United States on all of his income even though only thirty percent was earned here.*

Today in the Eighties, his scandals wouldn't be scandals; his beliefs and the freedom to speak out in disagreement with the government have been tested by more than one Hollywood star. But that was forty years ago, and by the time the early Fifties arrived, hysteria in the form of a McCarthy hurricane was blowing all over the United States. When Charlie and Oona sailed to Europe for a holiday, two days out they were notified that his re-entry visa to the U.S. "was being revoked on moral grounds."

Limelight (1952), was Charlie's last film made in Hollywood interspersed with **Monsieur Verdoux** (1947). Charlie felt that the latter had "moral value" while the critics labeled it as "either somber symbolism or sheer nonsense." **Limelight,** although praised by the critics—"Visitors to the theatres will find a Chaplin masterpiece awaiting them—" received few bookings outside of the major cities due to public resentment.

Whether it was pique or righteous indignation, Charlie stayed away for twenty years after the Attorney General's statement.

With Oona, he found the complete happiness he had sought. He had also been able to bring his mother over from England, and here she lived like royalty until her death. Oona, unlike his earlier wives, was the quintessence of what the "master" needed. They had eight children, and the marriage was in its thirty-fourth year when he died.

In 1924, Giovanni Papini wrote a bestseller, *Life of Christ*. This was the part Charlie wanted to play. Did he also attempt to play this part in real life? The company that had bought the movie rights was aghast when he said, "I'm the logical choice. I look the part, I'm a Jew, and I'm an atheist, so I'd

*Joan Thrush and Beverly Linet, eds., **Chaplin** (New York: Dell Magazine Publications).

Vital and active, Charlie with vital and active "Great Men of the Twentieth Century." top to bottom: With author George Bernard Shaw. 1940.
With India's leader Mahatma Gandhi. 1941.
With Prime Minister Winston Churchill. 1931.

President Franklin Roosevelt recommended a study of the cartoon, published in the *Washington Evening Star*, when he indicated he had little sympathy with the inquiry being conducted of the cinema industry by a Senate sub-committee. November 1941.

Charlie and 24,000 people rallied for Henry Wallace by waving a dollar bill to support the Third Party movement. Pregnant wife, Oona, shown in rally. Hollywood, 1948.

Charlie and film director Ingmar Bergman talk shop in Chaplin's hotel room in Stockholm, Sweden. 1964.

Accompanied by wife Oona, Charlie waves to well-wishers upon his arrival back in the United States after his self-imposed exile in Switzerland. New York, 1972.

Charlie (left) at Biarritz, France, with great Russian dramatic basso, Feodor Chaliapin, and his daughter, selected as "The Russian Queen of Beauty." 1931.

New York welcomed Charlie back with a giant banner outside the Philharmonic Hall at Lincoln Center. Over 2,800 fans, friends, and show business personalities attended the gala. The time had come to survey his reputation through his films rather than judge the man. 1972.

(l-r) Actor John Garfield, Chaplin, playwright Clifford Odets and his wife, Bette, and Oona O'Neill Chaplin, at Fire Island. Photo taken of Chaplin the next to last summer he spent in the United States before his self-imposed exile in Switzerland. 1951.

Charlie and Oona in London looking over his most recent book. Pictured here three years before his death. 1974.

After a twenty-year absence, Charlie returns to the United States to accept his special award from the Academy of Motion Pictures and Sciences. Proudly, he displays his "Oscar," in Los Angeles. 1972.

Near Lake Geneva, at a small cemetery in Corsier-sur-Vevey, Switzerland, friends and family attend funeral services for "The Little Tramp." 1977.

Unknown persons dug up and stole the remains of Charlie Chaplin, later returned, but their reasons remained unknown. Switzerland, 1978.

be able to look at the character objectively. Who else could do that?"*

Charlie was not Jewish. But he could be whatever or whomever he wanted to be when he wanted—a dictator, a child, a tramp. The running thread of his life appears to be his propensity for living the role of the trampled tramp who gets his licks in, but who is not the total martyr. That would bore him and us. Yet the thread of martyrdom stitches the man Chaplin: as a saint in laughter, he was loved; as a saint in speech, he was sacrificed.

He did return to the United States in 1972—mellowed, aging, less agile. He needed no award as the Bible needs no favorable review, but he accepted the special "Oscar" as the "apology" offered him; the statue was an attempt to color a lily with gold paint.

He died, age 88, in his sleep on Christmas Day. At his request, he was buried in Switzerland with "no crowds."

What remains is the timeless artistry of the man. "Works of art stand so alone that they can not be approached by criticism. They can only be approached by love."**

CHARLES CHAPLIN
Died: December 25, 1977
Corsier, Switzerland

*John McCabe, **Charlie Chaplin** (New York: Doubleday & Co., Inc.).
**Garcia Lorca.

Chaplin, wearing the insignia of the K.B.E., after being knighted at Buckingham Palace by Queen Elizabeth. With his family in his London hotel suite, (l-r) son-in-law, Nick Sistovaris; daughters, Annette and Josephine; wife, Oona; son, Christopher; and daughters, Geraldine and Jane. 1975.

Chaplin with Marie Dressler in **Tillie's Punctured Romance.** 1914. Originally a Broadway play, the film made screen history as the first full-length (six reels) comedy. It was Dressler's first movie role and Chaplin's last at the Keystone Company.

(l-r) Charlie, Edna Purviance, and Leo White in **A Jitney Elopement,** a 2-reeler. 1915. Purviance became Chaplin's leading lady from 1915-1923. This film was written and directed by Chaplin for Essanay, who gave Leo White the wonderful name of Count Chloride de Lime!

Chaplin and Scraps in **A Dog's Life,** (1918) his initial film for First National. Considered a minor masterpiece, it was Chaplin's beginning of "thinking about comedy in terms of structural sense." The film parallels the lives of the Tramp and the dog.

Chaplin and Jackie Coogan in **The Kid.** (1921). One of its many features was Chaplin's attempt to honestly depict the cruelty by authorities to waif-like children; drawn from his own childhood, of course.

Charlie in **Shoulder Arms,** (1918), his third film for First National, three reels. This is considered one of his finest films. It was released a few weeks before the armistice (WWI), and Charlie feared it might offend. But the difference between his film and the serious war dramas was, in Chaplin's role, all a dream.

Chaplin in **The Gold Rush.** 1925. In this film he added the contributions of Mother Nature to life's problems and conflicts, usually reserved just for societal ones.

Charlie Chaplin and Paulette Goddard in **Modern Times.** 1936.

Chaplin as Hynkel, Dictator of Tomania, in **The Great Dictator.** 1940. With anti-Semitism at its peak, Chaplin's boldness in producing the film in which he portrays an heroic Jew, took great courage. The popularity of the film continued to grow as interest was kept alive in Hitler's Germany.

A family affair from **Limelight.** 1952. (l-r) Chaplin children, Michael,6; Josephine, 3; and Geraldine, 7½, watch organ grinder as Chaplin looks on.

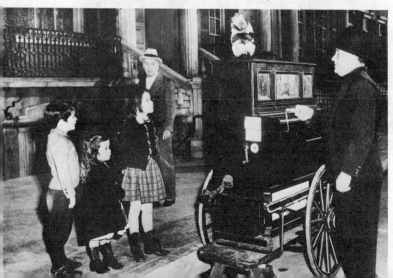

Chaplin and Claire Bloom in **Limelight.** 1952. Of all of the leading women with whom he played or attempted to "pygmalionize," only Claire Bloom went on to genuine distinction as an actress.

Charlie stabs at six-tiered birthday cake during a surprise party on the set of **A Countess From Hong Kong.** Center, actress Sophia Loren and next to her, Chaplin's son, Sydney; Wife Oona(rear) and assorted Chaplin children look on. England, 1966.

Chaplin's four million dollar "Swan Song," **"A Countess from Hong Kong."** "Cygnet" Marlon Brando takes direction from the master. 1966.

Julius Henry Marx—kept an air rifle next to his bed and shot at howling dogs. Alias—Groucho who quipped, "Extension 4-8-2 eh? Sounds like a cannibal story." Shown here in 1972.

GROUCHO MARX

Born: October 2, 1890 New York, New York

"Peesie-Weesie" material was a standard technique in burlesque for years. Composed of a series of doggerel verses, it enabled an act to pump audiences for laughs endlessly. On tour the Marx Brothers met another performer who gave them their nicknames.* Had he written a "Peesie-Weesie" it might go like this.

**Show biz Art Fisher played a game
Of changing everybody's name.
When he met the brothers four,
He ripped off nicknames by the score.
Peesie-Weesie—Peesie Weesie,
Then the four increased the score,
Adding Zeppo to the lore.**

Chico—Leonard 1887-1961
Harpo—Adolph, Arthur 1888-1964
Groucho—Julius 1890-1977
Gummo—Milton 1893-1977
Zeppo—Herbert 1901—1979
Manfred—first son, died.

The boys legalized these names, signing all contracts and legal papers thusly. Their father handled their name change by always calling each "darling." Their mother fought valiantly against the change. It was one of the few battles she ever lost. For she, and she alone, was the driving force behind the boys. She was a mixture of martyr, matrix, marvel, and monument.

German-born, Minnie Schoenberg Marx, was a slim, auburn-haired beauty of eighteen when she married Sam Marx. Her father, who lived with them until he died at age 101, was called Grandpa. He had been a magician in Germany, where in a covered wagon, he and his family trudged the countryside hoping to eke out a living. His wife played the harp and could pick up a few pennies playing in a dance band after his performance. But usually, at the point of starvation, the family was forced to troop home and send the children out to work. Minnie did not think show business was so great, and for a long while fought against her "boys" going in that direction. But her

brother, Al Shean with partner, Ed Gallagher, later became one of vaudeville's biggest acts. And Al had even abandoned his succesful pants pressing business to achieve this! So ultimately, Minnie gave in and pursued a show biz life for her otherwise unsuccessful children.

Alsacian-born Sam Marx, her husband and the boys' father, although considered a fine man, was nevertheless, as impractical as any man could be. In their shabby flat on New York's east side, behind the kitchen, sat his worktable, a pair of shears, and bolts of cloth. Sam, who couldn't sew, was a tailor. Instead of a measuring tape, he "eyeballed" the customers, all of whom were loyal friends who seldom reordered. Having cut the cloth, Sam then sent it out to a bushelman to finish. When the "poys" (an accent of the first order) were rich enough, Sam became a sartorial delight (others fashioned his clothes for him), and the "poys" nicknamed him "Frenchie."

Minnie Schoenberg Marx, age 16, as she looked a few years before her marriage. She died in 1929.

Sam Marx, father of the famous "poys" as he called them. His delightful German accent was as famous as his strudel.

*Kyle Crichton, **The Marx Brothers** (New York: Doubleday & Co., Inc.).

This is supposed to be (according to Groucho) the first picture he had taken. In Germany, age five, while visiting his mother's family. The two little girls are his cousins, and the child with the soleful look is Chico. 1895.

The frantic, frenetic home and street life of the Marx Family with its incessant, uproarious commotion and unbelievable events, all form the foundation of the Marx Brothers' scripts and characters. Groucho, the bogus WASP (probably Jewish); Chico, the pushcart peddler (Italian); Harpo, speechless (dropped out of school in the fourth grade), obviously had nothing to say; all of these characters were drawn from life as they knew it: a life where everyone was so poor that it did not seem merciless. Their kitchen was the meeting ground for friends and neighbors who'd drop in for coffee and gossip. The apartment also housed Minnie's sister Hannah, her daughter, and Grandpa. Minnie was addicted to poker, Sam to pinochle, and the boys to flying around and to flying pigeons from the roof. Always on the verge of a mishap, looking like quadruplets as youngsters, they traveled in a pack, furthering the confusion. Only Zeppo, the toddling baby, was excluded from the madness.

Their school record is a record in itself. Only Groucho loved the written word. Chico had a flair for mathematics, but the flair found its way into gambling, not geometry. Once he even hocked a pair of pants Sam had cut, and when Minnie and company rushed to the backroom to cut another pair, they found that he had even hocked the shears; either to cover a bet or to make another one. He was the recipient of the 25¢ piano lessons. Ultimately his ability and un-usual technique astounded and confounded every music critic and player in the world as the public acclaimed him as "great." His ability was not limited to his fingers but ran as far down as his legs and feet. He could move faster than anyone else towards a "chick"—hence, the name Chico (not Cheeco).

Harpo, apocryphally, had a first-grade teacher who loved him so much that she wanted to keep him there until she could legalize her feelings. He worked in the local grocery store and hoped to be a butcher one day. At first he only butchered the harp, but later became the most famous harpist since Orpheus twanged his lyre. He was self-taught, never learned to read music, and could play any musical instrument invented within a matter of hours. Like Chico, he demonstrated every wrong way to play the instrument and went on to great fame and more public acclaim. Hence, Harpo.

Gummo, having survived rheumatic fever, was the frail, sickly son. Minnie was quick to seize this bit of providence and put him in charge of Mr. Hummel, the rent collector. While the family hid, Gummo would answer the door and present his pathetic face, fading frame, and high squeaking voice to the rent-hounder Hummel. Pushed too far, Gummo could produce a tear, which would propel Hummel back down the stairs. Later, Gummo grew big and strong and had the second best voice in the family, after Groucho. He was addicted to his gum-shoes (rubbers), which he only removed when it rained so as not to ruin them. Hence, Gummo.

Groucho was Minnie's big hope for making it in show biz. His early experiences were tinged with sadness and frought with fear that he couldn't always do what Minnie wanted; fear that he would fall into disfavor.

Aged 10, he was already singing soprano in Gus Edwards' vaudeville troupe. Aged 15, he was sent on the road with another youngster and an older man. The former absconded with the twelve dollars Groucho had managed to save, and the leader, Mr. Le May, absconded with their salaries, leaving Groucho stranded in Denver. The landlady

The last photograph of the four brothers and "Papa," taken two years before Sam Marx died.

Marx Brothers doing their version of a Highland Fling in front of Grauman's Chinese Theatre. (l-r) Groucho; Harpo; Chico; Sid Grauman, owner of the theater; and Zeppo. Hollywood, 1933.

found him sobbing in his room, gave him two dollars, and pointed him in the direction of a job. No matter what life was like in New York, the family was a family, and fifteen year-old Groucho was frightened without them. He was further frightened by the job he got: delivering groceries by horse and wagon over mountainous roads so steep that if the horse slipped, he could fall two thousand feet into an abyss. Nightly, he would awaken screaming from nightmares of falling. Finally, he saved enough money to return home. Food for the trip, he found through his wits. He was constantly being sent out for jobs, out on the road, out for interviews for plays, acting jobs about which he knew nothing. He would come home starving but bravely protesting, "I'm all right, Mom."*

After years of trial and error, Minnie finally declared, "If there is going to be an act, then it's going to be *our* act." From that moment on, acts were sketched with the boys, herself, her sister, her brother-in-law, outsiders—whomever and whatever worked. She moved the family to Chicago where she became a fulltime agent. Still a pretty and lively girl, the bookers felt sorry for her and for the dismal acts she was trying to book. But they also liked her, and they liked Sam's cooking and the card games.

When they took to the road, Sam was supposed to sell cloth to augment their income. The boys were usually dressed in short pants and high socks to look "schmall" as Sam would say. This would enable them to buy half-fare train tickets or convince landladies that the room price should be less, considering there were only a few children. After they were known as The Three Nightingales, The Four Nightingales, The Six Mascots, The Marx Brothers & Co.: In a Potpourri of Song, Wit, and Dance, they (Groucho and Chico) concocted a tabloid **Fun in Hi Skule** and **Visiting the Old School Ten Years Later.** Groucho was the teacher and without direction or pattern, the others were the students.

From the family location known as 4512 Grand Boulevard, Minnie sent them into the provinces from whence they would re-

*Ibid.

23

turneth neither rich nor openly resentful. In Waukegan, they "broke up" the house violinist, Benny Kubelsky. To the end of his life, he would "fall down" whenever he remembered their skit. *He* became Jack Benny.

All of this Marxian melodrama took place before WWI. After the war, brother Al (Shean) was coerced into writing a new sketch for his nephews. On a piece of butcher's paper, he wrote, **Home Again,** the blueprint for their future. They worked, were fired, reworked, and were rehired; but **Home Again** began to click. Gummo had dropped out, Zeppo was in. Finally in 1924, they were hired for a musical, **I'll Say She Is.** They took Broadway by the proverbial storm.

Writer and critic Alexander Woollcott fell under some sort of hypnotic spell and remained there until his death probably extolling the brothers with his last breath. Although the origin of "break a leg," said to performers instead of "good luck," did not begin with Minnie Marx, nevertheless she took it quite literally. Opening night she was carried to her seat by the "poys." A fall during a gown fitting had resulted in a broken ankle.

I'll Say She Is was followed by **Cocoanuts** and **Animal Crackers.** These were committed to film in the east, but the year **Monkey Business** came out, 1931, the brothers hit Hollywood. Zeppo quit after **Duck Soup** and became an agent like Gummo. Their classic films were made in the early Thirties, then they remained idle from **Go West** (1940) until **A Night in Casablanca** (1946). After **Love Happy** (1949), they broke up.

Unfortunately, Minnie Marx died in 1929 before their fame had spread to international proportions.

Groucho, as a single, went on to fantastic fame through radio and television. His show, "You Bet Your Life," later packaged as "The Best of Groucho," was once the highest rated show in the country and, in its fourteen year history, piled award upon award. The prankster with the painted on mustache became a mock emcee with a real mustache. He went from film roles in which he picked on the upper-classes, to teasing the middle-class contestants with his invec-

24

(l-r) Zeppo, Chico, Groucho, and Harpo prior to filming **Duck Soup.** Upon completion of the movie, Zeppo quit, leaving Three Marx Brothers. 1933.

Groucho, always a devotee of baseball, shown here as the catcher on the team, formed by the show in which he was playing. Circa 1932.

Groucho and first wife Ruth Johnson Marx at a party given by Hal Roach to celebrate his 20th anniversary as a film producer at his Culver City studio. 1933.

Melinda mugs with her father, Groucho, during a vacation in New York City. 1956.

Groucho with his third and last wife Eden Hartford (l) being greeted in New York by his daughter Miriam (Mrs. Gordon Allen) en route to a summer playhouse production, **Time for Elizabeth.** Both Mr. and Mrs. were to appear in the show, which Groucho had co-authored. 1957.

Film industry bigwigs welcome Governor Adlai Stevenson. (l-r) MGM president, William Goetz; Stevenson; producer, Dore Schary; and Groucho. 1952.

tiveness. The camera close-ups began to expose the real face of Groucho whose private-self and public-self were so fused by being confused that one began to wonder what it meant to deal with him. As he made the insult an art form, many hailed him as one of the greatest media comedians of all time.

His personal life reflected the dizzy disaster of his early life. In 1920, he married Ruth Johnson, a dancer from **Home Again.** The marriage lasted until 1942 and produced two children: daughter Miriam and son Arthur. Second wife, Catherine Gorcey, ex-wife of Leo Gorcey of **Dead End Kids** fame, he wed in 1945 and divorced in 1950. An incident involving their only child, Melinda, was highly publicized by a letter written by Groucho. A country club, known to exclude Jews, prevented Melinda from going swimming. The club's president received a letter in typical rapier Marx tone from Groucho (and why not), but it also included a typical Marxian retort—observation, "Melinda is only half-Jewish so why can't she go in up to her waist?" One can only ponder the necessity for jocularity in the face of such obtuseness.

He married for the last time in 1953, aged 63, to Eden Hartford, aged 24. After their divorce, and after squiring young women about, he hired secretary-companion Erin Fleming. And thus begins the final Marx Brothers script. She was appointed his guardian and guardian of his estate. Her importance to him was displayed when he refused to attend a function in Washington, D.C. because she was ill; "I won't go anywhere without her," he said, even though he was to present the Smithsonian Institution with Marxian memorablia.

In March of 1977 while confined to his home following a hip operation, an unpleasant court battle began to rage instituted by son Arthur revolving around Ms. Fleming. The testimony went two ways. She was accused of "exerting baleful influence over Groucho, even threatening his well-being." Or, "she was the only reason he clung to life." The court appointed close friend Nat Perrin as temporary conservator and then

Groucho, spring of '76, a year before his death shown with: (l-r) Cindy Williams of TV's "Laverne and Shirley;" James Bacon, author of book Groucho is holding; Henry (The Fonz) Winkler of TV's "Happy Days."

Erin Fleming and Zeppo Marx seen in corridor of Superior Court in California after testimony in "custody" suit over Groucho. Said Zeppo, "It would kill him (Groucho) if his long-time companion Erin were taken away from him. He loves her." 1977. Zeppo was barred from funeral of his brother after defending Ms. Fleming.

Barbara Sinatra (3rd from left) was formerly married to Zeppo Marx. As Barbara Blakely, model and dancer, she wed Zeppo in 1959. Shown here with the Sinatra clan (l-r) Frank, Jr.; daughter, Nancy; Barbara; Frank Sinatra; his mother Dolly; and daughter Tina. 1976.

(l-r) foreground, Arthur Marx, Groucho's son, with wife Lois, and their son, Andrew, seen leaving the mortuary after making funeral arrangements. 1977. Arthur, a successful writer, collaborates with Robert Fisher for television's "Alice." Marx and Fisher also wrote **The Impossible Years** and **Minnie's Boys,** both Broadway successes.

for the final solution, the judge moved the courtroom scene to Groucho's sickbed in Cedars-Sinai Hospital. With Groucho's approval, grandson Andrew was made conservator; the Bank of America was appointed conservator of Groucho's multi-million dollar estate.

Groucho Marx was about to leave this world the same way he came in—amidst competitive *tummel.*

It is public knowledge that Groucho was difficult to get along with. Called "an impossible husband, wounding father," yet his son said, "He was a sentimentalist but rather you find him dead than let on."

Hector Arce in his authorized biography* of Groucho, wrote about "his rage against women, revenge against his mother, and a lot of extraordinary joyless screwing." To wit, astute daughter Miriam added, "I do everything to fulfill my father's feelings about women. He hates them, and I prove him right." Miriam reportedly had bouts with booze, drugs, and a stay at the famous Minninger Clinic.

Writers and friends have tagged him as cruel, coarse, lecherous, and a "domesticated curmudgeon"—perhaps only Groucho really knew the "Magic word."

His theory about comedy was no theory, "If it gets a laugh, leave it in." By his own admission, he couldn't stand letting anyone get the last word, and so he wrote his own epitaph, "I hope they bury me near a straight man."

In a sense his funeral services were as iconoclastic as the real Groucho and the entertainer Groucho. Zeppo, the only surviving brother, was excluded from the services because he had defended Erin Fleming. She conducted her own memorial service.

In the beginning on 93rd Street, as a child, he was in the center of a battle for survival, for approval. In the end, aged 87, he was in the center of a custody battle, usually reserved for a child. And in between—?

GROUCHO MARX
Died: August 19, 1977
Los Angeles, California

*Hector Arce, **Groucho** (New York: G.P. Putnam's Sons).

(l-r) Chico, Groucho Marx, and Walter Woolf King in **A Night at the Opera.** 1935.

Typical Marx Brothers publicity poses in the Thirties.
(left) **Room Service** (right) **A Night at the Opera**

(l-r)Maureen O'Sullivan, Allan Jones, Groucho, Chico, Harpo Marx in **A Day at the Races.** 1937.

Chico, Harpo, and Groucho Marx in **Room Service.** 1938.

Douglas Dumbrille, Margaret Dumont, and Groucho in **The Big Store.** Margaret Dumont was perhaps the most electrifying character comedienne in the history of film. 1941.

Groucho (l) and Jimmy Durante (1893-1980) give NBC-TV contestant their approval for show, **T-Venus Chorus.** 1953.

Famous song team (l) Oscar Hammerstein and (r) Richard Rodgers fake a "You Bet Your Life" with Groucho as they prepare to celebrate the 11th anniversary of their first collaboration, **Oklahoma.** New York, 1954.

Groucho and Carmen Miranda in **Copacabana.** 1947. Sēnorita Miranda died in 1955 at the age of 38.

For eight years, he said he was "39." Shown here when he was really 39. Handsome, sweet, and kind—and funny. Jack Benny, 1933.

JACK BENNY

Born: February 14, 1894 Chicago, Illinois

AUTHOR'S PREFACE:

One balmy night in Los Angeles, I announced to my husband and children that I was about to take to my bed with flu. Sympathetically, they tucked me in, closed the door, and went downstairs for dinner. Within seconds the phone rang. Here is the conversation verbatim.

"Hi, Pat."

"Hi, Joan."

"What are you doing?"

"I just got into bed with flu."

"Well, you'll have to get sick tomorrow. Daddy needs a date."

"So?"

"So, Mother doesn't feel well, Daddy wants to hear Isaac Stern, and he wants you to go. He'll pick you up in an hour. Bye."

She hung up before I had a chance to reply. Thoughtfully, I walked downstairs and said to my husband,

"Do you mind if I get sick tomorrow?" Unperturbed he waited for more.

"Well—Mr. Benny needs a date—to go to Pasadena to hear Isaac Stern and the Trio."

"What are they playing?" asked my husband the amateur musician.

"The Archduke and the —."

"Of course, you can get sick tomorrow!"

An hour later the limo pulled up with my date, Jack Benny.

Because he was always chilly, he didn't notice that I was bundled up like an Eskimo. And because he was the "King of Hypochondria," I didn't mention being flubound.

"Hi, Mr. Benny," I chirped.

"How come you call me Mr. Benny when the whole world calls me Jack?"

"Because you are my best friend's father and who goes around calling an old "—the 'd' trailed off and reaching for another word—" out of respect." But he had caught the drift. He gave me one of those looks, put his hand to his cheek, and uttered, "W*E*LL, I Never—."

I never called him Mr. Benny again. Instead I called him Mr. Kabelefsky: a mixture of his real name and a favorite composer.

Feeling somewhat subdued from a fever rising into the hundreds, I was able to stand aside and observe the evening. Southern Californians are quite accustomed to celebrities; most natives never even turn around when one walks by. But from the moment we stepped out of the car until the end of the evening, the audience had its eyes half of the time on the stage, the other half of the time on Jack Benny. Without saying a word, their adoration and love for this wonderful, gentle man was clear. It was unusual and exciting and not commonplace in the world of Hollywoodites.

The next day I did take to my bed. The flu lasted longer and probably was a rougher case than usual because of the previous night's outing. But it was worth it.

To the memory of that night and many others, I dedicate this chapter—with love.

Joan Benny and the author on New Year's Eve. Beverly Hills, California, 1965.

Jack Benny was born Benjamin Kubelsky, son of Orthodox Jewish immigrant parents who had fled the European pogroms. Both parents settled in Chicago, but later his father, Meyer Kubelsky, opened a business in the small town of Waukegan, Illinois, where he and his bride, Emma Sachs, lived and raised two children, Benny and Florence.

On his sixth birthday, Benny was given a violin and told by his father, "Practice." Although the young Benny did practice, becoming quite proficient, he was not diligent. He was a scamp, a cutup, a dreamer, a nonstudent, and ultimately he was expelled from school in the ninth grade due to unaccountable absences. One of the few areas in which the older Benny felt insecure was his lack of formal education. And yet this worked for Jack. He desisted from taking a public view on politics; he worked equally well with Democrats or Republicans. And his manner of speech, although gramatically correct, was never condescending. He was always considered a man of the people.

As a teenage "dropout" he picked up work around Waukegan playing violin in dance bands for about $1.50 a day and later got jobs in "pit" bands in theaters. In one job he met Cora Salisbury, leader/pianist, who suggested that they form a duo and go on the road. The theater where they were working had closed, and the lure of the road was quite appealing to the young Benny. The idea was not quite so appealing to his father, but finally he said, "Okay. Three months or else!" And so in September of 1912, aged 18, "Salisbury and Kubelsky: From Grand Opera to Ragtime" hit the road. Benny never returned to Waukegan except to visit his family.

Cora made it quite clear that they were to make serious music. Although Benny never got to open his mouth, still a problem arose. Who would have thought that the name Kubelsky could account for it? But it did. An established violinist, Jan Kubelik, for whatever reason, felt threatened and forced Benny to use another name. He chose Benny K. Benny, hence "Salisbury and Benny." After a year of touring, Cora had to return to Waukegan to care for her ailing mother, but Benny now knew he had found his calling. He loved traveling, he loved the road, he loved show people, and he liked the steady income. He found another pianist, Lyman Woods, and together they toured for the next five years. Benny became Bennie; he thought it sounded classier. The five years, although hard work, proved to be the training ground for Benny. He acquired poise, stage presence, and began to "feel" audiences. The tour was marred by the early death of his mother in 1917 at the age of forty-seven.

Three weeks after his mother's death, Bennie joined the navy and once again became Benjamin Kubelsky. The navy proved to be a turning point in his career. David Wolfe, director of the Navy Relief Show, needed someone to play the orderly to an admiral; someone to say a few lines. Benny got the role and was so good that by the time the show opened, his part had grown a lot larger. This was the first time he had ever talked on stage, but he was good and after the war he knew what he would do.

As a single, back on the vaudeville circuit, he called himself, "Ben K. Benny: Fiddle Funology." Once again his name became a problem. Vaudeville star, Ben Bernie, accused him of "trying to cash in on *his* name." Taking the first name of a comic he greatly admired, Jack Osterman, and returning to his own nickname, Benny, he became Jack Benny. So one might say, he was born in 1920.

In January 1921, as "Jack Benny: Monologist," he debuted his new routine at Proctor's Fifth Avenue, New York City's spot for new acts to "break in." Sime Silverman, founder, editor, and publisher of *Variety*, which has become the show biz bible, favorably reviewed Jack's opening. By the end of 1921, he was on the circuit, playing the big houses and now billed as "Jack Benny: Aristocrat of Humor."

Those days were rough and tough. They were days of trial and error. Benny did not have money to hire writers and did not rely on standard gags from joke books. Instead he began to rely on his judgment; his ongoing life turned funny for the audience. If he failed to get a laugh, he'd repeat the line and look—I dare you not to laugh. This became a famous Benny *schtik* which was later refined to include the arms across his chest with one hand on his cheek. He acquired an amazingly accurate sense of timing and an understanding of his audiences.

By 1928-29 Jack had established himself not only as a great monologist but as an impeccably funny m.c. His diction, voice projection, mannerisms, all had been refined. His wardrobe and manner of dressing was as impeccable as his on-stage taste. He was the

first "on-screen m.c.," signed to a six-month contract by Louis B. Mayer (MGM). It was a short-lived film career, but he would return to the screen in later years.

Meanwhile Jack Benny, the man, had fallen in love with a young dancer, Mary Kelly, introduced to him by another rapidly rising comic team, George Burns and Gracie Allen. For four years Jack and Mary waltzed around the circle of matrimony until Jack finally confided in his father that he wanted to marry a Catholic. Aging Meyer did not deliver another "or else" but understood his son's feelings. Mary's family was not as liberal. She sent him a "Dear Jack" telegram informing him that she had married someone else. But fate was kind, for he was to meet and marry Sadye Marks. Together they would become lifetime friends of George and Gracie (Mr. and Mrs. Burns) as well as lifetime mates. Their marriage lasted forty-eight years—unheard of in the tradition of Hollywood marriages. George and Gracie also had a long-lived marriage until her death in 1964.

CLOSEST FAMILY FRIENDS

Jack Benny and Gracie Allen (Burns). 1937. Gracie died in 1964.

George Burns and Mary Livingstone Benny. Beverly Hills, 1969.

(l) Joan Benny, daughter of Jack and Mary, and Sandra Burns, daughter of George and Gracie. Beverly Hills, 1951.

Jack first met Sadye when she was thirteen years old. Zeppo Marx had inveigled Jack into a Passover dinner at the home of the Marks family in Vancouver, promising girls. Jack's idea of "girls" did not include a thirteen-year old, and so the first meeting of Jack and Sadye was not "love at first sight." Five years later their paths crossed again in Los Angeles. Jack was suffering from the Kelly catastrophe and Sadye was engaged to a nice young man. Their courtship reads like a Marx Brothers script, but they did marry on January 14, 1927.

Mary and Jack and their only child, Joan Naomi. Circa 1935.

Much to the bride's dismay, she discovered that she had married a traveling Don Juan. Always a ladies' man, always an adorer of women, Jack had former girlfriends in every town waiting for him. In her book*, Sadye is deliciously candid about her jealous feelings, and how she dealt with "Jack the Don."

Subsequently, Sadye joined the act as Marie Marsh, playing a dumb girl. It was not until 1932, when writer Harry Conn wrote in a part for a "Girl From Plainfield, New Jersey"that she became Mary Livingstone. Well, at least it wasn't "Mary Kelly!" Under the name of Mary Livingstone, she became an integral part of the famous radio show as well as indispensable in making decisions vis à vis their rapidly rising income.

In New York playing in **Vanities** for Earl Carroll, Jack was now earning $1,500 a week.

*Mary Livingstone Benny and Hilliard Marks with Marcia Borie, **Jack Benny: A Biography** (New York: Doubleday & Co., Inc.).

A far cry from his original $1.50 a day in Waukegan. In 1932, Ed Sullivan invited Jack to be a guest on his interview show. Radio was "in," and Mary knew it. And she knew that Jack had to be "in" on it, too. His appearance on the Sullivan show at her insistence, was a huge success and led account executive Doug Coulter to dangle a contract in front of him for his own radio show: "Canada Dry Ginger Ale Show and the Canada Dry Humorist."

1934 was an auspicious year for the Bennys. In October, under the sponsorship of General Foods, they went on the air (NBC) for Jell-O. The association lasted for eight seasons. The time slot was Sunday night at 7:00 p.m., and Jack Benny held that slot for an unbelievable twenty-one years. Don Wilson, the announcer, was added as the second member of the Benny radio family, and their off-network family also had an addition. Daughter Joan Naomi arrived in June of the same year. Many years later, Joan enlarged the family by presenting Mary and Jack with four lovely grandchildren: Michael, Maria, Bobby, and Joanna.

The personal side of Jack Benny's life was as velvety smooth as his velvet voice. Writers have tried to diagnose and explain the reasons. Perhaps the answer lies in how Jack saw the direction of his life: its aim and direction always toward his career. He let what he considered unimportant issues go the way others wanted them to go. Hiring brother-in-law Hickey was okay with him; it pleased Mary and didn't interfere with his goals. When he kept agent Irving Fein for almost thirty years, despite Mary's indifference, it was done because it was good for his career. Writers liked to point out how he lived in the non-lavish quarters of his home because "he was a simple man." If more lavish quarters had been good for his work, you can believe he would have used them.

His indifference to non-essentials is pointed up by the removal of the dining room chandelier. It had hung over his head for years and years, but it was eight years after its removal that he noticed it was gone.

Except for a mild case of diabetes and a huge case of hypochondria, his life was devoid of bad health. Mary, too, was relatively free of any serious illness except for fainting spells caused by low blood sugar. But according to daughter Joan, "Mother could and did faint at will." Perhaps a diminuendo in power and a constant fear of "live" performance were contributing factors to her low blood sugar.

As long as one understood the Benny makeup, it was easy to get along with him. His friends and fellow workers must have instinctively understood this, as most were a part of his life for many, many years.

"He was an egoist," said Joan, "but not egotistical." He was concerned with his looks and his clothes, yet he had true, honest humility. And this quality is the one that is recognized and appreciated by the public as well as friends. You really can't fake it. Audiences can psyche it out. Jack's total self-involvement, while remaining loving and giving, is the key to opening the door of his sustained success. Sooner or later everything crept into the Benny scripts.

And so in writing the life of Jack Benny, one must turn to the career of the man. Or the man who made the career.

He glided from one medium to another, vaudeville to radio to television, as smoothly as his gait walking on stage. To understand this, it is necessary to understand that his career always came first. This is not to say that he was not a generous man with his time and, yes, with his money, but his thoughts—perhaps those thoughts of the young dreamer back in Waukegan—were on his work and what made his work succeed. For example, he knew when and how to instigate his stinginess, but he knew when to take it out. Only other comedians were still making reference to it long after he had quit using it. The same thing with his age joke about being eternally 39. As he aged, he dropped it from his material, yet others kept it in their repertoire. He had an uncanny sense of what worked.

It seems to me that the most successful shows, either on radio or television, the shows with longevity, are the ones whose stars are people you would invite into your home. Sitting around in your living room

Jack Benny, after being 39-years old for eight years, turned 40. But he didn't think 40 was as funny as 39. Shown here in 1958, makes him actually 40, twenty-four years ago; and this makes him the only man ever to have taken twenty-five years to go from 39 to 40.

(l-r) Jack Benny with actor Tyrone Power (died 1958) and his French star wife, Annabella. Hollywood, 1946.

Jack Benny and Gary Cooper (died 1961). Hollywood, 1958.

with your family is a private affair. And so in this privacy, you only will include someone with whom you'd share your life, hospitality, and privacy. Jack Benny was that kind of person. And the people on his show were of equal quality.

Who could resist Dennis Day? Naive and young with a voice like an angel. Or raspy good-hearted "Rochester," Eddie Anderson. Or charming vocalist/drummer bandleader Phil Harris. And all of the others that came and went with the shows.

Another Benny secret of success was his lack of fear in giving his co-performers good lines. Many times he played straight-man to their gags; he was a reaction comedian not a joke-telling one. Johnny Carson put it this way, "If *other* people on your show are good, it makes *you* better." No matter how good or how famous the other Benny players became, it was not a threatening situation to Jack. He instinctively knew this strengthened *him*. It was always called or referred to as "The Jack Benny Show."

The one medium that eluded him in superstardom was film. Somehow the real flavor, the Benny zing, did not come off. At Paramount (1940) he made **Buck Benny Rides Again,** which made money, but one tends to remember his outlandish fifty-pound cowboy suit more than the film. At

Emmy winners (l-r) Bob Hope, Jack Benny, Barbara Hale, and Raymond Burr. Hollywood, 1959.

Representing over 200 years in show business, veterans prepare for NBC-TV's "The Big Time." (l-r) George Jessel, Eddie Cantor, George Burns, and Jack Benny. Hollywood, 1959.

Twentieth Century-Fox (1941) he played in **Charley's Aunt** where his comedic talent really flowed forth. And made big money. For United Artists (1942) he made **To Be or Not to Be** with pal Carole Lombard. But it was director Ernest Lubitsch whom Jack praised. He considered him a genius and perfect for directing him. Said Benny, "No comic can be great in films without two things: a great story, which gives him a character to play, and a great director." Somewhere within those words were his thoughts about the artistic lack of achievement in his other films. He made about twenty-eight in his lifetime.

JACK BENNY AND FRIENDS THROUGH THE YEARS

Vacationing in Puerto Rico, Jack and 84-year old great, Pablo Casals, try a little "Mary Had A Little Lamb." 1961.

Celebration for entertainer George Jessel (seated); George Burns, lighting candle; Jack Benny, leaning on table. (2nd row, l-r) Milton Prell, Mrs. Prell, Nancy Reagan, Gracie Allen, Mary Livingstone, Cyd Charisse. (rear l-r) Ronald Reagan, Ronnie Burns (son of George and Gracie) and Groucho Marx. Las Vegas, 1960.

Stars who entertained during WW II get together with Jack Benny. (l-r) front row: Merle Oberon, Kay Francis, Anna Lee, Carole Landis, Bob Hope, Jinx Falkenberg, Judith Anderson, John Garfield, Frances Langford. (l-r) back row: Andy Devine, Mitzie Mayfair, and Jerry Colonna. Los Angeles, 1943.

Musicians all, but better known as actors. Shown here rehearsing for Jack Benny's television show. (l-r) violinist, Benny; saxophonist, Fred MacMurray; clarinetist, Tony Martin; cornetist, Dick Powell; banjoist, Kirk Douglas; and drummer, Dan Dailey. Hollywood, 1954.

His first CBS telecast was in October of 1950, even though he continued his weekly radio show until 1954. Then he decided to concentrate on the new medium with twenty half-hour shows per season switching later to a weekly feature. In 1958, he was presented with an "Emmy" as television's finest comedian.

In 1964, the show returned to NBC for one season. Then the seventy-year old Jack spent his time doing commercials, guest spots, and prime-time specials of his own.

Until the end of his life, he continued to work in Las Vegas and other big time show palaces in this country and around the world. He had performed endlessly for the GI's during WW II and was many times honored for his generosity. His performances with leading symphony orchestras were famous for "saving Carnegie Hall" and other worthwhile endeavors. He tried to do justice

JACK BENNY THROUGH THE AGES

Jack Parr (r) credits Jack Benny with his discovery in 1947. Shown here, the first time the two Jacks appeared together on TV since that time. Hollywood, 1959.

"Tonight" TV host, Johnny Carson and close friend of Jack Benny, paid him a surprise visit during Benny show in Las Vegas. 1970.

Benny with junior Sinatra (Frank, Jr.), as they prepare for television show. Hollywood, 1962.

Benny with the senior Sinatra (Frank), as they discuss script for television show. New York, 1951.

musically to Mendelssohn or Berlioz, but a Heifetz he wasn't. On the other hand, Heifetz isn't much of a comedian.

But it was back in Waukegan, in June of 1959, that the ultimate honor was bestowed. In a brief ceremony, Benny Kubelsky picked up a gold-plated shovel and broke ground for the Jack Benny Junior High School.

The last time I saw him was in August of 1974. The 9th of August to be accurate. He was working in Connecticut, and as I walked into his hotel room he plunged right in, "Well, what do you think? Should I do the show tonight?"

This was the day President Nixon would or would not resign.

"How can I, or should I, go on and be funny when this could be one of the most traumatic days in the history of our country?" he continued.

The entire day was spent trying to make a decision. Mary called many times from Los Angeles, and those around him tried for different solutions. He was so deeply concerned: concerned for the family and people around Nixon and for the people of the United States.

The decision to go on was finally determined by the amount of cancellations. Only twenty-eight were phoned in, otherwise the house was sold out. After an early dinner, we went to the theater. I sat in the dressing room watching as he applied the pancake makeup. He had never looked so frail before; so vulnerable. The mirror reflected a disturbed face on the world's funniest man.

There was no way to anticipate what he would do on stage. The orchestra played "Love In Bloom" as he walked on. He did not glide; his gait was different. He raised his arms for the applause to stop. Quietly he said, "I have never openly discussed politics, and I'm not about to do it now. I have been an entertainer all of my life. That is all I know. The fact that you are here tonight means you have come to see me do what I do. And so, that is what I will do tonight—entertain you."

He walked off of the stage as the people rose to their feet. The strains of "Love In Bloom" started again, and Jack Benny made his usual entrance. The audience, still applauding, stayed on its feet for several minutes; some had tears in their eyes. There was little doubt that each person, in his own way, was being affected by this time in history and wondered about the eventual effect, individually and collectively.

Jack Benny who always gave 100% of himself, gave 120% that night. For a few hours he made us laugh: laugh at him, with him, and laugh at ourselves. And that's what it is all about. Isn't it?

I knew, yes—I knew, I would never see him again. I kissed him goodbye and called him "Jack."

He died four months later; the day after Christmas from cancer of the pancreas. It is safe to say that the whole world mourned his passing.

Benny lines, like Jack Benny, are immortal. Perhaps the most famous one is:

Hold-up Man: "Your money or your life."

Jack: Long pause ("In fact, one of my longest.")

Hold-up Man: "Quit stalling—I said your money or your life."

Jack: "I'M THINKING IT OVER!"

And so he did for eighty years.

JACK BENNY
Died: December 26, 1974
Los Angeles, California

38

He called her "Doll," and she called him "Doll." Shown here Jack and Mary in their forty-fourth year of marriage. London, 1971.

Pallbearers Gregory Peck, Frank Sinatra, and Milton Berle are all but obscured by the reflections on the glass to the door of the mortuary as they wait for the funeral services to begin for their friend, Jack Benny. Hollywood, 1974.

Jack Benny was filmdom's first "on-screen m.c." Shown here in Metro Movietone's two-reeler, **Songwriter's Revue,** he hosted different composers who played and sang a musical number for the film. Notably Arthur Freed, ten years prior to becoming a famous producer, sang his own composition, "Wedding of the Painted Doll." 1929.

(l-r) Fred Allen, Mary Martin, and Jack Benny recreating the famous "Allen-Benny Feud" from radio days (1937), for the film **Love Thy Neighbor** in 1940. The feud started when Fred Allen asked ten-year old violinist, Stewart Canin, a guest on his radio show, to please explain to Benny just how to play the instrument. Allen hoped that Benny would bite, respond, and thus enlarge Allen's radio audience.

Cecil Cunningham and Jack Benny in **Artists and Models.** 1937.

Preserving the "stingy" myth, Jack poses with his personal 1 cent slot machine in Las Vegas. Before he left, he netted 23 cents on his original 5 cents investment. Flamingo Hotel, 1958.

Jack Benny and his radio family. (l-r) Jack, Andy Devine, Blanche Stewart, Don Wilson, Mary Livingstone, Kenny Baker, and Phil Harris. 1937.

39

Jack Benny and Eddie "Rochester" Anderson in **Buck Benny Rides Again.** 1940.

Jack Benny playing the Bard's **Ham**—let in **To Be or Not To Be.** 1942.

"I'm An Old Cowhand—," Jack Benny and Gene Autry on radio. Circa 1940's.

Jack Benny, Charles Coburn, and Ann Sheridan in **George Washington Slept Here.** 1942.

Jack and Eddie "Rochester" Anderson prepare the famous Benny Maxwell on the "Jack Benny TV Program." 1951. Rochester died in 1977.

(l-r) Bing Crosby, Jack Benny, and George Burns reliving the good old days of vaudeville on "The Jack Benny Program." 1954.

Dennis, "Yes, please," Day, who replaced Kenny Baker; Margaret Truman, the President's daughter; and Jack on his radio show. 1955.

President Harry S. Truman, then 75, and Jack prepare for a 15-minute segment on the Benny TV Show when Jack was taken on a tour of the Truman library. Independence, Missouri, 1959.

41

Buster Keaton, it was not his face that was funny, it
was his presence and what he presented on the
screen that was funny. 1955.

BUSTER KEATON

Born: October 4, 1895 Piqua, Kansas

Joseph Frank Keaton, VI was nicknamed "Buster," by Harry Houdini, the great (probably the greatest) escape artist. Buster's actor parents, Joseph and Myra Keaton, toured for many years with the Houdinis, Harry and Bessie, in the primitive mid-Western form of entertainment known as medicine shows.

Myra, a comic actress, a cornet player, enhanced her position by becoming the first woman saxophonist (after it was invented) in the United States. Joe combined his great athletic prowess, which lasted into his seventies, with an instinctive feel for getting a laugh. This reached its ultimate when he included Buster in the act.

Like his godfather, Buster could not be restrained. When it became obvious that he could not be penned in, that babysitters were fruitless, Myra gave up and took Buster to the theater. Like candy to other children, being on the stage was Buster's treat. At nine months, he crawled on stage, tugged at his father's trousers, and got his first laugh. By age three, he was billed in the act as "The Human Mop." Playing straight man to his father, he was hurled about in what seemed like inhuman treatment, but to Buster it was "a piece of cake."

Behind the disguise lurks escape artist, Harry Houdini, who nicknamed his godchild, "Buster." Shown here, 1925.

Although the Keatons did well on the hayseed circuit, Joe was too talented and ambitious to perform for the yokels. At the turn of the century, they set out for the big time in the big city. After a minor engagement in a show that folded, they found themselves hungry and cold and faced with what seemed like an even greater problem: according to the law and the Society for the Prevention of Cruelty to Children, their Buster was underage. As soon as Buster could pass for age seven, which he did at age five, the father-son team set out on a tour of eastern cities, which climaxed with a sensational success back in Manhattan.

Myra dropped out of the act but held her own by producing two more children; Harry Stanley in 1904 and Louise Dresser in 1906. Neither child attempted a stage or screen career, being content to remain not in obscurity, but not in the limelight either. This writer met Louise many years later and found her enchantingly funny with a great deal of Buster-isms in her humor.

When the Keatons had earned enough money, they bought a summer home in Lake Muskegan, Michigan in 1909. Adventures at the lake provided Buster with much of the material he used later in films. At fourteen, Buster was not only an experienced driver of automobiles but exhibited unusual mechanical ability. He installed a gasoline engine in their twenty-five foot steam engine boat.

Despite the frivolity and joy at the lake, the Keaton marriage and the Keaton act were undergoing radical changes. After several aborted attempts, Myra finally left her husband, as Joe by now was drinking heavily. She was unable to cope with the anger he displayed and felt that Buster was endangered on stage by Joe's lack of control during these times. Furthermore, Buster's talent had grown to the point where he had become the comic and Joe, the straight man. As much as Joe loved his son (and vice versa, Buster adored his father), such a come-down combined with the encroachment of time and age which limited his athletic prowess must have been hard to bear. The act finally dissolved in 1917.

43

Buster had little difficulty finding work on his own. His reputation guaranteed about three hundred dollars a week salary, a handsome amount in those days. However, in New York he gave up the large pay for a smaller amount when he accepted producer Lou Anger's offer to join his client, Roscoe "Fatty" Arbuckle's movie company. Second only to Chaplin, Fatty was a leading comic film star and producer, who owned his own company. Two facts here are noteworthy regarding Keaton. First, his interest or rather uninterest in money; and second, despite being exposed to and cautioned by Chaplin and Arbuckle, Keaton never owned his own company. Both these failings were to cost him a lot later on.

Before Buster abandoned the stage for films, in typical Buster fashion, he thoroughly checked out the apparatus that would reflect his art. He spent hours examining the camera's mechanism: how the rotating shutter was synchronized with advancement of the film by sprocket and claw. And the Kleig lights commanded his attention: the clock mechanism used to push the carbon rods slowly forward as they were consumed by the electric arc between them. This study led to future quotes about him such as, "a skilled film director and editor and a brilliant engineer." With his new-found knowledge, Buster marched into the business of making movies.

Buster was made for silent comedy, or vice versa. The deadpan expression which had evolved from the stage formed the basis of his screen character. When the audience saw that he enjoyed himself, he didn't get any laughs, but the frozen face did. To this he added his original gags and stunts, always performed by himself. He abhorred the use of stuntmen, process shots, miniatures, or any other substitutions for the "real thing." Because he was a great acrobat with unusual strength, he could do his own stunts. It was his presence, not a funny face; what he did, and how he did it, that defined his genius. From the moment he joined Arbuckle (1917) and walked in front of a camera, he made screen history.

Peers in the industry were making inroads into film as an art form. Chaplin was making a statement in **Shoulder Arms;** Dis-

ney attempting a feature rather than gag cartoons. And so Buster in **The General** (1926) incorporated his gags into the story-line of the film. Shot on location, **The General** boasts some of the most elaborate trappings ever mounted for a film comedy. "Brimming with gags, these comedy sequences are built into the story, not added onto it. The timing and arrangement of many shots involving moving trains, camera positioning, and the like are flawless. The film is one of Keaton's milestones."*

Buster in **The General.** The real co-stars of his films, not people, but mechanical devices. These he understood and "they" understood him. 1926.

Roscoe "Fatty" Arbuckle functioned for Buster as his father had, both in life and in artistic work. Keaton performed in Arbuckle's studio from 1917 to 1920 as a featured player and assistant director, second only to Arbuckle. "Fatty" was forcibly retired from films after the "mysterious death" of actress Virginia Rappe. Circa 1920.

* Leonard Maltin, **The Great Movie Comedians** (New York: Crown Publishers).

Sadly, Fatty Arbuckle fell from stardom after being charged with murder. Even though he was acquitted, the public did not re-embrace him. He died in 1933 from an acute heart attack, complicated by obesity and alcohol. Chaplin survived his disfavor by self-exile in Switzerland. Buster did not fare as well as Chaplin but did not totally self-destruct as did Arbuckle.

In 1939, Alice Faye and Don Ameche portrayed Mack Sennett and Mabel Normand prototypes in **Hollywood Cavalcade.** Buster, with Faye, co-starred in a typical silent comedy recreation. Shown here, the original Mack Sennett, creator of the Keystone Cops, looking at a picture of Mabel Normand, artful comedienne. Of all of Sennett's gifted pupils, only Normand and Chaplin went on to become great and creative artists in their own right. Sennett, shown here. 1958.

In 1921, he married glamorous Natalie Talmadge, script girl and budding starlet in Fatty's company. Before their divorce, in 1933, the couple had two children; Joseph Talmadge (VII), born in June 1922, and Robert, born in February 1924. Natalie never achieved the prominence of her two star sisters, Norma and Constance; but she managed to star in stripping Buster of his money and further reducing his paternal status by legally changing the children's names to Talmadge. Buster's own parental security had fostered a certain naiveté and trusting attitude. His full force went into his work, not the machinations of others.

Following the demise of his marriage, the diminution of his money, and shortly after the making of **The General,** his producer and surrogate father Joe Schenck sold his contract to MGM. Schenck reportedly had offered Buster his own studio (1920), but Buster asked only for "a thousand dollars a week and 25 percent of the net." Joe Schenck was not Joe Keaton, so his paternal protectiveness was nonexistent. He gener-ously gave Buster what he asked for — an allowance — and proceeded to make for himself between a million and ten million on each of Buster's films, which cost less than $250,000 to make.* And *en passant*, they were also brothers-in-law. Schenck was married to Norma Talmadge.

Buster's work was personal. Each and every crew was handpicked, and their work was done together film after film. Not so in the vastness of the MGM acreage and arid attitude. Slowly his decline at MGM and his personal decline into alcoholism began (1933). However, no matter how devastating his films and later 2-reelers for Educational Picture Shorts and Columbia Pictures Shorts were, there was always one element that could not be overlooked. Buster was in them, and Buster could not be bad. Despite his pleas to use his own material and retain control over his work, MGM turned a deaf ear, and Buster backslid. Throughout the Forties, he made token appearances as walk-ons or in spineless supporting roles, but for-tunately for the "Human Mop," television was just around the corner. Skid row and sanitoriums finally lost out to Buster's su-preme strength of will.

In 1940, he married Eleanor Norris. Loyal and admiring, she gave him the support to rebuild. This time the money was not frit-tered away on villas and mansions but in-vested in the San Fernando Valley where Buster had wanted to live many years ago. There he was so beloved that in the Sixties he was given the honorary title of Mayor of Woodland Hills, a section of Los Angeles.

During the Fifties, Buster agreed to a summer stock production of **Merton of the Movies.** Character actress Jane Dulo met the Keatons at this time and became their life-long friend. Jane played with Buster in **Mer-ton** and played a lot of bridge with them be-tween performances. Bridge and baseball were Buster's pastimes: neither was ever subject to Buster's ridicule. Miss Dulo's per-spicacious statement, in spite of and despite his plight, reveals the true character of the man, "He was a man of genius, good taste, never vulgar, with a great sense of satire which dealt with people. He showed the plight of man from royalty to tramp."

*Rudi Blesh, **Keaton** (New York: Macmillian).

Buster and his first wife, Natalie Talmadge, married in 1921. Shown here in 1930.

Buster celebrates his 51st birthday in Paris with wife Eleanor. 1946.

"The Gentle Monster," Boris Karloff in "Frankenstein" makeup, crosses home plate in a benefit baseball game. Catcher Buster Keaton feigns fright. Los Angeles, 1940.

In the Sixties, recreating silent film vignettes, Buster did a series of commercials for Simon Pure Beer. From there he went into industrial films, along with more commercials, notably a comedy travelogue for the National Film Board of Canada, **The Railrodder.** Simultaneously, a second crew was filming Buster's filming: a portrait of an artist at work. The result was a documentary called **Buster Keaton Rides Again.** Fortunately for those who were too young to have seen the early Buster at work, it is now preserved on film.

Chaplin and Keaton have been compared, analyzed, and thoroughly worked over *ad nauseam* and *ad infinitum*. Apples and oranges do not compete for a first prize in taste; a contest between Keaton and Chaplin seems equally tasteless and fruitless. Their art remains. It is enough.

Meanwhile back on the farm in San Fernando Valley, the aging, successful Buster was enjoying weekends at the bridge table. With his wife Eleanor, sister Louise, and friend Jane comprising the nucleus. This writer was invited to join the foursome. I found him a tenacious competitor, and not one who ever enjoyed losing. One of his remarkable traits was his lack of bitterness. Later in life when his sons applied for reinstatement, he and Eleanor agreed with no

trace of rancor or acrimony. The same quality exists in his films.

Like his father, in his seventies Buster still had inordinate strength, and still maintained his wonderful sense of humor. There was in the household a St. Bernard by the name of Junior. Whenever Buster was losing and I was about to win, this 150-pound benign beast would find his way onto my lap. No matter what Jane would say, I know Buster trained Junior to do what he couldn't do—intimidate the guest.

Often when Buster was missing Eleanor told us that he could be found in the toy department of the local department store, talking with children or examining the latest mechanical toy. One day during our bridge game the doorbell rang. Eleanor found two nine-year olds pleading, "Please Mrs. Keaton, can Buster come out and play?"

The seventy-year old Buster grinned from ear-to-ear as he bounced out the door to play baseball with his friends. We understood.

It was bridge and baseball he adored. It was kids he loved.

Buster Keaton
Died: February 1, 1966
Los Angeles, California

Actor Donald O'Connor (l) played Buster in **The Buster Keaton Story,** with the famous "Stone Face" acting as technical adviser. 1956.

Buster peruses script for **It's a Mad, Mad, Mad, Mad World,** as Sid Caesar laughingly looks on. Hollywood, 1962.

Buster, almost 70, still strong and agile, squeezed into the grandfather clock for film, **Pajama Party,** quipped, "If only that pendulum would stop scraping my back." But he didn't smile. Hollywood, 1964.

Buster Keaton in **Our Hospitality,** his second feature film. These features followed his work in short subjects, first with Fatty Arbuckle (1917-1920), then shorts written and directed by Keaton (1920-1923). **The Three Ages** preceded **Our Hospitality,** both released in 1923.

Finding his way in the Fifties, Buster appeared in Las Vegas with (l-r) Buster, Paul Whiteman, Rudy Vallee, and Harry Richman in a number called "The Newcomers of 1928." Shown here rehearsing their act. 1958.

Buster and Eleanor Keaton en route to Europe aboard the U.S.S. **United States.** 1948.

Buster in **The Navigator,** his fourth feature film, a 6-reel, top-grossing comedy of its time. Keaton shared director's credit with Donald Crisp. 1924.

Buster in **Huckleberry Finn** at age 65. Others are (l-r) light heavyweight boxing champion, Archie Moore; Andy Devine; Eddie Hodges; and Buster. 1960.

Buster Keaton in **Sherlock, Jr.,** his third feature, which he directed. Buster plays a film projectionist who dreams himself into the picture's action as he sits in the projection room. The backgrounds change from his "real" existence to his "dream" happenings. The skill of the cuts is so extraordinary that one can not detect the trickery. 1924.

Buster Keaton in one his finest features, **The General.** Although the film has its quota of gags, these are built into the story, not added onto it. Shot on location in Oregon, the sequences were some of the most lavish and spectacular ever seen on the screen up until that time. 1926. (For the uninitiated, **The General** was a train not an officer.)

Buster in **Go West.** 1925.

Buster Keaton (l) and Charlie Chaplin in **Limelight.** In the film the two clowns attempt a comeback. This was Chaplin's last film made in the United States. Exhibited in New York City in 1952, it was not officially released until 1953.

Indomitable Buster two years before his death, in **Pajama Party,** with Bobbi Shaw. 1964.

ARCHETYPAL ACTORS

ACTORS

THE MEN

Men acquire a particular quality
by constantly acting in a particular way.
Aristotle

John Barrymore, "I'm fifty years old and I want to look like Jackie Cooper's grandson." His answer to a cameraman who wanted to know how to light the famous face. 1930.

JOHN BARRYMORE

Born: February 15, 1882 Philadelphia, Pennsylvania.

John Sidney Blythe Barrymore was born into America's first family of the theater, preceded by brother Lionel Blythe in 1878, and by sister Ethel Mae in 1879. Their parents, Georgiana and Maurice, both actors, left the responsibility of Jack's (so-called by his family and friends) upbringing to the matriarch of the family, grandmother Louisa Lane Drew. She was America's leading actress and the first female proprietor of a theater, Louisa Drew's Arch Street Theatre. Madam Drew, called "the Duchess" by her family, could boast that President Abraham Lincoln had handwritten a letter of thanks to her before he was assassinated by actor John Wilkes Booth, who had trod the boards of her theater. Although actors were regarded as social inferiors, Louisa saw to it that she and her family were seen as equals by Philadelphia's "main line" society.

In contrast to the managing women of the family, Lousia and Georgina, the men of the Barrymore family were charming, dashing figures, but all too weak in character. Jack's maternal grandfather, John Drew, Sr., was a successful Irish comic who had died of alcoholism at age 34. John Drew, Jr., Jack's uncle, was the leading American actor of his time, but also addicted to the bottle. Maurice, Jack's father, was reduced to vaudeville from the legitimate theater and died of syphilitic insanity.

When his mother met an untimely death, Jack's upbringing passed into the hands of yet a third woman, sister Ethel. It was she who saw to his conversion as a Catholic and later, supported him. She saw to it that he got small roles in the theater until he made it on his own.

As a boy, John showed great promise in his academic work. As an athlete, he could master any sport. Yet once he excelled, he became bored and dropped it. This restlessness was a trait that would be with him forever. The one career he wished for—art—eluded him. Realizing he could not earn a living as an artist, he was drawn into the "family business" to support himself. "Acting," he stated, "is not an art. It is a junk pile of all the arts." His poor opinion of the stage was prompted by the stunted state of the American theater before World War I. Plays followed two unvarying formulas: embarrassingly unfunny farce or melodrama garnished with a heroine tied to the railroad tracks. Bound by this insipid prescription, John ignored the content of the plays and displayed his charm and physique to the adoring women who crowded the matinees every Wednesday.

During his late teens and early twenties, chasing these adoring women became his challenge and prime preoccupation. His off-stage reputation as "Broadway's Lothario" was billed in bigger letters than that of the theater's marquee. His involvement with Evelyn Nesbitt brought him within a hairline of a nasty episode which ended with her outraged husband shooting and killing architect Stanford White.

In 1910, at the age of 28, John married seventeen-year old stage-struck socialite Katherine Corri Harris. This set a pattern of not only loving, but marrying younger women. Perhaps he sought to avoid woman's domination, so much a part of his upbringing. He may also have wished to escape a repetition of his first sexual experi-

Georgie Drew Barrymore and her talented offspring: Lionel, John, and Ethel

51

John Barrymore in his youth. He climbed many self-made mountains in his career. He also climbed nature-made Mont Blanc, the highest peak in Switzerland on his first and only attempt at mountaineering. And never repeated the feat.

ence. Seduced by his step-mother when he was fifteen, he bore the guilt of this encounter all of his life. Even though he had confessed this to his closest friend, Gene Fowler, Fowler desisted from mention of it in his biography of Barrymore.*

John's theatrical touring prevented close intimacy with wife Katherine, but when he was home he wanted a quiet domestic life not the limelight theatrical life she craved. The marriage ended in 1917.

John's development as an actor was sparked when he met Edward "Ned" Sheldon, an American playwright. Sheldon honestly tried to create a statement in his plays, a protest against racial oppression, social injustice, and corruption by officials. He and John could discuss other things outside of the theater like art, music, literature, philosophy, and architecture. John began to see the theater as an art form. He had already proved his surface glitter on the stage. Now he could bring into focus the second requirement of an actor, intelligence. The depth was brought out by Sheldon.

His first thoughtful foray on stage, de-

*Gene Fowler, **Goodnight Sweet Prince** (New York: Viking Press).

spite a bad case of stage fright, was in Glasworthy's **Justice.** Encouraged by Sheldon to do this, and after ten years of "commercial" successes, he was rewarded by rave reviews for his risk at honest acting. *The New York Times*, 1915, reported, "For Barrymore the first night of **Justice** was a milestone. By his simple, eloquent, deeply touching performance as young Falder, he arrested the attention of the city and gained overnight a prestige which is priceless in the theatre, a prestige all his work in trivial entertainment would not give him. It is what the theatre can bestow on those who serve it loyally. This comes to a player whose years in the theatre have been lackadaisical."

In the early 20's, it is doubtful that Barrymore ever studied Freud, yet he understood Hamlet—perhaps in his own instinctual fashion; an echo of his first sexual experience with his stepmother. Shown here as that young man who portrayed the very essence of male sexuality—far from the "pretty boy" image.

John's sporadic screen career had started in 1913 when he signed with Famous Players-Lasky. His debut was in **An American Citizen** (1914). But it was his dual role in **Dr. Jekyll and Mr. Hyde** (1920) that brought him international acclaim. That year also brought him a second wife.

Using the pen name of Michael Strange with literary pretentions, she persuaded him to perform her play, **Claire de Lune,** a work of derivative drivel. It was roundly panned by the critics and only survived by virtue of

John's name. Her real name was Blanche Oelrichs Thomas; Thomas, the name of her ex-husband Leonard. John and Blanche had one child, daughter Diana, born in 1921.

Diana, at age 20, made a successful Broadway debut and then arrived triumphantly in Hollywood with a $1,000 a week movie contract. Worshipping her father, who alternately petted her and ignored her, she proceeded to try to find a replacement for him in her various husbands as her talent ran downhill to the accompaniment of narcotics and alcohol. In 1960, two years after the release of a film based on her autobiography, **Too Much Too Soon,** in which Errol Flynn played her father, she died from an overdose of barbiturates and alcohol.

(l-r) Errol Flynn, who played Barrymore on the screen, and his wife Nora. John Decker, artist, whose studio in Los Angeles was the meeting place of good friends, Barrymore, W.C. Fields, and author Gene Fowler. Said Fowler of these friends, "Men who lived intensely, as do children and poets and jaguars." And (extreme right) Dr. Thos. Flynn, Errol's father, all aboard Flynn's boat **Zacca.** 1946.

One of the great figures in the American theater, producer/director Arthur Hopkins (right) who worked with and taught Barrymore, "Honesty! Honesty! Honesty! That is all we want. Do things the way they should be done!" said Hopkins, who stood above the phony and contrived. Seen here (l-r) with actress Dorothy Gish, actor Louis Calhern, actress Mady Christians. The award being presented was for distinguished performances in the Hopkins produced play, **The Magnificent Yankee.** New York, 1946.

John and daugher Diana in his Hollywood home a few months before his death. 1942.

In happier times for the family, Diana Barrymore clowning with her famous father John (r) and her equally famous uncle, Lionel. New York, 1942.

Diana Barrymore, John's daughter, arriving at City Hospital in an unconscious condition from an overdose of sleeping pills. Boston, 1955. Miss Barrymore committed suicide at the age of 38 in 1960. Playwright Tennessee Williams sent 2,000 violets to cover the casket.

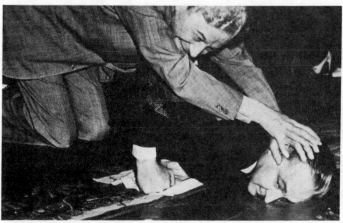

Others may leave their footprints on the sands of time or in the cement at Grauman's Chinese Theatre. John Barrymore, assisted by owner Sid Grauman, leaves his famous profile. Hollywood, 1940.

John (l) and Lionel (r) Barrymore clown for radio host/singer Rudy Vallee during rehearsal for his show. 1941.

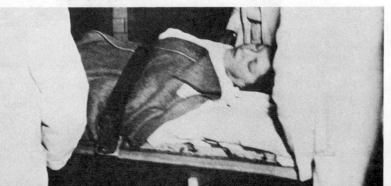

The marriage to Blanche began to wane, but their divorce did not become final until 1928. In the interim, guided by Ned Sheldon, John was put in touch with three great figures in the American theater: Arthur Hopkins, producer and director; Robert Jones, scenic designer; and Margaret Carrington, who became his voice and dramatic coach.

Under Hopkins' direction, John starred in Broadway's greatest hits in 1918: **Redemption** by Tolstoy, brought to this country via the Yiddish Theatre; and **The Jest,** written by Ned Sheldon, also featuring brother Lionel. The first Shakespearean play John attempted was **Richard III.** Despite the public's attitude that Shakespeare was a bore, restricted to the intelligensia, Hopkins and Barrymore decided that **Richard III** was a play, not a petrified parcel of antiquity. Wisely, Hopkins cast the play with actors like John who had never performed Shakespeare before, thus avoiding the florid "Shakespearean style" the public detested.

But **Richard III** was only prologue to **Hamlet.** Many consider Barrymore's portrayal of Hamlet the greatest performance ever of the greatest play in the English language. This was no accident on the part of Barrymore; erudite research yielded the wisdom of critics and scholars throughout the ages of the Bard's most noteworthy play. But careful preparation was not enough to mark his Hamlet as truly unique. With penetrating insight, Barrymore brought forth a new interpretation of a truth, previously concealed by public prudishness: Hamlet's gnawing jealousy of his step-father was evoked by love for his mother; a love tinged with incestuous undertones.

Barrymore's Hamlet was celebrated by perceptive critics, condemned by the literal minded like G. B. Shaw, but wildly applauded by the public. He played 101 performances, breaking the 100-performance record set by actor Edwin Booth. The play set an American record for box office receipts: $5,938 for a single matinee.

Three years after its New York opening, Barrymore took **Hamlet** to London. The very idea of an American **Hamlet** in England with its three hundred year old tradition of Shakespearean theater was regarded as such effrontery that no backer would put up the money to produce it.

So John invested his own and reaped a $10,000 profit. In such sensational fashion he taught the British about their own poet laureate's **Hamlet;** that Shakespeare could no longer be regarded as dead literature. But for Barrymore it was finished. As he had conquered and departed in his early school years, so he did again by seeing no point to the constant performances demanded by the theater. **Hamlet** was the summit; why bother with mole-hills?

Instead, the movies, which could be preserved, offered the opportunity to create one peak performance and then walk away until the next one.

In 1924, he costarred in **Beau Brummel** with Mary Astor, his protégée. She was an actress of classic beauty and very much in love with the "Greatest Actor" with the "Great Profile." With a few notable exceptions, the Barrymore films were a tribute to triviality, but the fee he received, such as $76,000 per film from Warner Bros., was enough to keep him in the life-style he adored. He bought expensive yachts and built a mansion worth millions replete with eleven gardeners.

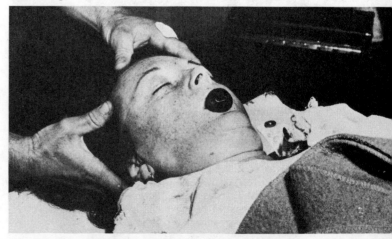

Beautiful actress Mary Astor, now 75, shown here after a suicide attempt. 1951. Ex-dancer Joan Casparis also attempted suicide the same night as Miss Astor, all of which seemed to involve Miss Astor's fourth husband, Thomas G. Wheelock. Mary Astor had been in love with John Barrymore, was his protégée, and co-starred with him in **Beau Brummel.** 1924.

Dolores Costello Barrymore and their children, Dolores Ethel Mae and John Blythe, Jr. 1937.

Unfortunately, Hollywood's world of film had few creative artists like Hopkins and Sheldon. Instead, it was bossed by tasteless dollar diggers. And so, Barrymore who was an interpretive genius, not a creator, fell into the means of providing himself with luxury, nubile women, and a way of satisfying his exhibitionism, forsaking the creative directors and writers that were necessary for his worthy talent.

In the late Twenties, the hey-day of his movie making, he lost interest in Mary Astor and became enamoured of budding starlet Dolores Costello. Despite objections by her former-movie-idol father Maurice, they were married November 24th, 1928. Two children were born to the couple: Dolores Ethel Mae, "Dede," in April 1930; and John Blythe, Jr., in June 1932. Dede became an obscure housewife. John, Jr., although offered many theatrical and movie roles, eventually

John Barrymore, Jr. with Betty Garrett in **The Shadow on the Window** 1957. Junior's attempt at an acting career was bungled through drugs, drink, and vagrancy.

The Barrymores, 1932. (Left to right front): Mrs. Lionel Barrymore (Irene Fenwick), Lionel, Ethel, Mrs. John Barrymore, (Dolores Costello), holding their daughter, Dolores Ethel, John, holding John, Jr. (Rear): John, Ethel, and Samuel Colt, children of Ethel.

Barrymore's $448,000 hilltop mansion, which he called "that Chinese Tenement." The "tenement" had among other things, two garden houses, a skeet range, a bowling green, and three swimming pools. It was put up at public auction. 1939.

John and third wife Dolores Costello on their wedding day. Her father, Maurice, a former movie idol, objected violently to Barrymore as a suitor, but John managed to charm Mrs. Costello, Dolores's mother, who divorced her husband (Maurice) and happily accepted John, age 43, as her son-in-law. Her daughter Dolores was 19 years old. Shown here, November 24, 1928.

Barrymore and his fourth wife, Elaine Jacobs shown here rehearsing **My Dear Children.** 1939.

bungled them through his capriciousness, drink, drugs, and subsequently jail. His troubles with the law made headlines until he finally faded into middle-aged anonymity.

John Barrymore's degeneration has been an American legend. Repeatedly diagnosed as an alcoholic, having started to imbibe at age 14, he was unable to stop. Edema, swelling of the tissues, caused by excessive drinking, was responsible for his appearance later in life. He did not run to fat; he became swollen. But worst of all was a deterioration in his judgment and self-control, plus a severe memory loss. Filming **Hat, Coat, Glove** in 1934, he could not remember a single line and had to be replaced.

Various attempts at "drying out" were failures as was a futile trip to India in search of Far Eastern mysticism techniques. Only by sheer genius of his acting technique was he able to continue performing with the help of prompting cards for films and his amusing ad-libbing on the stage. He could not stop drinking.

During one of his "drying out" episodes in New York Hospital, he met a young student journalist who, also, had dramatic aspirations, studying at Hunter College. Elaine Jacobs, often called a brassy New Yorker, became his fourth wife. Biographers have been incessantly cruel towards her charging that she married him to further her own stage career, ignoring the fact that this could be possible along with genuine love for Barrymore. The two can go hand-in-hand as say Kathy Crosby and Bing or Lauren Bacall and Bogie. Recently at a dinner party she told me that Barrymore wanted to return to the stage, after a fourteen year absence, in **Macbeth**. But in view of his condition, she knew he would fail and therefore suggested another vehicle, **My Dear Children**, with a less demanding role, which he did.

In the battering Miss Jacobs, a/k/a Elaine Barrie, underwent, many feel that there was an undercurrent of social and religious discrimination against her; most probably from the haughty Barrymores. Had John married a theatrical luminary or Blue Book baby, this would have been more palatable to them. The fact that their attempts at divorce were thwarted three times seems to demon-

strate there was feeling and need for each other that couldn't be resolved. She never married again. This writer found her charming and still quite beautiful and still full of deep affection for her husband. At present she is writing her own book about John. They were finally divorced in 1940.

John Barrymore had friends as diverse as W.C. Fields and Winston Churchill. He was one of the greatest figures in theatrical history, an incomparable lover to women, a swordsman and athlete, a wealthy playboy and yachtsman, a mountain climber, and a big-game sportsman. He was also a noted collector of antiques and **objets d'art,** a craftsman, designer, an erudite scholar of the English language and world literature, master of invective and imaginative profanity, but he was unsuccessful as a painter and a total failure as both husband and father. He will long be remembered.

John was the first of the three to die, then Lionel, and last, Ethel. Although John had made over three million dollars in his lifetime, equivalent by today's standards to ten times that much, he died owing money, and when he was taken to the hospital for the last time, he had all of 60¢ in his pocket.

He collapsed during a rehearsal for the "Rudy Vallee Radio Show" on May 19th, 1942. An appetite for the entire world and all of its goods, fueled by a thirst for alcohol, led to a slow death of his art and the final destruction of his body. He died of pneumonia complicated by gastric ulcers, cirrhosis of the liver, and chronic nephritis. The last rites of the Catholic faith were administered before he died, and then he was buried at the Calvary Cemetery in Los Angeles.

Pallbearers for John Barrymore. (l-r) W. C. Fields, E. J. Mannix, Gene Fowler (hidden from view in right column), John Decker, C. J. Briden, and Stanley Campbell. June, 1942.

A young Lionel Barrymore at MGM. Circa 1926.

Brother Lionel, unlike John, preferred the privacy offered by a movie career. His fifty-year career in films, commencing in the late Thirties, was played from a wheel chair: he had sustained a hip injury. Lionel had signed with MGM and remained there from 1926 to 1954.

Lionel, like John, had preferred another vocation, scenic design. But Grandmother Louisa made it quite clear that the stage was designed for him. He made his Broadway debut in **Sag Harbor,** in September of 1900. D.W. Griffith hired him as an extra for $10.00 a day as the first Barrymore took to the land of film. He made his feature film debut in Griffith's **Judith of Bethulia** (1914).

Lionel was an inventive, curious man who found many outlets for his varied talents. He is partially credited with the invention of the boom microphone. As a director at MGM of sound tests, he found the stationery "mikes" unsatisfactory and so tied one to a fishing pole and held it above the actors. He published a novel and composed a tone poem, **In Memoriam,** dedicated to John, which was performed by the Philadelphia Orchestra in 1944.

He married twice. First to Doris Rankin in 1904. They had one daughter, Ethel Barrymore II. He was divorced and remarried in 1923. This time to actress Irene Fenwick, who died Christmas eve, 1936. The next day John substituted for him as Scrooge in **The Christmas Carol,** his annual radio show.

Lionel gave new meaning to the term "character actor". Even as an older man his appearances were not just "cameo" spots to revel in past glory, but were full of "a seasoned star graciously delving into his reservoir of experienced talent to bolster a production's impact on the public."* He

*James Robert Parish and Ronald Bowers, **The MGM Stock Company** (New York: Arlington House).

received an "Oscar" in 1931 as the alcoholic lawyer in **A Free Soul.**

For many years sister Ethel was considered the First Lady of the American Theatre. Her three-year performance in **The Corn is Green** (1940's), playing Mrs. Moffatt, was memorable. As a girl, she had hoped for another career, as a concert pianist, but followed the family tradition—the theater. She was a beauty who captured the heart of Winston Churchill and refused his offer of marriage. She did marry once: in 1905 to socialite-stockbroker Russell Griswold Colt. They had three children: Samuel Peabody, John Drew, and Ethel Barrymore. Ethel legally divorced her playboy husband in 1923, but as a devout Catholic she knew she could not and would not ever marry again.

In 1944, she won an "Oscar" for her best supporting role as Cary Grant's cockney mother in **None But The Lonely Heart.** She received three additional Academy Award nominations, thus going from First Lady of the Theatre to Reigning Grand Dame of the Cinema.

She died of a heart attack, aged eighty, in her Beverly Hills home. Ethel was buried in the family mausoleum at Calvary Cemetery beside her brothers.

John, Ethel, and Lionel appeared together in 1932 in **Rasputin and the Empress**—the first and only film they did ensemble. Scene stealing had reached its peak and talented director Boleslavsky, adapter of "Method Acting" to film, had little control over these three. The film was ruined by the competition of their collective colossal egos. In a monument to over-acting, scene stealing deteriorated into hammy exhibitionism.

The family's three hundred years in the theater came to an end after the deaths of John, Lionel, and Ethel. The Royal Family exists no longer. Put another way, in Ethel's trademark—"That's all there is. There isn't any more."

JOHN BARRYMORE
Died: June 1, 1942
Los Angeles, California
Lionel Barrymore
Died November 15, 1954
Los Angeles, California
Ethel Barrymore
Died June 18, 1959
Beverly Hills, California

In 1938 MGM came up with the **Dr. Kildare** series, featuring Lionel Barrymore as the crochety but loving medico. The role took on greater importance after the studio bounced the original "Dr. Kildare", Lew Ayres, for his pacifist stand during WW II. Seen here, Lionel in a scene from **Dr. Kildare's Wedding Day,** circa 1944. Note fifth from left, a very young Red Skelton.

Grande Dame Ethel Barrymore lunching with a very young actor Robert Montgomery and Major Edward Bowes of the famed **Major Bowes Radio Amateur Night Show.** New York, 1933.

Lionel and Ethel reunited for the first time in 21 years for the motion picture, **Main Street to Broadway.** Hollywood, 1953.

The Three Barrymores appearing together for the first time in **Rasputin.** Lionel, behind the chin foliage as "The Mad Monk," Ethel, as the Empress, and John as a Russian prince. 1944.

Barrymore and Dolores Costello, his third wife and leading lady in these films: **The Sea Hunt** and **The Sea Beast** (1926); **When A Man Loves** (1927); and **Show of Shows** (1929). Shown here in **The Sea Beast.**

Barrymore made **The Sea Beast** in January of 1926. In 1930, he did a remake titled, **Moby Dick,** with Joan Bennett. Both films were made by Warner Brothers. In the original, shown here, George O'Hara played Barrymore's brother.

John Barrymore and Mary Astor in **Don Juan.** August 1926. Astor was his longtime protégée, and she was desperately in love with him, but they were never married. She went on to have a distinguished and lengthy career, appearing in **Hush... Hush, Sweet Charlotte** with Bette Davis in 1965 at the age of sixty.

After reprising **Moby Dick,** Barrymore turned his talent to the bearded bizarre **Svengali**, which co-starred Marion Marsh. They were reteamed the same year in **The Mad Genius;** Barrymore working for $30,000 a week plus a percentage for Warner Brothers. 1931.

(l-) Basil Rathbone as Tybalt fences with Barrymore as Mercutio in **Romeo and Juliet.** Leslie Howard (center) as Romeo looks on. Juliet was played by Norma Shearer. 1936. (**Romeo and Juliet** was first made by Vitagraph in 1908 against the background of New York City's Central Park Mall. In 1916, Francis X. Bushman and Beverly Bayne, the first screen "love team," played the star-crossed lovers.)

Barrymore and Greta Garbo in **Grand Hotel.** 1932. Everyone at the studio (MGM) was prepared for the "battle of the century" when the two stars faced the camera together, but respectful of each other's talent, they behaved beautifully. Barrymore was physically unable to accept the offer to play **Camille** (1937) with Garbo: one of her great roles; he was replaced by actor Henry Daniell.

(l-r) Katharine Hepburn, who made her film debut here, Billie Burke, and John Barrymore in **Bill of Divorcement.** 1932. Many consider this Barrymore's finest film work.

Barrymore and Carole Lombard in **Twentieth Century,** a screwball romp in which he decidedly romped and ————. 1934.

(1-r) Anne Baxter, Barrymore, and Mary Beth Hughes in **The Great Profile.** It was sad to see Barrymore parody himself in this movie. 1940.

Barrymore and Frances Farmer in his next to last film, **World Premiere.** 1941. At this point in his life he could no longer be counted on to carry his own — ill and unable to remember lines. He died a year later.

Boris Karloff, né William "Billy" Pratt, in his native London. "It's not true I was born a monster," he said. "Hollywood made me one." 1958.

BORIS KARLOFF

Born: November 23, 1887 Dulwich, England

In 1931, Universal Studios assigned James Whale the task of directing **Frankenstein.** Mary Shelley's classic 1816 novel had been scheduled for production yearly since 1920 when the studio first purchased the rights. Actor Lon Chaney had frowned on the part of the Monster feeling it was "a bit too strong" and opted instead for **The Hunchback of Notre Dame.** Bela Lugosi, **Dracula**'s star, was not quite so fussy, but studio head, Carl Laemmle, Jr., was and refused Lugosi the part. Laemmle thought British actor, Leslie Howard, would be right but director Whale said, "No." He had his eye on Karloff, a non-contract player, and after several other actors had tested, Whale set about to make the test with Karloff. But first makeup man Jack P. Pierce had to fashion the Monster, build the Monster—after he had done some research.

He discovered that there were six ways to open the skull and selected the easiest one, figuring that the mad doctor in the film would also select the easiest way. The cut would be made straight across the top of the

skull, and the stolen brain would be dropped in, like a cake in a box. Hence, the Monster's head appeared square and flat. A scar across the forehead with metal clamps as fasteners showed how the parts were held together. The two metal studs in the sides of the neck were the inlets for the electricity that charged the Monster; lightning was to be his life force. Further research revealed that when the Egyptians buried criminals alive, their hands and feet were bound; thus, when the blood turned to water, it flowed to their extremities stretching their limbs to an abnormal size and inflating the face. Makeup man Pierce encased Karloff's hands in plaster, darkening the fingertips with shoe polish to give a half-dead appearance. The arms were made to appear longer by simply shortening the sleeve length. To stiffen the legs, he covered them with two pairs of pants bolstered with steel struts. The feet were enlarged with asphalt-layers's type boots which raised Karloff's normal height of five feet, eleven inches to seven feet, six inches. His face was a mass of cheesecloth over which layers and layers of makeup were applied. Pierce used a greenish-grey color to emulate the skin tone of a dead man and the deep pores, acne-look, was the result of the cheesecloth as it sopped up the color. The eyes presented another problem: how to make him appear unintelligent. He cut shapes of half-moons from rubber and glued them onto Karloff's eyelids. Pierce called them "lizard eyes." If one fleck of the makeup fell into Karloff's eyes, it caused him great pain. Needless to say, the hot lights and summer shooting schedule did cause this to happen. The makeup job took about five hours to apply and two hours to remove.

It was not Pierce, but Karloff who gave the character's eyes the appearance of intense suffering. Karloff said, "I saw the character as an innocent one. A pathetic creature who, like us all, had neither wish nor say in his creation; and certainly did not wish upon itself the hideous image which automatically terrified humans whom it tried to befriend. The most heart-rending aspect of the creature's life, for us, was his ultimate

A dual celebration for Karloff on the movie set. His 51st birthday and the birth of his daughter. Hollywood, 1938.

desertion by his creator. It was as though man, in his blundering, searching, attempts to improve himself, was to find himself deserted by his God."*

No matter how Karloff, Pierce, Whale, or Laemmle saw or interpreted the Monster, the result, called a horror film, established a valuable commodity for itself and other studios. Although **Dracula** had come first, this genre of movie had no title until **Frankenstein.** In England, it was given the new rating of H—Horrific: only persons over the age of sixteen would be admitted.

And yet, according to Karloff, "It was the youngsters who wrote me saying, 'It was a dirty shame what those cruel men did to you.' That was very significant and perceptive." And, "Over the years thousands of children wrote, expressing compassion for the great, weird creature who was so abused by its sadistic keeper that it could only respond to violence with violence. Those children saw beyond the makeup and really understood." For, once upon a time, Boris Karloff had been a child, too.

Born William Henry Pratt, he was the ninth child in a line of seven brothers and a step-sister. His father, Edward Pratt, had spent his life in the Indian Salt Revenue Service and intended his sons to follow his example of a life in the diplomatic corps. Six of the seven older brothers did exactly that. But brother George, under the surname of Marlowe, went on the stage. Their mother, Eliza Sara Millard Pratt, died when Billy, as he was called, was only seven. Their father had died when Billy was just five. It was his

step-sister, Emma, who raised him. And any other brother who happened to be home on leave would try to influence the young Billy and share in his upbringing. Billy appreciated their brotherly concern, but despite an attempt at consular work, he had fallen under the influence of George, the actor. In 1896, playing the role of the Demon King in **Cinderella,** Billy knew that the theater was what he wanted.

When he reached age twenty-one, he was given a small inheritance left by his mother. He flipped a coin to determine whether he would set sail to Australia or Canada, and Canada won. And so in May of 1909, he left England, feeling very much the black sheep of the family. It would be twenty-four years before he returned, but he would come back as a white knight.

Life in Ontario was hard. Wages were so small, twenty-five cents an hour, that he went from job-to-job trying to improve his standard of living. The British public schools had given him fine manners and refined speech, but had not prepared him for ditch-digging, farming, laying concrete, and other backbreaking tasks. But Billy was not a complainer; he did what he had to do to further his dream of being on the stage. And ultimately it was this hard training that sustained him when he was out-of-work at the studios and accounts for the longevity of his career into his eighties. For even then, as a cripple, he continued to work.

In 1910, with a few dollars in his pocket, he answered an ad in *Billboard* for an experienced actor. He was accepted by mail, not through audition, and boarded a train to join the Jean Russell Stock Company in Nelson, Canada. It was on the train that Boris Karloff was born. Taking the last name from one of his mother's Russian ancestors, he then plucked a suitable first name out of the air; Boris sounded right to him.

His official stage debut, 1911, was in Molnar's **The Devil.** He faked his way through learning stage terms, directions, and the art of applying makeup. His good size and boney looks gave off a villainous effect, and so he became very popular as the villain in their various productions. He

*Denis Gifford, **Karloff** (New York: Curtis Books).

lasted two years with the company before he once again found himself broke and unemployed. After more time spent in hard labor at odd jobs, he answered another ad in *Billboard*, but this time he had experience.

For the next two years with the Harry St. Clair Players, Karloff did solid repertory melodramatic farces. He was in 106 different shows in fifty-three weeks. He said he was a "quick study" and that "quick studys" got the longest parts. He tried his luck in Chicago in 1914, but found work impossible to get, so returned to the St. Clair Players. When the group disbanded in 1917, Karloff found himself in Los Angeles. Although he had never considered movies, he enjoyed the bit assignments and extra work in addition to the day-laborer jobs.

Universal hired him for one week to be a member of a mob and a Mexican soldier in Douglas Fairbanks's movie, **His Majesty the American.** The next ten years were spent playing foreign-looking villains in exotic lands. He played a Mexican, a French-Canadian, Arabian, Apache, Egyptian, and even what he had been—a "north-woodsman." By now he was in his thirties, had an agent, and more money in his pocket than he had ever known, about $150 a week. He was ready to enter the "talkies" and marriage. His first wife, Helene Vivian Soule, was a blond dancer known as Pauline. Her husband playfully called her "Polly." They were married in 1923 and divorced in 1929. All that is known about Polly is that after the divorce she supported herself as an artist. When Karloff achieved fame, she refused all interviews saying that, "as an artist I wish a fellow artist success."

Karloff, like Lon Chaney with whom he had become friends, was a very private person. His marriages (3) and divorces (2) did not make juicy gossip for the papers; any suffering or misdeeds remained within the confines of the Karloff home.

In speaking about Lon Chaney, Karloff recalled the advice given to him, "Seek individuality and try to find something that no one else can do." Karloff was being billed by Universal as the "New Lon Chaney," but to Karloff there was only one Chaney. Both of

Lon Chaney in his famous role of Quasimodo in **The Hunchback of Notre Dame.** 1923.

Chaney, "The Man of a Thousand Faces," like Karloff, had risen to fame the hard way. Shown here as Erik in **Phantom of the Opera,** 1925.

Chaney's parents were deaf-mutes. Perhaps from this sorrow, he could depict the souls of afflicted people as he did in the roles of Quasimodo (**The Hunchback of Notre Dame)** and Erik, the deformed one (**Phantom of the Opera**). And then came Chaney's own struggle with throat cancer just after he had proved himself in his first and only talkie, **The Unholy Three.** He died at the age of forty-seven in 1930.

Karloff returned to the stage after a seven year absence, playing in three or four various dramas before appearing in the Los Angeles production of **The Criminal Code.** His luck held out, for when Columbia Pictures Corporation bought the screen rights, director Howard Hawks retained him for the film version. Finally stage actors were coming into their own. They were adept at taking direction, had good speaking voices, and could, in many instances, help the new breed of film directors. Karloff was asked by Hawks exactly how he had played a very important moment on the stage: it was a point in the play where imagination was the key, not a visual experience. And so, in the film, Karloff was allowed to play it the same way. To quote Karloff, "Imagination is the quality most needed in screen thrillers."

The success of **The Criminal Code** led Karloff to **The Mad Genius,** starring John Barrymore. But before that he had done three films for RKO-Radio and four for Warner Brothers. Karloff was a workhorse. He returned to Universal to play in another film (another villain), and it was there that director James Whale saw him and made the decision to test Karloff for the Monster.

Despite twenty years of acting, Karloff had never been under contract to any studio. He was finally placed under contract after, not before, the success of **Frankenstein.** The film changed his whole life; it changed the life of Universal as previous poor profits grew into the millions; it changed the entire industry as other major companies hopped on the "horror bandwagon," and it brought about the Pratt family reunion in England after twenty-four years.

However, the reason he was sent to England was not for a holiday but— what else?—for a film. And of course, it was after Universal had loaned him out to MGM for **The Mask of Fu Manchu,** and after he had completed **The Mummy** for Universal.

In the interim, he had remarried, this time to librarian Dorothy Stine. Together they had moved into a nicer home replete with a 400 pound pig, 5 dogs, egg-producing poultry, and vegetables and fruit grown by them. They just pottered around until the call came to go to England for the film, **The Ghoul,** released in 1933.

Boris Karloff and his second wife, Dot Stine, at the premiere of **Tovarich.** Los Angeles, 1937.

Karloff relaxing in his home in Coldwater Canyon with one of his five dogs. For the first time, he had financial freedom. Los Angeles, 1939.

Sara Karloff, age 16, daughter of Boris Karloff, named "Queen of the Grand National Junior Livestock Exposition" in San Francisco. 1954.

The intrepid gentle Monster finally faced his three remaining brothers, all quite successful in the Corps, and much to his delight, the brothers were proud of him and of his success. The reunion, after the ice was broken, was one "of deep understanding, a sense of well-being, and warm friendship."

Back in Hollywood, Karloff made four more movies before Universal realized that it had been a mistake to kill their Monster. And so they righted their wrong and conceived a script where the monster had merely been buried alive by the flames, not killed. **The Bride of Frankenstein** began shooting, but unfortunately Karloff fell and broke his hip. The then forty-eight year old actor agreed to a stuntman for the first time. The film made money and so—**Son of Frankenstein.** Another winner, but Boris took off his boots forever. Later **Frankenstein** films were made with Lon Chaney, Jr., Glenn Strange, and Bela Lugosi. Karloff was quoted as saying, "Every time they make another **Frankenstein** picture, I get all the fan mail. The other fellow gets the check!"

He did five horror films for Columbia Pictures without makeup, just darkened bushy eyebrows, before the call to Broadway and his beloved theater. For those of you who were around, can you ever forget his line in the first scene when another character asks him, "Why did you do that?" (Karloff had just murdered a man who had given them a lift in his car.) And Karloff, in the role of Jonathan, replies, "He said I looked like Boris Karloff!" The play? The unforgettable, **Arsenic and Old Lace.**

Unfortunately for film buffs, this line is lost as Raymond Massey plays Jonathan, and the humor of it pales.

63

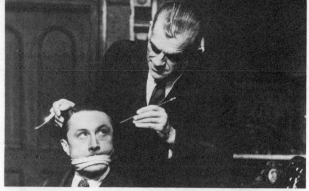

Karloff with Allyn Joslyn in a scene from **Arsenic and Old Lace.** New York, 1941.

Karloff and actor James Cagney at Screen Actors Guild meeting. Karloff was one of the original founders of SAG and served as a director for thirty years. Hollywood, 1940.

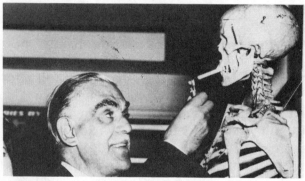

A friendly monster gesture by Karloff when he opened a crime book exhibition at the National Book League showroom. London, 1954.

Karloff and his third wife, Evelyn Hope Helmore, arriving in London. 1958.

(l-r) Robert Coote, director Buzz Kulik, Karloff, and Dan O'Herlihy rehearsing a scene for CBS-TV's Playhouse 90's first special, "To the Sound of Trumpets." 1960.

From 1940 to 1968 the Karloff craft turned to terror. To him horror was synonymous with revulsion; terror was synonymous with spine-tingling. Notable among this period was **Bedlam** done with Russian intellectual Val Lewton. The authenticity of the film was so appalling that Great Britain censored it on the grounds that it was too revealing about their infamous London madhouse.

Karloff's Broadway roles from '46 to '49 helped mellow his image in the public's eyes. He played Captain Hook and George Darling with Jean Arthur in **Peter Pan;** Gramps in **On Borrowed Time;** the kindly professor in **The Linden Tree.** But just as his image was changing, another sort of monster was being unleashed—television. And so from the depths of the studio vaults, his horror films were disinterred.

However, during the Fifties and Sixties Karloff's career became the most rewarding artistically and financially. His television series, "Boris Karloff Mystery Playhouse," "Thriller," and the British filmed "Colonel March," allowed him the range within his scope of what he had hoped to achieve in Hollywood. His frequent guest spots on other series furthered his image. He also made recordings for children, and at one point, as a disc jockey, read stories to children on the air, "live." Now he was tagged, "The Gentle Monster."

Crippled, tired, with bronchitis and arthritis, he forged on, making more and more films. The list remains incomplete, but researchers agree that Karloff appeared on the screen about four hundred times. He was eighty-one years old, minus one lung and inhaling oxygen as he sat in his wheelchair with a steel leg brace, ready to do four more films. He did not want to just sit around and do nothing until the end came. He wanted to do what he loved best—act.

Finally in 1968, with his third wife, Evelyn Hope Helmore, whom he had married in 1946 after his divorce, he returned to England. For three months he fought for his life in a British hospital until the end came quietly for the beloved monster.

The funeral was private, and his ashes were buried in the Garden of Remembrance in his native land.

BORIS KARLOFF
Died: February 2, 1969
Sussex, England

Karloff and Zita Johann in **The Mummy.** 1932. For the first time, Universal Studio billed him as KARLOFF; just his last name which ranked him alongside Garbo.

Evelyn Keyes and Karloff in **Before I Hang.** 1940. Karloff, as Dr. John Garth, seeks a cure for death, but everything gets confused as the players romp through a homicidal holiday.

Anne Revere and Karloff in **The Devil Commands.** 1941. Despite the flimsy sections of the film, Karloff rises above them to give a tender performance as the grief-stricken husband trying desperately to contact his dead wife through spiritual means.

Susanna Foster and Karloff in **The Climax.** 1944. The film was a remake of the 1930 version and utilized the refurbished set from Lon Chaney's 1925 **Phantom of the Opera.**

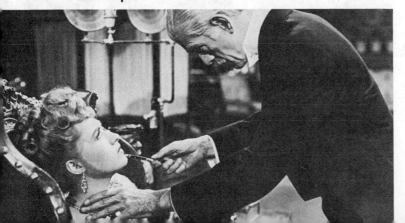

Henry Daniell and Karloff in **The Body Snatcher.** 1945. Bela Lugosi and Karloff had one major scene together, which is considered one of their finest.

Karloff as "Captain Hook" in the Broadway production of **Peter Pan,** co-starring Jean Arthur. 1950.

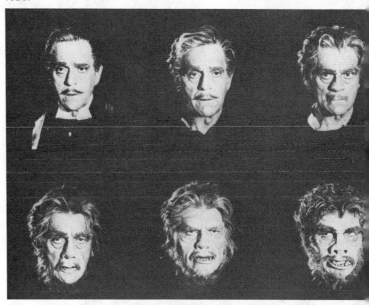

Karloff's makeup transformation from Dr. Jekyll to Mr. Hyde in Robert Louis Stevenson's classic case history of the schizophrenic's metamorphosis. Makeup artist was Bud Westmore who had taken over from Jack P. Pierce, creator of the "Monster" makeup in **Frankenstein.** This for the film, **Abbot & Costello Meet Dr. Jekyll & Mr. Hyde.** 1953.

Viveca Lindfors, Jean Pierre Aumont, and Karloff, now confined to a wheelchair with arthritis and a steel leg brace, in **Cauldron of Blood.** 1967. The film made in Spain, was not released in the United States until 1970, after Karloff's death.

Humphrey Bogart as Sam Spade, private detective, in **The Maltese Falcon,** displayed his sex appeal and then tragic toughness as he sent his love to jail. A whole new genre of detective stories was thus created. 1941.

HUMPHREY BOGART

Born: December 25, 1899*, New York, New York

Humphrey DeForest Bogart was the first of three children born to Dr. Belmont DeForest Bogart and Maude Humphrey. Both parents were third generation Americans who lived quite comfortably on New York's then ultra-fashionable Riverside Drive. Dr. Belmont had a moderate practice but could easily be swayed to lay down his stethoscope and pick up a hunting rifle, fishing tackle, social slippers, or his first love, to take the helm of a boat. The latter hobby he passed on to Humphrey who was given a sloop on his eighth birthday. As an adult Humphrey always owned a boat when he could afford one. Sadly, Dr. Bogart's paternal image began to falter as he bacame a morphine addict desperately trying to mask the pain of arthritis. He and his wife were not as careful in masking their marital problems. They fought openly and often as did Humphrey with his first three wives. Ultimately, Dr. Bogart sought refuge as a ship's doctor. He died at age 55 leaving vast debts. He also left his son with a scar and slight lisp, the result of a hard slap across the mouth when Humphrey was a youngster.** This, of course, led to the famous Bogart speech delivery and added to his sexy on-screen appeal.

Maude Humphrey was a magazine illustrator who had studied abroad. More often than not, she earned a yearly salary greater than her husband's. She gave Humphrey his first bit of exposure by using him as the model for the Mellin's Baby Food label, known as the "Original Maude Humphrey Baby" drawing. She was an early believer in freedom for women; an outspoken lady both at home and in public (as was Bogart's third wife, Mayo). One suspects that the marriage was kept intact for propriety's sake

* Conflicting birthdates appear in various biographies attributed to the Publicity Department at Warner Bros. Studio: January 23, 1899 or December 25, 1900.

Joe Hyams, **Bogart & Bacall (New York: Warner Books).

Humphrey's education in private schools was routine for privileged boys. At prep school he managed to get expelled. Because he was scantly educated and unqualified for work, he joined the Navy during WWI. When he returned after a two-year hitch, he was just as much at sea as he had been for the past two years. He was offered a job by the father of a close childhood friend. William Brady produced plays and always had his hand in some sort of entertainment or exhibition type endeavor. Bogart always maintained that theater was the farthest thing from his mind, but at that point in his life he had little choice and less funds. And as life progressed it was always his good fortune to have his friends come to the rescue. His social position offered good contacts.

He began his career in the theatre as an errand boy, then stepped in as stage manager during a crisis; and finally walked on-stage as a Japanese valet with one spoken line in the play **Drifting.** He was now 23.

Heaven only knows what William Brady saw in Humphrey, who by his own words, at that time would rather be drinking with his friends, but Brady kept pushing him, on-stage and off. Ultimately, he was rewarded for his perspicacity and patience as he did live long enough to see Humphrey become a big star and fine actor. Humphrey had several false starts in the theater and several balks in Hollywood. His career took a big

Bogie, born into Blue Book Society, uninterested in a theatrical career, became a legend. Here he looks the part of the socialite.

leap with the help of his friend, playwright Robert E. Sherwood. Sherwood wrote a small part for Bogart in his upcoming play, **The Petrified Forest,** which was to star British actor Leslie Howard. But producer Arthur Hopkins (see Barrymore, Chapter 6) saw Bogart in the more important role of Duke Mantee, the killer on the lam. And Howard agreed with him. The play opened in 1935, and now Humphrey (age 36) was finally headed somewhere.

Warner Brothers Studio had Edward G. Robinson in mind for the Mantee role in the film but was forced to take Bogart when Howard threatened to quit if he did not play the part. The film launched one of the biggest personalities on the screen. Hollywood tagged him "Bogie," and the name stuck, with the public as well as his friends.

He started at Warner Brothers with a salary of $400 a week. After his success in **Forest,** he was raised to $650. As the years went by he kept getting raises until around 1947 he was making several hundred thousand dollars a year.

Although his portrayal of Mantee was outstanding, the next few films were rather desultory until George Raft and Paul Muni both refused to play the aging gangster in **High Sierra** (1941), and again Raft refused **The Maltese Falcon** (1941). Bogie stepped in and made a great success of each. By 1943, he was ready for **Casablanca** with Ingrid Bergman, Claude Rains, and "Play it Again, Sam" Dooley Wilson. As Rick, the owner of the café, Bogie fully evolved his tough-man image with romantic undertones and his ability for comedic exchanges. One of the more famous ones:

Rains: "What's your nationality?"
Bogie: "I'm a drunkard."

Off-screen, Bogie wasn't exactly a drunkard, but he could and did drink — a lot and a lot. Back in New York he had been a frequent visitor to the speakeasies and later to the more posh clubs after the repeal of Prohibition. He was known to be high-spirited with an equally high-spirited temper, and in those early days when he was merely playing at acting he was more of an elbow-bender than a hard study. Not until the De-

68

Humphrey Bogart and the first of his four wives, Helen Mencken, whom he married in 1926, just about the time this photo was taken.

Second wife, Mary Phillips Bogart leaving court after divorcing Bogie. She said, "He wanted the freedom of a single man." At right, a friend, Mary Baker. Los Angeles, 1937.

Bogie and his third wife, Mayo Methot, after their marriage ceremony. The wedding night was described as "a drunken debacle" which marked the beginning of the era of "The Battling Bogarts." California, 1938.

Bogie on the air with host Milton Berle (l) and Lt. Charles Shea, Congressional Medal of Honor recipient, on Berle's show "Let Yourself Go." New York City, 1945.

Bogie on record to protest the tactics of the House UnAmerican Activities Committee. (l-r) June Havoc, Bogie, and Betty Bacall. Washington, D.C., 1947.

Bogie and Betty Bogart on board their boat **Santana** in Toyon Cave, the then newest playground for the Hollywood colony. Santa Catalina, California, 1947.

pression when the stock market collapsed and the banks closed did he really have to buckle down and work. His gray pallor (hangover telltale) was not make-up but when combined with his creased, wrinkled eyes and whiskey-scarred voice, it all added up to appeal — sex and public.

Of Bogie's four marriages it might be said that one and two were mistakes, three was mayhem, and four was magic.

Number one was actress Helen Menken, 1926-28; number two was actress, Mary Phillips, 1928-1938. Number three was also an actress, Mayo Methot. She had appeared in several films after a brief stint on Broadway. She was the daughter of a sea captain, which gave her and Bogie something in common: their love of boats and water. But what they really had going for them was that Mayo could match Bogie drink for drink and fight for fight. One might conjecture that they had complementary neuroses. Their brawls and brawling were as legendary as Bogie's reputation as an actor. To add to the fun and games, they called everything "Sluggy"; their dog, their boat, their home, Sluggy Hollow. Unfortunately the whole thing turned into a debacle as Mayo slipped into chronic alcoholism and suicidal tendencies. The marriage ended when Bogie met Bronx-born Betty Joan Perske better known as Lauren Bacall.

Betty Bacall, as she is called by her friends, had arrived in Hollywood after years of hard work, no money, undeveloped talent, and fabulous looks. She had been a model and as such had caught the eye of director Howard Hawks, who was looking for someone to play opposite Bogie in **To Have**

And Have Not. Betty Bacall was the complete antithesis of any woman formerly in Bogie's life: in looks, background, attitude, and even religion. She was a social drinker and noncombatant. And she was eighteen. He was forty-three and one of the top stars in the world.

They fell in love during the filming of **To Have** and were married after Bogie was divorced from Mayo in 1945. Their life together had all the charm and luster Hollywood had to offer, and together they became one of Hollywood's most famous couples on-screen and off. Brawlin' Bogie settled comfortably into married life, probably a wish from early childhood, and became the father of two children. Son Stephen was born in 1949, and daughter Leslie Howard was born in 1952.

Bogie's career kept zooming, and in 1951 he was awarded an "Oscar" for his performance in **The African Queen** playing oppo-

On the left—an 80-pound perch. On the right — the lady who caught it (Lauren Bacall); and in the middle —middleman Bogart. Lake Albert, British Uganda, 1951.

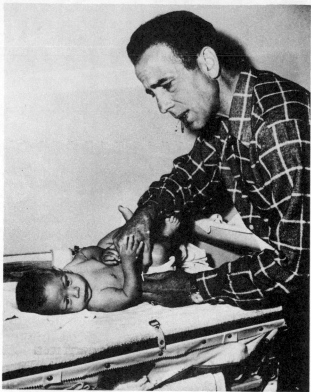

Bogie diapering his first child, Stephen Humphrey Bogart. The Bogarts met and fell in love during the filming of **To Have and Have Not,** in which Bogie played the role of Steve; hence his son's sentimental name. 1949.

Bogie (age 55) and his two children, Stephen and Leslie (named for actor Leslie Howard) and wife Lauren Bacall (29) at home in California. 1954.

Back from deepest Africa after completion of **The African Queen,** (l-r) Lauren Bacall, who kept her husband company; Bogie; and co-star Katharine Hepburn. London airport, 1951.

Bogie wins an "Oscar" for **The African Queen.** (l-r) Bette Davis accepting for Kim Hunter (Best Supporting Actress, **A Streetcar Named Desire**); presenter, George Sanders; Karl Malden (Best Supporting Actor, **Streetcar**); Greer Garson accepting for Vivien Leigh (Best Actress, **Streetcar**); Bogie, Best Actor; and presenter Ronald Colman, Hollywood. 1952.

Lauren Bacall went on to further fame after her husband's death, both on film and on the stage. Shown here after another achievement, her book **Lauren Bacall By Myself**, Alfred Knopf Publishers, at a party celebrating its publication with son, Steve. New York City, 1979.

Rumors once flew that Lauren Bacall would marry close friend of both Bogie and her, Frank Sinatra. But she married Jason Robards, Jr. (1961), and they had a son, Sam. The night that Bogie died, Sinatra was so broken up that he could not perform. His pal Jerry Lewis went on for him at the Copacabana. Sinatra and Betty shown here at the preview of his film, **Pal Joey**. Hollywood, 1957.

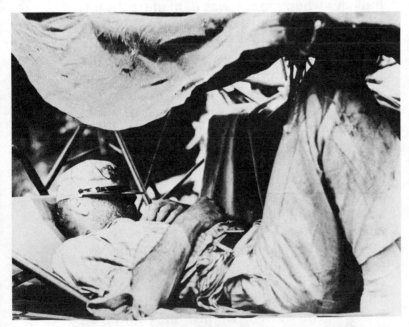

Bogie: "If I ever catch the rotten, dirty sneaking thieving son-of-a-cameraman who took this shot, I'll tear his larcenous heart out, I'll push his bloody nose in like it was a panda's. A guy can't even catch some shut-eye in peace without some rotten, dirty, sneaking, thieving . . . " Africa, 1951.

Rev. Kermit Castellanos, associate Rector of All Saints Episcopal Church, conducted brief religious services. Instead of a casket, this scale model of Bogie's famed 55-foot yawl, **Santana**, was placed before the altar as cremation was held simultaneously at Forest Lawn Cemetery. California, 1957.

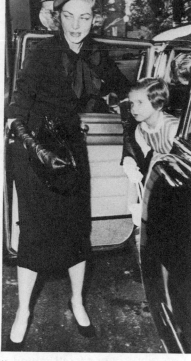

Actress Lauren Bacall, widow of Humphrey Bogart, assists their children at their father's funeral. (l) Stephen, age 6; (r) Leslie, age 4. Beverly Hills, 1957.

Friends say goodbye to Bogie. (l-r) Sylvia Fine Kaye and her husband Danny Kaye; Veronica Passani Peck and her husband Gregory Peck. Funeral services were held at the All Saints Episcopal Church. Beverly Hills, California. 1957.

site Katharine Hepburn. Both she and Spencer Tracy were close personal friends, first of Bogie and later of Betty. Tracy and Bogie had originally met when Bogie went to Hollywood in the late Twenties. Two other notable films in the Bogart list are **The Treasure of Sierra Madre** (1948) and **The Caine Mutiny** (1954). His last film, **The Harder They Fall** (1956) was roughly his seventieth film.

Lauren Bacall went on to a highly successful screen career. Later she was a smash on Broadway, first in **Cactus Flower** (1965) then **Applause** (1970). Originally, the film, **All About Eve** (1950), which starred Bette Davis and Anne Baxter. Lauren Bacall played the Davis role in the musical stage version. In 1981 she triumphed again on Broadway in **Woman of the Year**.

Maude Humphrey Bogart lived to be seventy-five. Bogie's youngest sister, Catherine Elizabeth died at age thirty-three. Mayo died at the age of forty-seven from acute alcoholism.

Bogie's other sister, Frances "Pat" Bogart had married Stuart Rose, and it was Mr. Rose, a story editor at Fox Studio, who arranged for Bogie's first screen test back in the days when money was tight and jobs impossible to get. But Fox dropped Humphrey deciding that he just didn't have it, and he returned to New York in 1933. Fox's folly thus became Warners' windfall.

In 1956, Bogie was stricken with throat cancer. The operation for removal of a malignant ulcer in the esophagus revealed that the lymph glands had been attacked, and they were removed. He lost the fight for life a year later.

To Have And Have Not brought Bogie and Bacall together. His years with her were certainly the eleven happiest years of his life. Whether you are a film buff or not, sixteen words from the film surely have passed your ears.

Bacall: "You know how to whistle, don't you Steve? You just put your lips together and blow."

HUMPHREY BOGART
Died: January 14, 1957
Los Angeles, California

At the age of 36, Humphrey Bogart made an impact on the screen recreating the role of Duke Mantee, killer on the lam, the role he played on Broadway. (l-r) Leslie Howard, Bette Davis, Bogie, and Dick Foran in **The Petrified Forest.** 1936.

By 1938 Bogie's career was zooming with the release of **Swing Your Lady, Crime School, Men Are Such Fools, Racket Busters, Angels With Dirty Faces**; and **The Amazing Dr. Clitterhouse**, shown here.

(l-r) Humphrey Bogart, Bette Davis, and Geraldine Fitzgerald in **Dark Victory.** 1939. In 1931, Bogie's fourth film, **Bad Sister**, introduced Bette Davis to screen audiences.

(l-r) Humphrey Bogart, Erin O'Brien-Moore, Dickie Jones, Ann Sheridan, Dick Foran in **Black Legion.** 1937.

(l-r) Humphrey Bogart, George Raft, George Tobias in **They Drive By Night.** 1940.

The film starred Errol Flynn and Mirian Hopkins, but Bogart was about to take a giant step forward the following year. (l-r) George Regas, Bogart, Moroni Olsen, and Paul Fix in **Virginia City**. 1940.

(l-r) Dooley Wilson ("Play It Again Sam"), Humphrey Bogart, and Ingrid Bergman in **Casablanca.** This film made Bogie king of the Warner Bros. lot and catapulted him into the top ten box-office attractions. 1943.

Bogart and Ida Lupino in **High Sierra**. Fortunately for Bogie, both Paul Muni and George Raft turned down the part. 1941.

(l-r) Humphrey Bogart, Peter Lorre, Mary Astor, and Sydney Greenstreet in **The Maltese Falcon**. Again, George Raft declined the role and Bogart took over. Playing detective Sam Spade, Bogie became a top star. 1941.

Bogie and "Baby" Lauren Bacall in **The Big Sleep**. He called her "Baby," but Warners pushed her into fame as "The Look." 1946.

Lauren Bacall and Bogie in their first film together, **To Have and Have Not.** They opted for "to have," and she became his fourth wife. 1944.

Bogart and Tim Holt in **The Treasure of Sierra Madre,** which was directed by John Huston who directed his father, Walter Huston, also in the film. 1948.

(l-r) Bogie, Van Johnson, Todd Karnes, and Robert Francis in **The Caine Mutiny.** Bogart gave one of his finest performances as the paranoid Navy Captain Queeg. 1954.

Eleanor Parker and Humphrey Bogart in **Chain Lightning.** 1950.

Bogie, Martha Stewart, and Gloria Grahame in **In a Lonely Place.** 1950.

(in background) Dewey Martin, (l-r) Bogie, Martha Scott, Richard Eyer in **The Desperate Hours,** which was Bogart's next to last film. 1955.

Bogie and Katharine Hepburn in **The African Queen.** He was nominated for and won an "Oscar" for Best Performance. 1951.

Bogie's last film, **The Harder They Fall,** with Jan Sterling. 1956. Stricken with throat cancer, after twenty-six years of film making and over seventy films, he died a year later. Director and friend John Huston said, "There will never be another like him."

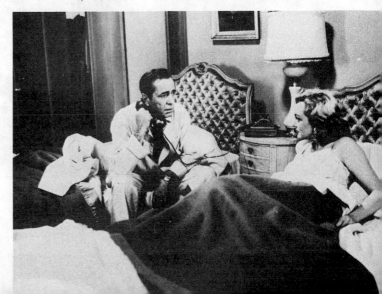

"Spencer Tracy, you're the best damn actor I ever saw," said fellow actor/director George M. Cohan, quoted by writer Damon Runyon.

SPENCER TRACY

BORN: April 5, 1900 Milwaukee, Wisconsin

The label or status tag, "actor's actor," (dancer's dancer, singer's singer) is bandied about as much as the word *genius*; and generally it is applied without the real meaning having been explored or investigated. Spencer Tracy wore this plaque, so inscribed. When applied to Spencer Tracy, its meaning stems from Tracy the man, Tracy the person—not Tracy from a Method school of acting or any other well of teaching. Tracy, the actor, was played by Tracy the man, self-styled and conceived. The simplicity of his formula was extremely complex in its execution. If one views his films thirty years apart, what is seen is the same actor doing the same thing only doing it better.

Perhaps he deviated once from his method in **The Old Man and The Sea.** Critics concurred that "he didn't even bother to act." His peers disagreed as they nominated him for a sixth Academy Award, Best Actor honor. He was definitely his own man, his own person. He brought this to Hollywood and remained tenaciously true to what he had created. He was this sort of actor; he was this sort of growing child and later, young adult.

As a child, the youngest of two boys, he labored through parochial schools and a military academy without direction—only distinct likes and dislikes. He joined the

Spencer Tracy at the age of twelve in his native Milwaukee, Wisconsin.

Navy with childhood pal William J. O'Brien (actor Pat) and survived basic training only to be left at the pier in the Norfolk Navy yard as the war (WWI) ended. Back in Milwaukee, he continued his education partially financed with a $30.00 a month pension from the government. He went on to Ripon College as a pre-med student and, there he found his "calling."

Encouraged to join the debating team, Tracy found a good outlet for his tenacity. He developed a good memory and a presence, both of which contributed to his ultimate success. For example, in 1939 in **Stanley and Livingston,** he delivered a 442 word speech without any difficulty and with a presence in a medium that does not lend itself to lengthy speeches.

His acting also began at Ripon where he played the lead in **The Truth** and in a one act play, **The Valiant.** During his second year of college, using **The Valiant** as his vehicle, he auditioned for New York's American Academy of Dramatic Arts and was accepted. Eighteen years later in 1940, he returned to Ripon to accept an honorary degree.

His father, John Edward Tracy, the general sales manager of a truck company, abandoned all hope of his younger son following in his footsteps and agreed to pay his tuition in the New York school, but Spence had to finance the rest. His pension, wits, and roommate, Pat O'Brien, would carry him through, as he launched into acting.

Money was always a problem for both young men. Just when they were at the end of their monetary rope, they got jobs with

Spencer Tracy (l) and author Ernest Hemingway discussing the latter's Nobel and Pulitzer Prize winning novel, **The Old Man and the Sea,** which they hoped to land as successfully on film as the Cuban fisherman, played by Tracy, landed his prize fish in the film. Casablanca, Cuba, 1956.

the Theatre Guild's **Rossum's Universal Robots** (1923), called **R.U.R.,** and appeared onstage as robots. They received a salary of $15.00 a week, and Spencer Bonaventure Tracy was christened — actor.

From 1923 to 1930, Tracy worked in as many stock companies and as many plays as he could, as he was hired, as the plays opened and closed. Similar to actors working today in "soaps," it was learn your lines, forget your lines, and start over as the companies put on at least two plays a week. It was difficult yet satisfying; rewarding not so much monetarily but certainly emotionally.

During the run of **The Gypsy Trail** (1923) in Cincinnati, Ohio, he married his only wife, actress Louise Treadwell. They had met earlier in another company, and when the play folded they joined the Stuart Walker Company that opened **Gypsy.** The following year their first child, John, was born. Ultimately Louise would give up her acting career and devote herself to the founding and work of the John Tracy Clinic (named for John who had become deaf) dedicated to deafness in children. The clinic, opened formally in 1943, has received world-wide acclaim for its recognition of the problems associated with deafness in children. And Louise was honored for her early insight into the problems and for doing something about them.

The beautiful people of the Golden era of Hollywood. (l-r) Clark Gable, Spencer Tracy, Robert Taylor, and William Powell representing about $10,000,000 worth of "he-talent" on the MGM lot. 1937.

As Spence wended his way from New Jersey to Michigan and back again, one of his most ardent fans was George M. Cohan. Tracy actually played the same role that Cohan had played in **The Song and Dance Man** (1925) and did a couple of other shows under the aegis of producer Cohan. But it was Tracy's performance in the role of Killer Mears in **The Last Mile** that finally brought him the recognition he had been working towards. The play opened on Broadway in 1930 and shortly thereafter Hollywood, in the form of Fox Films, crooked its finger. Tracy left the play for a short time making his first film, **Up The River,** with another newcomer, Humphrey Bogart. Spence and Bogie became life-long friends. Coincidentally, Bogart's third wife, Mayo Methot, had gained stage recognition when she played opposite Cohan in **The Song and Dance Man.** The long arm of coincidence also stretched itself in connection with **The Last Mile.** Seated in the audience one night was another aspiring actor who was "wiped out" by Tracy's performance. So much so that when he was offered the Killer Mears role in the West Coast production he wanted to turn it down. In fact, he had almost made up

Tracy and his wife Louise Treadwell Tracy arriving in Honolulu for a Hawaiian vacation. 1936.

Spencer and Louise Tracy and their son John in their box at the Midwich Country Club near Los Angeles, California. 1939.

his mind to open a haberdashery store in New York City. But he accepted the part and left for California, where he landed a contract at MGM after having been seen in the play. Clark Gable was the actor. And so when Tracy had finished his run-of-the-play contract in **Mile,** he joined Gable and Bogart in Hollywood, and the Golden Age of Movies with three kingpins began its ascent.

Neither Hollywood nor Fox Films understood the tiger (Tracy) they had by the tail. Although he was a hard worker (and drinker), words such as uncooperative, cantankerous, and stubborn flew around. That's what Fox thought it had; Tracy thought he had bad roles. He lasted through his three years at Fox (1935) and then joined Gable at MGM. Along the way Spencer's second child was born, Louise, called "Susie," and the Tracys moved into a house in the valley on twelve acres away from the spotlight of active Hollywood and Beverly Hills. Gable would do the same thing when he married actress Carole Lombard.

Papa Tracy with daughter "Susie" on the set of **I Take This Woman,** which co-starred Hedy Lamarr. Hollywood, 1939.

Under the "parentage" of MGM's mighty L.B. Mayer, Tracy became a part of the Golden Thirties and Forties and the studio's star system, but only insofar as he was part of that era. He was never a part of what it stood for. To go back to the opening statement about Tracy being his own man, own person, he maintained this despite and in spite of the comings and goings of the studio's brainstorms about how its "stars"

should behave. Men in the garb of "press agents" were usually responsible (after long memos from LBM) for building the star image, but not with Tracy. From all reports, he not only did not have a press agent, but wouldn't have paid any attention if one had been assigned. Gable was molded by the studio, and each divorce, subsequent marriage, etc. was highly publicized according to studio vision. Bogart and Bacall became a part of Hollywood's fashionable and highly visible "Rat Pack" with Sinatra at its head, but Spencer Tracy lived his life his way, and at his pace. His philosophy and his ground rules worked for him, and if you got along with him (at work or otherwise) you played by his rules.

He climbed Mt. Olympus, Greek home of the gods, and stayed atop. Hard working, thoroughly professional, he made over seventy films, and every film had his all. If a picture was not successful, as **Edward My Son** (1949), it was not a bad picture just an unsuccessful one. Tracy usually ran the gamut of accepting a role, doubting his decision, pulling out, changing his mind, and then giving his best. He made about thirty films before his breakthrough and recognition in **Fury** and **San Francisco** (1936) which gave him star status; the latter gave him his first "Oscar" nomination. But it was his portrayal of Manuel, the Gloucester Portuguese fisherman in **Captains Courageous** (1937) that catapulted him to the status of legend. Ill the night of the Awards, Spencer sent Louise to accept the golden statue for him. He was nominated nine times and won twice with back-to-back films: the second was **Boys Town** (1938). His first color film was **Northwest Passage** (1940), and in the same year he became even more colorful when a twenty-seven year relationship with actress Katharine Hepburn was formed while they were filming **Woman of the Year.**

If the point of Tracy's being his own man has not been made, then the relationship with Hepburn should solidify the Tracy personage once and for all.

The Tracys had been estranged (in their way) for many years. Hepburn and Spence obviously had an attraction for one another

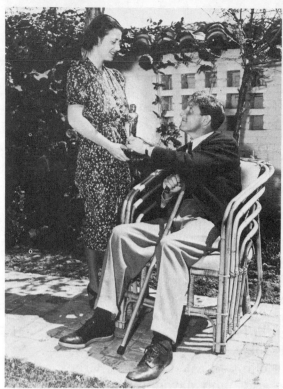

Mrs. Tracy presents "Oscar" to Spence upon his return home from the hospital. This was his first win. 1938.

Top honors for film in 1938 went to Bette Davis for **Jezebel** and Tracy for **Boys Town.** Sir Cedric Hardwicke (r) made the presentations at the awards dinner. 1939.

Top honors for 1937 films went to Luise Rainer for **The Good Earth** and to Spencer Tracy for **Captains Courageous.** (l-r) MGM chief, Louis B. Mayer; Luise Rainer; Louise Tracy, accepting for Spencer; and director and then president of the Academy, Frank Capra. 1938.

Director Edward Dmytryk (**The Mountain**) and Tracy admiring their "Silver Spurs" awards, the "Oscars" of Western movies for their work together on **Broken Lance** (1954). Here they are shown, after the fact, as they had been in Europe shooting **The Mountain** when the presentations were made. Hollywood, 1956.

Katharine Hepburn and her niece, Katharine Houghton, who played her daughter in **Guess Who's Coming To Dinner.** 1966.

An unbelievable line-up of stars, all paying rapt attention to the master, Spencer Tracy, on the set of the zany **It's A Mad, Mad, Mad, Mad World.** (l-r) Edie Adams, Sid Caesar, Phil Silvers, Dorothy Provine, Ethel Merman, Milton Berle, Dick Shawn, Terry-Thomas, Mickey Rooney (front), Buddy Hackett, Jonathan Winters, Spencer Tracy, Peter Falk, and Eddie "Rochester" Anderson. 1962.

Producer Leland Hayward (left) and Spencer Tracy star of **The Old Man and the Sea** wish director Fred Zinneman (center) good luck as he prepares to leave for Peru to shoot the catching of the giant marlin, which is the principal episode of the story. It took over six years to bring the film from the screenplay author Peter Viertel's typewriter to the finished product with a change of directors in mid-stream to John Sturges. Release date, 1958.

Close personal friend of Tracy, Supreme Court Justice William O. Douglas talks with actress Marlene Dietrich and Spencer on the set of **Judgment at Nuremberg** in Hollywood. 1961. Justice Douglas had been in Germany when the War Crime Trials had been conducted after WW II.

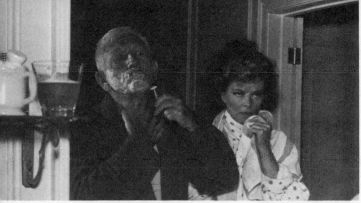

Twenty-five years after their first meeting and nine films together, Tracy spoke to Hepburn in their final film as if he were summing up their lives together and his feelings — what an old man remembers about having loved, being loved. The film, **Guess Who's Coming to Dinner.** 1967.

James Stewart (top) and Frank Sinatra were among the pallbearers at the Requiem Mass for their friend, Spencer Tracy. Hollywood, 1967.

Mrs. Tracy, estranged from her husband, being escorted from the Requiem Mass by studio chief, Howard Strickling who was also a close personal friend of Clark Gable's and grandson John Tracy, Jr. Hollywood. 1967.

and a chemistry that produced one of the great tandem teams on the screen. Off-screen, they went their own way together and set their own course of action. Unlike Gable's five marriages and Bogart's four and all of the other in-between action, Hepburn and Tracy left the press and the public at the altar. Only after his death did she begin to speak, and this was done when and how she wanted—forty years after the fact.

Spencer Tracy did not play the game, and in Katharine Hepburn he found another non-game player. Professionally, he left the game court of MGM in 1954 and became a free-lancer. His first film was **The Mountain** (1956) for Paramount Pictures. Two films later, he made the controversial **The Old Man and The Sea.**

He returned to Broadway during the summer of '45, and in the fall opened in Robert E. Sherwood's **The Rugged Path.** But the path was indeed rugged, and the play closed after eighty-odd performances. It was his last Broadway venture.

Meanwhile after **The Old Man and The Sea,** he bounced back with **The Last Hurrah,** directed by John Ford, and this put him back on everybody's favorite list. After this film he did five more, three of which brought him Academy nominations: **Inherit the Wind** (1960); **Judgement at Nuremberg** (1961); and his last film, **Guess Who's Coming to Dinner** (1967).

In 1963 his health had begun to decline, and so he took off for a year after being hospitalized for a lung condition. His red hair had turned totally white and the face magnificently lined and etched by the acid of time. He was known for his refusal to wear make-up. He let his audiences see his face develop and age as his acting did.

It was obvious to the cast and crew of **Guess Who's** during the filming that he was seriously ill, yet he completely dominated the film. Tenacious to the end, but with the clarity of an actor's actor who understood what he was about.

Three weeks after completion of the film, he died. Brendan Gill of *The New Yorker* magazine said, ''Mr. Tracy gives a faultless and, under the circumstances, heartbreaking performance.''

Tracy and the word unique, in its true definition — different from all others; having no like or equal —were brothers. And the era of picture making also qualifies for the same word. The stars produced at that time are gone; the era is gone; picture making as it was known then and as we see it now will never return.

SPENCER TRACY
DIED: June 11, 1967
Hollywood, California

Spencer Tracy and Bette Davis in **20,000 Years in Sing Sing,** during his early days for Fox Films. 1932.

Playing the role of Manuel, the Gloucester Portuguese fisherman, Tracy won his first "Oscar" in **Captains Courageous.** Shown here with Freddie Bartholomew. Critics agreed that their performances were superb as the young brat evolves into a man through the philosophy of Rudyard Kipling's sentimental fisherman. 1937.

Tracy and Loretta Young in **A Man's Castle.** Still under contract to Fox, he was loaned to Columbia for this in 1933.

Finished with Fox Films, MGM launched Tracy into star status in **Fury,** which was successful at the box office and had the full weight of Louis B. Mayer behind it. His next film, **San Francisco,** brought him his first "Oscar" nomination. Shown here with co-star Sylvia Sidney in **Fury.** 1936.

Playing a cab driver who marries an immigrant (Luise Rainer), Tracy made this film and one other, **They Gave Him a Gun,** in 1937 following **Captain's Courageous.** (l-r) Regis Toomey; Janet Beecher, with back to camera; Irving Bacon; Spencer Tracy; and Luise Rainer.

Tracy and Rita Johnson in **Edison, The Man.** 1940. Earlier MGM had made **Young Tom Edison** with Mickey Rooney. Now Tracy picks up where Rooney left off playing Edison from age 25 until his death at age 84. A feat only Tracy could have brought off.

Tracy and Katharine Hepburn met for the first time in 1940. Shown here in **Keeper of the Flame,** their second film together. 1942.

Tracy and Swedish actress Signe Hasso in **The Seventh Cross,** one of the few films that Tracy allowed makeup to be used on his face. As the pale anti-Nazi who has escaped from a concentration camp, Spence felt he needed a little help. 1944.

(l-r) Tracy, Irene Dunn, and Van Johnson in **A Guy Named Joe.** Johnson was in a serious auto accident during the filming of this, and Tracy insisted that they shoot around him rather than replace him. 1943.

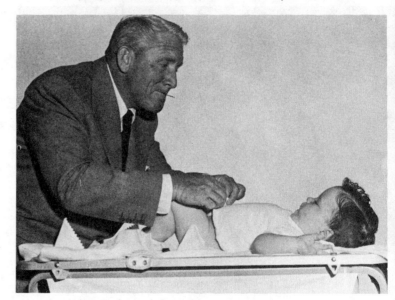

As a sequel to **Father of the Bride,** Tracy made **Father's Little Dividend.** Mother was played by Joan Bennett and daughter played by Elizabeth Taylor. 1951.

(l-r) Tracy, Mervyn Johns, and Deborah Kerr in **Edward, My Son.** Filmed in England, it did not enjoy a big success. 1949.

Tracy and Hepburn in their seventh film together, **Pat and Mike.** 1952. Tracy had by now made such memorable films as **Stanley and Livingston** (1939); **Men of Boys Town** (1941); **Dr. Jekyll and Mr. Hyde** (1941); **Tortilla Flat** (1942); and **State of the Union** (1948).

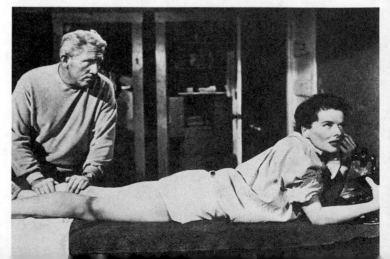

Tracy received his fifth Academy Award nomination for this film, **Bad Day at Black Rock.** 1955. Shown here with Ernest Borgnine, this film was Tracy's last for MGM.

Tracy and Marlene Dietrich in **Judgment at Nuremberg,** which originally was a TV "Playhouse 90" production. 1959. Tracy delivers a thirteen minute, forty-two second summation speech, topping his ten minute speech in **Inherit the Wind.** The whole speech was shot in one take using two cameras simultaneously, allowing Tracy full concentration and full range without interruption. 1961. Tracy received his eighth "Oscar" nomination for this film.

Tracy in Ernest Hemingway's **The Old Man and The Sea,** in which he was the only star appearing on-screen in almost two-thirds of the film as well as doing off-screen narration. In 1958, he won his sixth Academy nomination for this film.

Tracy in his next to last film, **It's A Mad, Mad, Mad, Mad World,** which was a mad, mad, mad, mad, "chase" comedy, and the cop —Tracy as Captain C.G. Culpeper. 1963.

(l-r) Gene Kelly, Dick York, and Spencer Tracy in **Inherit The Wind** for which Tracy received his seventh "Oscar" nomination. Playing opposite co-star Frederic March (William Jennings Bryan, alias Matthew Harrison Brady) Tracy (Clarence Darrow, alias Henry Drummond) had a chance to pit his skill against another skillful trouper. 1960.

Sidney Poitier, Tracy, and Katharine Hepburn in **Guess Who's Coming to Dinner,** Spence's last film and "an important contribution to motion pictures." The performances of all three stand the test of time as they remain superb and full of conviction. 1967. Tracy received his ninth "Oscar" nomination for this film.

It happened one night in Hollywood on February 27, 1935. The "King's" peers crowned him Best Actor for his performance in **It Happened One Night,** now a movie classic.

CLARK GABLE

Born: February 1, 1901 Cadiz, Ohio

Clark Gable and his father, William Gable. Shown here in court where Clark was accused of fathering a child in England. The claimant, Violet Norton, was deported. Father stands by son. 1937.

"All the world's a stage, and all the men and women merely players: they have their exits and their entrances; and one man plays many parts, his act being in seven stages . . . "

Clark Gable's seven stages are best delineated through his female alliances and feminine influences: a mother, one step-mother, and five wives — mothers of another sort. The exits and entrances of the other players (a cast of hundreds) played their parts; some returned for encores; many played one scene and went into another play.

The first ten months of Gable's life were spent in constant companionship with his ailing mother, Addie Hershelmen Gable. Although bedridden a great deal of the time, she kept her only child with her: fondling him, playing with him, and caring for his every need. When she died at the age of 31, she left a void in his life he would try to fill for the rest of his.

His father, William Gable, found a suitable replacement, Jennie Dunlap, and married her a year and a month after the death of his first wife. In the interim, Clark was tended to by his mother's relatives, who doted on him as much as she had done; and then he was put in the care of Jennie. She, too, devoted all of her time to the only child she would ever have. Most of his young friends never knew that she was not his natural mother. She taught him about books and to make music, hoping someday he might even be a musician. She kept him meticulously clean and neat; a trait he would keep forever, even to the point of extremes. Whatever would become of Clark, one thing Jennie knew — he would not follow in his father's footsteps.

Will Gable was a hard-drinking wildcatter who made certain — whenever he was at home — that his only child would not be a sissy. Clark's lifetime interests of hunting, sports, and mechanics were developed through and with his father whom he alternately adored and despised. It was more the work that his father did, the abject poverty, and later the sixteen-hour day of hard labor that he disliked. Later, when Will abandoned the non-producing oil fields and bought a dirt farm, Clark (like Scarlett) vowed he would never be a part of that life. He would not labor nor languish in dirt, and when he made money he would save half of everything he made.

He quit high school in his third year and headed for the big city — Akron. He didn't know what he would do, but he surely knew what he wouldn't do. He was 18 years old when he saw his first movie in Akron. He also attended the theater for the first time. Now he knew what it was he wanted to do. He managed to get work in the local stock company, but the Depression forced him back home which had become Big Heart, Oklahoma. He stuck it out until the end of 1922, then headed west, and a ten-year separation from his father.

In Portland, Oregon, he managed to attach himself to the Astoria Stock Company. Clark was always comfortable with women, which now worked favorably for him, and he had his own "macho manifesto," which made him okay with the guys. He fell in love with the company's ingenue, Franz Dorfler, but her career was very important to her, and so she rejected his proposal of marriage. He then turned to Josephine Dillon, a teacher and coach, seventeen years his senior, who told him he *could* become an actor. Naturally he married her (1924) and accepted the martyr-type molding Josephine had in mind for him. Unfortunately for her, she fell in love with her Adonis. But true to her word, she kept at him, grooming him for her ultimate (and his) goal — Broadway.

Clark Gable's first love came to light during the Norton paternity suit in 1937. But he had fallen in love with actress Franz Dorfler, shown here with Assistant U.S. Attorney Jack Powell, in the early 1920's in Oregon. She rejected his proposal of marriage, and he turned to coach Josephine Dillon whom he married. Miss Dorfler testified on Gable's behalf. 1937.

Josephine Dillon, Gable's first wife, remembers as she looks at photograph of him taken while he was making his first film playing an extra bit. Shown here in 1960.

Gable's second wife, Ria (center) chatting with Claudette Colbert and Clark. 1932.

Josephine believed in work, and work he did. He played in various stock companies and made endless tours. He made a name for himself playing in Houston; first, second leads, then when the lead quit the company, Clark took over and became something of a matinee idol. Meanwhile Josephine was in New York cajoling producer Arthur Hopkins to give Clark a part in **Machinal** which starred Zita Johann. And meanwhile, Clark had attached himself to wealthy Ria Lucas Langham, also seventeen years his senior, with a ready-made family of two children.

His New York debut, 1928, was not auspicious, drawing reviews such as "Woolworth Romeo" and "vigorous and brutally masculine." Ria followed him to New York and began to refine her "zircon in the rough." She taught him how to dress, how to order and what to order in the posh restaurants, in other words what she was selling, he was buying. Naturally, she would be his next wife — stage four. Josephine went back to Hollywood and floated in and out of Clark's financial life thereafter.

Unable to get work in New York, Clark, Ria, and family returned to California where a big break was waiting for him. He played Killer Mears in **The Last Mile** in the West Coast production, having seen Spencer Tracy in the role on Broadway. Audiences that once rejected him, now sat upright as the "he-man" quality of Gable snarled out at them from his stage-cage; and agent Minna Wallis was quick to sign him on. Agents, secretaries, publicity people, directors, etc. plus the never-ending supply of women, these were the players: all important to him, and he was always important to them.

Minna Wallis got him a part in **Painted Desert** despite the fact that he had never been on a horse. But never let it be said that Gable was not a worker, a fast study, and considered a true professional throughout his film career. He learned to ride and learned to like the $750 a week he was earning, saddle sores et al. This was a far cry from the 50 cents a week he earned during the summer of his first job. After his initial film appearance, he was still thinking about the theater until Minna got him a one-year

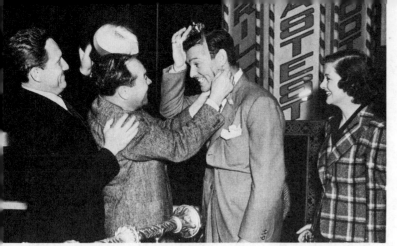

The original Killer Mears, good pal, Spencer Tracy (l) and close friend, MGM bigwig, E. J. Mannix, crown Gable, who played Killer Mears (1930) on the West Coast, on his birthday. Myrna Loy looks on. Hollywood, 1938.

contract at MGM for $650 a week. This was the beginning of a twenty-three year association with MGM where Clark Gable rose to unbelievable heights as its number one star and made millions for the studio and its head Louis Burt Mayer.

He made **The Easiest Way** which starred Constance Bennett and Robert Montgomery. He had his two front teeth (gold) fixed and went into **A Free Soul** with Lionel Barrymore who won an "Oscar" for his performance. Barrymore had long been in Gable's corner and many years before had tried to talk him into a film career. Gable garnered a few thousand fan letters from the film, and MGM went into high gear as it prepared its property for **Sporting Blood,** Gable's first starring role. The year — 1930 — and by 1937 there would be no bigger star in the heavens (or on earth) than Clark Gable.

By the time he won an "Oscar" (1935) for his performance in **It Happened One Night** with Claudette Colbert, also an "Oscar" winner, he had for the first time security — personal and financial. It was time to move on and find mother, stage five.

Perfection came wrapped up in blonde, beautiful, talented, gregarious, sports-loving, rich, star — Carole Lombard. And the final touch, she needed to *give.* Every motive in her life would be devoted to making her husband (after she got him) comfortable and happy. The other players, Ria, Marion Davies, Joan Crawford, etc., bit the dust, and in the case of Jean Harlow, it was **The Red Dust.**

Carole and Clark bought twenty-two

Skeet shooters meet on the Beverly Hills estate of John Barrymore (l) with Clark Gable, his guest. Known as MGM power. 1934.

(l-r) Norma Shearer Thalberg who had over forty films to her credit and whose husband, Irving Thalberg, is credited with discovering Gable; Mr. and Mrs. Ed. Mannix, MGM exec and close friends; and Gable at a birthday party for Marie Dressler, MGM star, then age 62. Hollywood, 1933.

On his thirty-sixth birthday in 1937, young MGM star Judy Garland sang a specially composed song for the occasion, "You Made Me Love You." L.B. Mayer cried, Gable was touched, and the song went into the film **Broadway Melodies of 1938,** where Judy sang it to a photo of Clark. Years later (1949) said Gable to Garland, "Goddamn brat. You've ruined every one of my birthdays. They bring you out from behind the wallpaper to sing that song, and it's a pain in the ass."

Gable and Carole Lombard in their first public appearance after Ria Gable announced her intention of a divorce. With them, Howard Strickling, publicity director for MGM and lifetime close friend of Gable's. 1939.

acres of land in the valley where every conceivable convenience was installed along with animals and fowl, making their ranch workable. The "valley" unlike Beverly Hills, was remote and allowed them privacy and "space, to do their thing:" parlance of the Seventies but applicable to the Thirties.

In 1939, Gable began the immortal marriage, and be began the immortal film **Gone With the Wind.** At first he was reluctant to play Rhett Butler, just as he had been reluctant to play Fletcher Christian in **Mutiny on the Bounty.** But **Bounty** brought him an "Oscar" nomination (he lost to Victor McLaglen in **The Informer**), so despite his fear of appearing as a "dandy" not as a "he-man," he agreed to play the role. In fact, fans across the nation practically dictated to the studio who would play the part. His major mistake was in not getting a percentage of the film. Always cautious about money, he did not realize until his break with MGM (a sort of parent) that he could have been earning a lot more money through percentage and through participation as a producer. But MGM was his family, and just as he had been the kingpin in his real family, he would not disturb the *status quo.* If Will Gable was a formidable father, alongside L. B. Mayer he was a pussycat.

In 1942, Carole Lombard Gable was killed in a plane crash. Friends, relatives, co-workers stood by and wondered if Clark Gable would survive. Psychologists have had a field day examining the "whys and wherefores." But Gable had been a survivor from the time his mother died, and he would remain a survivor. And as before, he would find the best way for him to survive. World War II gave him his *raison d'etre* and provided a script — a background — in which he could play a real-live hero. He enlisted as a non-com, went through the grueling Officer's Training School, managed to win the respect and camaraderie of his fellow army buddies, and emerged a hero with ribbons, medals, and prestige. This turning point in his life displayed the true guts in the character of Gable. Never a character actor on-screen, although he often wished he could emulate his idol Spencer Tracy, he played himself throughout this ordeal.

Lionel Barrymore (seated) being feted on his 61st birthday by MGM luminaries. (l-r)Norma Shearer and Rosalind Russell, Mickey Rooney, Robert Montgomery, Gable; MGM mogul, Louis B. Mayer, and Robert Taylor. Barrymore was an early booster of Gable and may have been responsible for his initial screen test. Culver City. 1939.

Gable and third wife Carole Lombard at premiere of **Gone With the Wind** in Atlanta, Georgia. 1939.

(l-r) Vivien Leigh (Scarlett); Clark Gable (Rhett); author Margaret Mitchell; producer David Selznick; and Olivia De Haviland (Melanie) at the opening of **Gone With The Wind,** in Atlanta, Georgia. 1939.

Captain Clark Gable during a press interview. He had won the Air Medal for "exceptionally meritorious achievements" in five bomber missions in the European war (WWII) theatre when he manned a Flying Fortress gun. Washington, D.C., 1943.

(l-r) Capt. Gable; Mrs. Walter Lang, secretary to Carole Lombard Gable; actress Irene Dunn; and producer Louis B. Mayer at the launching of the 10,500-ton Liberty ship, S.S. **Carole Lombard.** Wilmington, California, 1944.

A quick look back at the cast of characters: (r-l) Doug Fairbanks, Jr. (married to Joan Crawford, who had a love affair with Gable and a long friendship); onlookers, Robert Montgomery and wife; Crawford; Doug Fairbanks, Sr. who married Lady Sylvia Ashley, Gable's fourth wife; Gable and his second wife Ria. 1932.

Relaxing on the slopes, Gable and friends take time off between films. His first after WWII was **Adventure,** with Greer Garson. The slogan was "Gable's back and Garson has him." (l-r) Mrs. Gary Cooper, Jack Hemingway, Ingrid Bergman, Gary Cooper and Gable. Sun Valley, Idaho, 1946.

Author Arthur Miller (Marilyn Monroe's husband) and Gable talking things over off the set of **The Misfits.** Nevada, 1960.

Gable and fourth wife Lady Sylvia Ashley Stanley, widow of Douglas Fairbanks, Sr. Gable had been a widower for about seven years (Carole Lombard) but not without numerous lady friends. Solvang, California, 1949.

Kay Williams Spreckels Gable, fifth wife of Clark, and their son, John Clark Gable, born after his father's death. Encino, California, 1961.

(l-r) Pallbearers Spencer Tracy; Robert Taylor; E.J. Mannix, close friend and MGM executive; Jimmy Stewart. Kay Gable and Chaplain Johnson E. West, USAF of March Air Force Base (center) leaving the church after military services for Clark Gable. Glendale, California, 1960.

Final resting place for Clark Gable inside the "Great Mausoleum" on the grounds of the Forest Lawn Memorial Park. He was entombed in a crypt beside the remains of his third wife, Carole Lombard, inside the mausoleum. Glendale, California, 1960.

After the war was over, he moved from female to female rather than from film to film. He yearned to be married again; to try and find that peaceful existence again. He was by now over forty, and despite efforts to appear young, he was getting flabby from hard-drinking and a bit frivolous in his motorcycle flights of speed — an innovation of the youth prior to *speed*.

Stage six was set in his search when he married (1949) Lady Sylvia Ashley, widow of Douglas Fairbanks, Sr., Mary Pickford's ex. Lady Sylvia appeared like a good choice as she enjoyed all of the things Clark did, but she enjoyed them on another level. She was chic, indoctrinated into British society, even though she was *low born* by their standards, but she brought too much change to the ranch where Clark was no longer the star. If their eighteen months of marriage did one thing, it taught Gable what he didn't want.

And so the final stage of his life was now set. He married Kay Williams Spreckels (1954), divorced, mother of two, and previously, a movie starlet. She was rich, beautiful, and had the one quality he needed — she, like Carole, would give him the attention he needed; together they would face the maturing years with peace and stability.

He allowed his age to shine through on-screen and off. He happily assumed the father role for her two children, something he had not been ready for with Ria's children, and now broken with MGM, he set off to make independent films as a free-lancer.

His last film, **The Misfits**, clearly showed the mature Gable. Playwright Arthur Miller many times discussed the maturity, expertise, and total control Clark Gable had over himself and his work. There, in the barren windswept land of Nevada, Gable was thrust into the neuroses of Marilyn Monroe; the disturbed methods of "Method" actor Montgomery Clift; and the nightly high jinx stunts of director, John Huston. Gable emerged as "the leader and guiding spirit of the production." He walked away from **The Misfits** feeling it was the second most important film (to him) in his life: **Gone With the Wind** was the first.

Clark Gable really had a good life. He achieved his desire to be an actor and achieved what he never dreamed of — as an actor, he reigned supreme; he had the love and devotion of many people; he made vast sums of money, which allayed his fear of poverty; and he was blessed with good health to the accompaniment of great physical beauty. The only thing he missed was the birth of his only child, a son, born months after his death.

In her book, *Long Live the King**, author Lyn Tornabene, sensitively and with great insight about her subject, put Gable's death into proper perspective, "Always the right man for each of his three public decades . . . glamor personified in the depressed Thirties, bereaved hero in the war-shaped Forties, Established American in the Eisenhower Fifties. He wouldn't have fitted into the violent decades that followed his death."

His death was not violent. He died quietly and calmly, and mercifully did not suffer from a lingering illness. He was buried in a crypt next to Carole Lombard.

CLARK GABLE
Died: November 16, 1960

* Lyn Tornabene, **Long Live the King** (New York: G. P. Putnam's Sons and Pocket Books).

Gable and Joan Crawford in his third film, **Dance Fools, Dance.** They had an on again, off again love affair but remained friends until his death. She said Gable had "more sheer animal magic than anyone in the world and every woman knew it." 1931.

Gable and Greta Garbo in **Susan Lenox: Her Fall and Rise.** This was their only film together (to the relief of all involved), but Garbo demanded him for the movie. The combination proved to be a Russian "Cleopatra" with an American "Little Caesar." 1931.

Gable and Claudette Colbert in **It Happened One Night.** Both won the "Oscar" for their performances. The feat was not repeated until 1975 when Jack Nicholson and Louise Fletcher both won for **One Flew Over the Cuckoo's Nest. Night** also captured Best Director, Best Film, and Best Writer. 1934.

(l-r) Lorraine Kreuger, Bernadene Hayes, Joan Marsh, Clark Gable, Paula Stone, Virginia Dale, and Virginia Grey, longstanding girlfriend of Gable's, in **Idiot's Delight.** Originally done on Broadway with Alfred Lunt and Lynn Fontanne, Gable filled the (role) shoes of "Harry, the hoofer" with amazing ease and great comedic talent. Norma Shearer was his co-star. 1939.

Twenty-one year old Jean Harlow, famous for her lack of underwear (as well as Norma Shearer) and Gable in movie **Red Dust,** considered quite erotic for its day. 1932.

Gable as Rhett Butler, Vivien Leigh as Scarlett O'Hara in **Gone With The Wind,** Gable's first Technicolor film (seven cameras). It was also his first "cry" on camera (maybe in life). He lost the "Oscar" to Robert Donat in **Goodbye, Mr. Chips.** Three directors were used: George Cukor, Victor Fleming, and Sam Wood. Fleming picked up the "Oscar" for Best Director, Vivien Leigh for Best Actress, and producer Selznick for Best Picture. 1939.

Gable glaring at Charles Laughton (in hat) in **Mutiny on the Bounty.** Gable feared playing the role of Fletcher Christian, because he thought it was unmanly. But he was talked into it, was nominated for an "Oscar," but lost to Paul Muni in **The Story of Louis Pasteur.** However, the film won Best Film and MGM made a lot of money. 1935.

Gable, Rosalind Russell, and Peter Lorre in **They Met in Bombay.** Not a noteworthy film, but the stars romped through the dismal script with professionalism. 1941.

Gable and Lana Turner in **Honky Tonk.** Writer Lyn Tornabene described them as "sex-kitten and tomcat," and that says it all. Jealous wife, Carole Lombard, was barred from the set. 1941.

Anne Baxter and Gable in **Homecoming.** This was made post WWII and after Carole Lombard's death. John Hodiak (real-life husband of Anne Baxter) and Lana Turner rounded out the cast. 1948.

Gable and Ava Gardner in **Mogambo** (1953), shot on location in Africa. Once Ava said she wanted to land the "King," but when he was free, she was married to —#1-Mickey Rooney; #2- Artie Shaw; and at this time #3- Frank Sinatra.

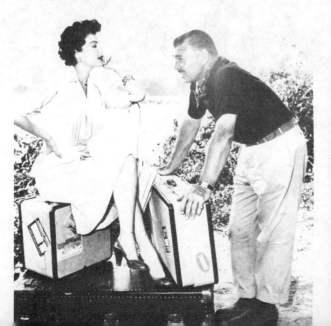

Louis Calhern and Gable in **Betrayed.** This was Gable's swan song with MGM after twenty-three years. The "King" didn't abdicate, he just took his crown with him. 1954.

Gable and Eleanor Parker in **The King and Four Queens.** Jane Russell, husband Bob Waterfield, and Gable formed a production company to make this film. It was considered "tawdry" and not worthy of the aging "King." 1956.

Gable and Burt Lancaster in **Run Silent, Run Deep.** Back in 1937 fans had seen Gable die on-screen in **Parnell.** Now, twenty-one years later, he died again in this film. 1958.

(l-r) Gable, Marilyn Monroe, and Montgomery Clift, (all deceased) in **The Misfits,** The "King's" last picture. The picture was an ordeal from beginning to end, but end it did finally on November 4th. Clark died twelve days later. 1961.

John Wayne, crimefighter, war-time hero, yes. But
first, last, and always, America's cowboy personified,
and its number one hero.

JOHN WAYNE

BORN: May 26, 1907 Winterset, Iowa

AUTHOR'S PREFACE

For the reader who has been following the text in order, my close friendship with Joan Benny Blumofe was established in the chapter on her father, Jack Benny. Therefore, it follows that during my life in Southern California, I would, through this friendship, meet many members of the film colony. Through Joan I met the Waynes. And throughout the years living in Los Angeles, I spent a good deal of time with Duke and Pilar, his third wife. As Chapter IV on Jack Benny commences with one of the many phone calls between Joan and me, so does this one. And my introduction to Duke.

"Spend the weekend playing bridge at the John Waynes? Are you mad? You know I'm a Democrat!"

"They're not interested in your politics, Pat, just your bridge prowess. They are real buffs and anxious to meet you. I'll pick you up in an hour."

And so I met the Waynes. Many times I've been asked—"Well, what about politics? What's he like?" Naturally, I formed my own, quite simple, opinion. To me, he was the product of his screen roles or his screen roles were the result of the man. They were as interchangeable as a palindrome.

He was kind to and appreciative of women. He was tougher on and towards men; he expected more, in a different way, from them. He was strong, unafraid, tough, could drink and brawl with the best; yet he was kind, gentle and devoted to his family. And he was loyal. One has only to peruse the film credits from his earliest to his later ones to see that the same names keep appearing and re-appearing through the decades. For example, character actor George "Gabby" Hayes appears in **From Riders of Destiny** *(1933), and eleven times til 1936. And in 1940, his name is still in a Wayne film. Ward Bond, Harry Carey, Harry Carey, Jr., and Yakima Cunutt (one of Duke's oldest and closest pals) are other examples. His loyalty can be labeled legendary*

In Europe during the 15th and 16th centuries, "morality plays" flourished. Their characters, the personification of good and evil, were usually involved with man's struggle for survival and for his soul. The greatest English "morality" was called Everyman. Europe's appreciation of Americana (ahead of ours) stems from this. John Wayne was the personification of Americana. When Walt Disney was trying desperately to understand why companies weren't lining up to buy Mickey Mouse series after the success of **Steamboat Willie**, *a very wise, show-biz veteran, Harry Reichenbach explained it, "Those guys don't know what's good until the public tells them."*

And John Wayne once said, "Nobody likes my acting except the people."

It amounts to the same thing.

Every generation will discover the mighty Western and will uncover and re-discover the Western's Everyman...John Wayne.

JOHN WAYNE

Marion Michael Morrison was tagged "Duke" long before he became John Wayne. The story goes that he and his dog "Big Duke" were inseparable, and so why not call them by the same name: one Big and one Little. "Big Duke" eventually went to dog heaven and "Little" became just plain "Duke" as he went on to heaven on earth.

In the beginning the "Dukes" lived in the desert town of Lancaster, California. Today with superhighways, Lancaster is just over an hour's drive from Los Angeles. But in those days it was a homesteaders' outpost, as barren as its neighbor the Mojave Desert. Little Duke hated it: hated the rough life and hated the snakes that abounded on Morrison property. But even as a child, he was proud and fierce and refused to give in to unmanly behavior.

Prior to moving to Lancaster, the family lived in Iowa. His father, Clyde, a pharmacist, was forced to move west because of bad health. Duke, aged five, his younger brother, Bob, and his mother, Mary, followed Clyde to the wilderness where they endured the rugged Lancaster life. Shortly thereafter, Clyde's health improved and the family moved to Glendale, just a spit away from the studios of Hollywood.

Although Duke participated in school plays, he was more famous for the plays he was making on the high school football team. But neither plays were his ultimate goal. He had his heart set on the Naval Academy in Annapolis, Maryland. However, there were other plans in store for him. The closest he ever got to the Academy was in an early film, **Salute** (1929), where he played the brother of West Point cadet, George O'Brien, with the typical rivalry between the two schools and their football teams. This, his third film, although of no consequence, put him close to director John Ford, who would play an important part in his life.

The wild Wayne spirit erupted after his rejection. Before settling into another school, he took off on an ocean liner bound for Honolulu. Wayne always loved the water. After he became successful, one of his own boats was a converted mine sweeper, *The Wild Goose*, which he used to entertain guests. He also used it for another Wayne sport, fishing expeditions.

Duke was a good student in school and only barely missed the cutoff at Annapolis, but was rewarded with a football scholarship at USC, the University of Southern California. There he distinguished himself on one of the Trojans' fine teams.

His father's business, as so many others,

Duke was always a good student, but his entrance to USC was on an athletic scholarship. Circa 1928.

John Wayne and director, John Ford. Wayne said, "Ford taught me **not** to act for the camera but to **react**." Ford died in 1973.

was failing during this Depression era, and so Duke jumped at the chance for a summer job. Western star, Tom Mix, an avid football fan, promised Trojan coach, Howard Jones, jobs for his boys if Jones got him good seats. And so Duke joined what is called "the swing gang" at Fox Studios. For $35.00 a week, the gang moved props, furniture, etc. from one set to another.

During one of his clean-up jobs on the set after the shooting was over, he was tossing the fake snow (corn flakes) off the tip of his broom when he was spotted by director John Ford. Ford used him briefly in three films in the 20's and one in the 30's. It would be another eleven years before Duke would get the call from Ford to make **Stagecoach,** the film that launched him as a star.

Meanwhile back on the back lot, John Wayne was born because Fox did not think Marion Morrison suited a gun-slinger-stuntman. Director Raoul Walsh, at the suggestion of Ford, put Duke in **The Big Trail** (1930) with another new face—Tyrone Power. Before Wayne left Fox, he made what he considered "the worst film I ever made," **Girls Demand Excitement** (1931). When Duke returned to Fox, twenty years later, he came back as a big star.

From the time he exited until Ford called him, his career moved up and down. At one point it went so far downhill that Duke called the Westerns "Z" films. But they were actually "B" films. He scraped along, grinding out one after another, until Republic Pictures was born in 1935, and the decision was made to upgrade its star and its Westerns. During this period Wayne was gaining in-

A typical barroom brawl with Duke in the middle of it. With close friend, Yakima Canutt, they perfected the on-screen fight technique. Shown here with Howard Keel as the Indian in typical fight scene from **The War Wagon.** 1966.

Duke taking a rest after shooting of above scene, obviously satisfied with the result. 1966.

DUKE ON THE RECEIVING END

The American Legion award for "serving the country in the proper manner in the pictures they have made." (l-r) John Wayne, Walter Pigeon, and Ward Bond. Miami, 1951.

Harvard University's **Lampoon** magazine invited the star to Cambridge. Ten-block parade route offered a few hurled snowballs along the way. 1974.

Frank Sinatra presents the Scopus Awards on behalf of the American Friends of the Hebrew University to Nobel Laureates Milton Friedman, (l) Dr. Baruch S. Blumberg, (r) and to actor John Wayne. Los Angeles, 1977.

valuable experience, and one "invaluable" person rode into his life: rodeo rider-stuntman, Yakima Canutt. Wayne learned how to really ride from him, how to fall off of a horse; he copied his gait and his speech; together they worked at perfecting the barroom brawls. The classic movie fight, which many think has never been improved on, was made in 1914, **The Spoilers,** between William Farnum and Tom Santschi. It was given a full reel so great was its authenticity. In 1922, Milton Sills and Noah Beery fought in the first re-make; in 1930, Paramount engaged Farnum and Santschi to coach Gary Cooper and William Boyd in the second re-make. By the time John Wayne and Randolph Scott got around to the third version, Duke and Canutt had been perfecting the fight technique. Today every battle reflects their years of work.

When John Wayne got the nod from John Ford in 1939, he was ready. The tradition of Westerns had been set with **The Great Train Robbery.** The first Western star, Gilbert M. Anderson, "Broncho Billy" as he was known on the screen, had established that the hero would be difficult to displace. In good times or bad, Westerns were known to play around the country successfully except in the top-grossing theaters of the major cities, where they were considered box-office poison. Until John Wayne. He became the nation's top male figure—favorite. Later two Westerns, not Wayne's, went on to become classics: **High Noon** and **Treasure of Sierra Madre.** The formula—quite simple, "It (the Western) remains the foundation for all complex storytelling rhetoric the movies have ever developed. Whatever the plot is saying, Westerns move."* But it was John Wayne who epitomized the American Western and its hero.

Richard Griffith and Arthur Mayer, **The Movies** (New York: Simon and Schuster).

Between scenes of shooting **The Townsend Harris Story,** director John Huston "acts" for John Wayne as he reads a letter from home. Said Duke, "He's the best actor on the set!" Kyoto, Japan, 1958. (Film released under title of **The Barbarian and The Geisha**)

WWII and John Wayne war films were almost inseparable. Shown here **They Were Expendable.** 1945.

"Hopalong" John Wayne maneuvering on crutches after he injured his foot in a fall but went right back to work. On location of **The Legend of the Lost.** Tripoli, Libya. 1957.

John Wayne with Panamanian leader Brig. General Omar Torrijos during the U.S. Senate Foreign Relations Committee meeting about naval passage rights in the Canal and clarification of the amendments to the treaty of U.S. defense. Wayne went to see what, then, Gov. Ronald Reagan, was talking about. Panama, 1978.

Big Duke on Little Merv's TV show — "The Merv Griffin Show". Circa late Sixties.

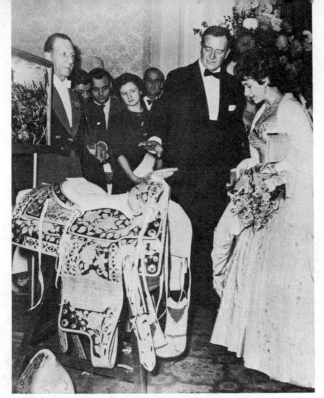

At the premiere of **The Alamo,** Duke presents Princess Margaret with a silver-mounted western saddle, crafted by a Texan. London, 1960.

Duke and wife, Pilar, leaving hospital after winning the first round of his bout with cancer. Los Angeles, 1964.

Bob Hope (l) joined by John Wayne and Bing Crosby for NBC-TV's presentation of "Texaco presents a Quarter-Century of Bob Hope." Hollywood, 1975.

Duke checking out the Technicolor-Panavision camera as co-director with Ray Kellogg in **The Green Berets.** 1968.

WWII and Wayne films seem as inseparable as Duke and his dog. One, **Sands of Iwo Jima,** brought peer recognition: an "Oscar" nomination. **They Were Expendable** and **Back to Bataan** were big money makers. By 1949, John Wayne had not been off the studio's payroll since 1929. He had gone from "Z" to "A" in more than twenty-two years of filmmaking.

In 1960, he produced and directed **The Alamo,** using his own money (reported to be in the vicinity of 12 million) and almost went bankrupt. So at age 52, he began to grind out more Westerns, and again became big, big box office. Duke turned to directing once more in **The Green Berets** (1964) at a time when Vietnam was a highly volatile subject. Despite its jingoistic slant, the film made money and caused one writer aptly to remark, "It should have been reviewed as a film, not the critic's view on the war." Both Johns, Wayne and Ford, have been called "too American" in their filmmaking from time to time.

101

Duke, Pilar, and their first child, daughter Aissa Maria, at age 6, in Honolulu, 1962. Aissa married Bruce Alan Berman in April of 1981 in Honolulu

At right Duke and his first wife, Josephine Saenz, in wedding photo. 1933. At left, Duke and second wife Esperanza Baur, applying for wedding license. 1946.

Duke and son Pat, age 15, on the set but in different films. Pat in **Mister Roberts** and Dad in **The Sea Chase.** Hollywood, 1954.

Duke and his youngest son, John Ethan, age 8, discussing the script of **The Million Dollar Kidnapping.** John Ethan made his screen debut playing Duke's grandson. Durango, Mexico, 1970. (This was Wayne's 144th film.)

Daughter, Melinda Ann, and proud Papa John, prior to the wedding of Melinda and Gregory R. Munoz. Hollywood, 1964.

Duke, 46, and third wife, Pilar Palette, 21, after the marriage ceremony held in the former home of King Kamehameha III in Kalua, Hawaii. 1954.

Duke waving from the Grand Marshall's car in the 84th Tournament of Roses Parade. Seated with him, wife Pilar and daughter Marissa. In front, son John Ethan and daughter Aissa. Pasadena, Calif. 1973. (USC beat Ohio State 42 to 17.)

Duke gestures, ''Go get 'em,'' to little Ricky Schroder, star of **The Champ** as Shirley Jones and Sammy Davis Jr. look on. This was Duke's first public appearance after his cancer surgery. He presented the ''Oscar'' at the Academy Awards for the Best Picture, **The Deer Hunter.** April 1979.

At 60, the big man was still going strong. He had licked cancer in 1964 when half a lung was removed. He was now heavier in bulk than most stars; his voice had grown huskier and more gravel-toned, but he was up there on the screen bigger than life. Finally he was rewarded with an "Oscar" for his portrayal of Rooster Cogburn in **True Grit,** considered by many to be his finest performance.

Duke married three times: each a Latin beauty. His first wife, Josephine Saenz, was the daughter of a Panamanian diplomat. They had four children, two sons and two daughters. Michael has been a producer on many of his father's films, while Patrick has played various roles opposite his dad. This marriage ended in 1946; the same year he married Mexican actress Esperanza "Chata" Baur, from whom he was divorced in 1953. In 1954 he married Peruvian beauty, Pilar Pallette, and started another family; Aissa, John Ethan, and Marissa. One day I asked Pilar about the meaning of Aissa's name, and she confided that she had made it up, but "don't tell Duke," she added. Yet had he known he would have enjoyed the joke on him. For his sense of humor was as big as everything else about him. When I asked him to endorse my first book, one on the subject of bridge, the card game, he readily agreed. But knowing how stuffy my Boston publisher was, he left out a word. His endorsement read, "You Can Play With Me Anytime." The publisher inserted the word "bridge" after "play." But it was typical of his humor.

Duke went into the hospital for routine gall bladder surgery, but it turned into a nine hour operation. He had had open heart surgery just the year before. The big man lost the last fight to cancer at the age of 72, but he went down swinging.

The day of his funeral I overheard someone say, "Somehow I don't feel as safe with John Wayne not around." Duke would have liked that.

JOHN WAYNE
Died: June 11, 1979
Los Angeles, California.

UCLA Medical Center spokesman, Bernard Strohm, at press interview where he revealed the news of Duke's spreading cancer. Sons, Pat Wayne (l) and Michael Wayne (r) stand by stoically. 1979.

One of the many tributes to Duke was a memorial luncheon held by Senator John Warner in the nation's Capitol. (l-r) Pat Wayne, Michael Wayne, Senator Warner, and his wife, Elizabeth Taylor. March 1980.

Behind every big grin, there's an even bigger sense of humor. At least it was so with Duke.

(l-r) George Bancroft, John Wayne, Andy Devine, and Francis Ford in **Stagecoach.** 1939. This film made Duke a star.

John Wayne in his eighth film, **The Big Trail.** 1930.

Duke in **Adventure's End,** his fifty-eighth film. 1937.

(l-r) Raymond Hatton, John Wayne, and Ray Corrigan in **Wyoming Outlaw.** 1939. In 1936, Republic Pictures started one of the best series of Westerns with **The Three Mesquiteers.** This photo is from one of the series which continued after Wayne returned to the studio. He had been on loan to Universal for five films.

(l-r) Ray Milland, Paulette Goddard, Susan Hayward, and John Wayne in Cecil B. DeMille's spectacular, **Reap the Wild Wind.** 1942.

John Wayne, age 38, and Ann Dvorak, age 33, in **Flame of Barbary Coast.** 1945. Butterfly ("I don't know nothing 'bout birthin' babies, Miz Scarlett.") McQueen was also in this film.

Louise Allbritton and John Wayne in **Pittsburgh.** 1942.

George "Gabby" Hayes, John Wayne, and Martha Scott in **In Old Oklahoma,** later titled, **War of the Wildcats.** 1943.

Charles Winninger, John Wayne, age 36 and Jean Arthur, age 35, in **A Lady Takes A Chance.** 1943.

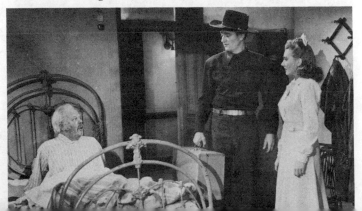

Don DeFore, Claudette Colbert, and Duke in **Without Reservations.** 1946.

John Wayne, Lauren Bacall, and Mike Mazurki in **Blood Alley.** 1955.

John Wayne and the beautiful Susan Hayward, who died in 1975, as they appeared in **The Conqueror.** 1956.

(l-r) Duke, Elizabeth Allen, Dorothy Lamour, and Lee Marvin in **Donovan's Reef.** 1963.

John Wayne and Rita Hayworth, then age 46, in **Circus World.** 1964.

John Wayne in **The Cowboys.** 1972.

John Wayne and Patricia Neal in **In Harm's Way.** 1965.

John Wayne and Ann-Margret in **The Train Robbers.** 1973.

Lauren Bacall and Duke in his last film **The Shootist.** 1976.

John Wayne in his "Oscar" winning performance as Rooster Cogburn in **True Grit.** He was tough, colorful, and up against tough competition with youngster co-star, Kim Darby, yet Duke stole the film right from under everyone's nose. 1969.

ARCHETYPAL ACTORS

ACTORS

THE WOMEN

The secret of success is constancy
to purpose.

Disraeli

Mary Pickford — America's Sweetheart, Queen of Hollywood, Film Heroine, Shaper of the Motion Picture Industry, Astute Business Woman. 1920.

MARY PICKFORD

Born: April 8, 1893 Toronto, Canada

When fifteen-year old Mary Pickford knocked on the door of Biograph Company, it was opened by their only director, David Wark Griffith, aged 33. Together and separately, they would lay the foundation of the motion picture industry. D.W. Griffith's work would turn the nickelodeon cheapness of flicks into an art form; Mary would create the star system, and with her second husband, Douglas Fairbanks, create America's Royalty. She was to become the most powerful woman in the history of film.

By the time she was five years old, Gladys Marie Smith (Mary Pickford) was on the stage where she assumed the financial responsibility for the entire family. And this would continue until her death.

Her father, John "Jack" Charles Smith, ran a candy counter in Toronto but barely managed to eke out a living. Little Gladys adored her father, who died when she was four, leaving her mother, Charlotte, a widow at twenty-four. Yet Charlotte was astute enough to recognize the potential of Gladys's good looks as a way out of their poverty stricken existence. By then two other children had been born, Lottie and Jack, Jr. Charlotte Pickford Hennessey Smith became the epitome of the term "stage mother" and remained the dominant force in Mary's life. Wherever Mary went the others followed, attempting similar careers; whatever Mary earned went into a common family money pot. Ultimately Mary made them all quite wealthy.

The first role Gladys played was a dual one: a girl in the first act, a boy in the last act. Little did she know that one day she would re-create the feat by playing **Little Lord Fauntleroy** and the mother in the movie of the same title, 1921. This stands as one of her finest performances.

After working in various stock companies for $10.00 a week, the family headed for New York City in 1900. Mary got work, and

Little Gladys Smith of Toronto before she assumed the grown-up responsibility of supporting her family. Canada, 1897.

by 1902-3 she was out on tour again in **The Fatal Wedding.** About the same time, a seventeen-year old Douglas Fairbanks and his mother had left Denver, also for the big city and a stage career. Another family with whom the Smiths were to become friendly, a mother and two daughters, was also in New York attempting the stage life, Dorothy and Lillian Gish.

By 1904, Gladys announced that she was through with touring, tired of cheap hotels and bad food, and that she was going to make it on Broadway. Through sheer determination and guts, she wangled an audition with producer David Belasco and wound up on the stage in **The Warrens of Virginia.** Belasco changed her name, plucking Pickford from Gladys's mother's assortment of names as well as Mary. Lottie and Jack also became Pickfords. Down the street, on Broadway, Douglas Fairbanks was also playing. He, too, had undergone a name change. Originally, Douglas Ulman, he took his mother's first husband's name of Fairbanks.

Within two years of her auspicious stage debut, she became, at age 15, too old to play children and too young to play ingenues. And so she turned to movies. Mary, as most serious stage actors, felt this work was demeaning. At the time only the poorer classes attended the nickelodeon flicks. One, they could afford it; and two, it was an escape from their otherwise dreary existences. The more affluent patronized the stage productions. And yet, it was these "poorer folk" who became discriminating about what they saw and whom they preferred seeing. They began to recognize the difference between a Griffith movie and an also-ran, and they demanded to know who the little girl with the golden curls was. Perforce, Griffith began labeling his films, and Mary insisted on billing: a first in the business. Throughout this book the reader will see the public's demands met, as in the case of Walt Disney and John Wayne, both of whom had tremendous public appeal long before the critics and studio heads acknowledged their work.

Meanwhile, back at Biograph, Griffith did Mary's makeup for her screen test, as two other Biograph employees stood by. Mack Sennett was one; and actor Owen Moore, who later became Mary's first husband was the other. Griffith had come to Biograph after twelve years as an actor and playwright. He, too, used another name, Lawrence Griffith, until he felt his work warranted his real name. This came about when the decision was made to have a director. Until then, the actors improvised the scripts as well as their costumes, applied their own makeup, and for $5.00 a day, just ambled in front of the camera following their improvised story lines. When Griffith moved from behind the camera and away from the lights, he became the director.

Mary, as an extra, played on-screen for the first time in **Her First Biscuits:** a 7-minute, split-reel, which took one day to shoot. Full reels took two days! At 16, she got her first leading part in **The Violin Maker,** and

They met in 1908 when she was fifteen and he was thirty-three. Now 28 years later, D.W. Griffith hands Mary Pickford a gold-plated box ticket for the 55th Annual Actor's Fund Benefit, which she had helped to establish. 1936.

Griffith, pleased with her work, gave her a contract for $40.00 a week.

By 1910, Mary had done 26 additional films, Griffith had made 142, and Douglas Fairbanks, Sr. had made Douglas Fairbanks, Jr. Most of the shooting was done in New Jersey where the terrain offered more contrast and allowed the restless Griffith to be more expansive. In the studio, he had already expanded his technique. He knew that moving pictures had to follow its own formula, not copy the one used on the stage. He had, by then, departed from the "one scene-one shot" method by changing the position of the camera. He had changed the actors' entrances and exits by having them walk directly toward the camera or enter from behind it. He did what is called cross-cutting or parallel editing—back and forth—to create tension. He had also developed close-ups, medium and long range shots, which in turn accounted for the public's changing demands. Now with close-ups, they could read the actor's thoughts, reflect on their expressions, and dwell on the faces they liked. Everything we take for granted today was revolutionary in 1909. Although the fade-out was the result of an accident, still Griffith and his camerman, Billy Bitzer, recognized its potential.

Now armed with his techniques, the restless Griffith took his company to California. There he made **Ramona** with his child star, Mary Pickford. Another first happened: the company paid the book publisher for the screen rights. The fee—$100.

Mary, besides her acting, had begun selling storylines to Biograph for $15.00 per. When they turned her down, she sold them to competing companies for $20 or $25 per story. Mack Sennett, aware of Mary's encroaching fame, paid her $5.00 per just to use her name on his scripts. When he approached her with a story about a lot of policemen running amuck, Mary refused. "Distasteful," she told him. Hence, Mary missed out on the Keystone Kops. It was one of her few errors in judgment.

One of her last films before she left Biograph was **The Informer,** which turned out to be the pre-epic for Griffith's great, but controversial, **Birth of a Nation.**

In 1912, Biograph broke up. Although Mary and Griffith had mutual respect for one another's work, their aims were not the same. His was on film for film's sake; hers, on being in control and emphasis on the star. Mack Sennett and young actress, Mabel Normand, went on to form Keystone, and Griffith went his own way. Mary returned to the stage briefly where she played **A Good Little Devil** with unknown Clare Boothe (Mrs. Henry Luce) as her standby.

Under the aegis of Adolph Zukor, founder of Famous Players, which later became Paramount Pictures and Paramount Co. as the distributor, Mary returned to film. Zukor bought the rights to **A Good Little Girl** and gave in to Mary's financial demands which started with $500 a week and then $1,000 a week. Zukor was a wise old bird, and he knew he had a star, even though the film was a disaster. Unlike the Griffith movies, this was static; they had tried to reproduce the stage version. But Zukor believed in the star system, and he believed in Mary. By the time **Hearts Adrift** and **Tess of the Storm Country** came out, Mary was firmly established as a big star. Zukor even had the know-how to put her name in blazing lights above the theater's marquee.

1915 saw **Birth of a Nation** open at $1.00 per ticket, and Mary Pickford's salary went to $4,000 a week against 50% of Famous Players total profit. And she met Douglas Fairbanks.

A year later, at the age of 23, she was the highest paid woman and the star who had the most control of her films. She formed Mary Pickford Famous Players and her own distributing outfit, Artcraft. She stayed with Zukor for five and a half years before starting her own company.

The Pickford image, the little girl with the golden curls, the little girl with the smudge on her face who defended the poor and underprivileged, the Cinderella image, first America's Sweetheart, then, the World's Sweetheart, was forced to retain this facade for most of her acting life. At age 24, she played a ten-year old in **The Poor Little Rich**

Mary in the Thirties.

Girl, one of her finest films. She played **Pollyanna, Rebecca of Sunnybrook Farm,** and in **Stella Maris,** she shrewdly played both the ugly, poor cockney girl and the crippled-confined-to-bed-for-life, wealthy girl. Sometimes, to keep the effect of her child-look, the furniture and actors were over-sized to make her look smaller.

But in 1919, it was again D.W. Griffith who really knew how to preserve the youthful appearance. He put black maline over the camera's lens and kept Mary Pickford, Lillian Gish, and others looking 12 when they were 25.

As shrewd as she was off-screen, apparently her mastery of pantomime and her non-saccharine portrayals on-screen were innocent. She was deprived of being a child in real life, and one can only surmise that she lived out on film all that she had missed as a toddler. Even her schooling was brief: six or seven months in a two-year period was all she ever received. Later, as an adult, she hired a French instructor who rode to and from the studio teaching Mary. Her desire to improve herself never quit. But still in the record books, one notes that Pickford played the little girl from 1917 when she was 24 until 1926 when she was 31.

In 1920, America's Sweetheart, now divorced from Owen, and America's All-American Boy, also divorced, were married. Douglas, with the help of youngster writer Anita Loos and her husband, writer/director, John Emerson, was established as the clean-living, muscles of steel. He was Mr. Average Man with Superman powers in roles such as **The Three Musketeers** and **The Mark of Zorro.** His abiding concern with his physicality and leaping hyena antics found an outlet that put him just a few rungs under Mary and Chaplin on film. Yet his finest contributions went somewhat unnoticed. When in 1919 he, Mary, Chaplin, and Griffith formed their own company, United Artists, it was Doug who brought in Joseph Schenk to head administrative affairs. And Schenk brought with him Constance and Norma Talmadge, Glora Swanson, Buster Keaton, and John Barrymore. In the Thirties, when things looked pretty bad in the industry, it was Doug who brought in Darryl Zanuck. And when Griffith began to fail, it was Doug who eased him out. He was also the first president of the newly formed Academy of Motion Pictures Arts and Sciences, 1927.

Doug had the famous "Pickfair" built for his bride as a wedding present. From there they reigned as America's Royalty. Their fame was world-wide, their studio one of the most successful, their love for one another could have been another movie script. Alas, just like a movie script, it did not end happily, but it did end dramatically.

Mary and Douglas were divorced in 1936. When Douglas lept into the arms of Sylvia Ashley, wife of Lord Ashley, Mary found solace in the arms of budding star, Buddy Rogers, who had appeared in the "Oscar" winning film, **Wings** (1927). America's Sweetheart married America's Boyfriend in 1937, and their film together, **My Best Girl,** established him as a star.

Douglas died in 1939, six months after Owen Moore, Mary's first husband, had died. Douglas died on Owen's birthday. Mary thought this was an omen of sorts as she was slowly becoming interested in spiritual meanderings and later Christian Science. Her original religious training had been as a Methodist and a Catholic.

The rest of her family all came to an early demise long before Mary. Charlotte died in 1927, but she did die rich. Sister Lottie married four times, lost her child, Gwynne, in a custody suit to Charlotte and Douglas, and died at age 42 (1936). Jack, Jr. married three times. His second wife was beautiful Ziegfeld girl, Marilyn Miller. Jack was 36 (1932) when he died of drugs and alcohol.

By 1923-26, Mary had begun to cut back on her filmmaking to only one a year. She made over two hundred in her lifetime. Because she owned most of her films, many generations of movie-goers have not seen her. However, this is being undone by Buddy Rogers now that she is no longer around. It was the advent of sound that encouraged her to finally give up. And al-

Mary Pickford and second husband, Douglas Fairbanks. Their romance and marriage set the world aflame, but sixteen years later, the flame burned out. 1925.

Surviving husband, Buddy Rogers, in front of Pickfair, built by Fairbanks as a wedding gift to Mary. After Mary's death, the mansion was put on the market for ten million dollars. Mr. Rogers planned to build a more modest home on the grounds. Shown here, 1980.

America's Sweetheart, Mary, married America's Boyfriend, Buddy, in 1937.

Still "Sweethearts" they were married 42 years when Mary died. Shown here, after 39 years, in their home. Beverly Hills, 1976.

though she won the coveted "Oscar" for her performance in **Coquette,** her first sound effort, she became discouraged with her next three sound films. Her last, at age 40, opened in 1933 as the banks were closing. Mary closed her career simultaneously.

She remained active in Hollywood life as a hostess, contributing to the foundation of the Motion Picture Relief Fund and the Motion Picture Country Home as well as being a founding member in the various organizations that protected writers: The Writers Club, The Screen Writers Guild, etc. She was extremely patriotic and gave her services and money to both world wars. She and Buddy made an attempt at the perfect marriage. During the mid-Forties they adopted two children; a son, Ronnie, and a daughter, Roxanne.

In 1965 at age 72, Mary Pickford finally wrapped it up. She literally took to her bed and except for some trips and special occasions, stayed ensconced there until her death. Hovering over her was her husband, eleven years her junior, who protected her from the outside world for which she had no use. Her mail was scrutinized and even unpleasant articles were removed from the daily newspapers before they were brought upstairs with her noon meal. A large glass of whiskey sat on her bedside table, which she would sip throughout the day in a room full of memorabilia and a mind full of memories.

Once in 1952, she had thought of a comeback. Her competitor, Charlie Chaplin was by then still hard at work, and Mary never wanted to take a backseat to Charlie. She withdrew on a technicality: she wanted her film to be in technicolor and it could not be arranged. In 1976, she was awarded an Honorary "Oscar" for her "unique contribution to the film industry and the development of film as an artistic medium."

In March of 1981, people gathered at the estate of Mary Pickford for the final disposal of some 2,400 pieces of memorabilia. The proceeds of the auction went to the Mary Pickford Foundation with a portion allocated to the Hollywood Historical Trust Fund. Among the vast collection there was a telegram from columnist Walter Winchell, dated March 13, 1941, with reference to an Errol Flynn escapade, "Ask him (Flynn) to stop goosing little Japanese girls. May get us into the war, by heck." Winchell, the clairvoyant, struck again.

Mary Pickford was eighty-six when she died. To her, the film industry had changed so much that by now she found it offensive. Gone were the days when signs such as "Ladies and children are cordially invited to this theatre. No offensive pictures are ever shown here." She liked it better in those days.

She was cremated, and then a private memorial service was held at Hollywood's famous Forest Lawn Cemetery. An era had really come to an end.

MARY PICKFORD
Died: May 29, 1979
Santa Monica, California

Mary Pickford signs Dublin actor Barry Fitzgerald (1888-1961) to a long term contract in 1937.

Janet Gaynor (l) won the 1927 "Oscar" for her performance in silent film, **Seventh Heaven.** Mary (r) displays her "Oscar," which she won in sound film, **Coquette,** in 1929. Both actresses shown here in their California homes. 1954.

(l-r) Dick Powell (1904-1963), Mary, and John Boles (1897-1961). 1938.

Mary in the center of things (holding flowers) as California honors Charles Lindbergh. (l-r) Douglas Fairbanks; Major C.C. Mosely; Mayor of Glendale, A.C. Kimblin; Mrs. Lindbergh; Mary and Lindy; and Dudley Stell, Chairman of the Day. Circa 1920's.

(l-r) Frank Sinatra, age 30; Mary; and husband Buddy Rogers. 1945.

Mary and her brother Jack whose playboy life-style eclipsed his short-lived acting career and mild attempts at directing. 1929.

Mary Pickford and rising young star, then 8-years old, Margaret O'Brien. 1945.

Authoress Elinor Glyn (**Three Weeks)** and Mary Pickford. Glyn also tagged Clara Bow the "It" Girl. Hollywood, 1926.

Mary gets a lift from William Holden in Nairobi, Kenya. 1961.

Famous group of past stars. (l-r) Al Jolson; Mary Pickford; Ronald Coleman; Gloria Swanson; Douglas Fairbanks; Joe Schenk; Charles Chaplin; Samuel Goldwyn; and Eddie Cantor. Hollywood, 1930's.

Lt. Buddy Rogers and Mary Pickford with daughter Roxanne, age 2. Hollywood, 1944.

President of the Academy of Motion Pictures Arts and Sciences, Walter Mirisch, presents Mary Pickford with her honorary "Oscar." She won her first one forty-seven years prior to this. It was the first "Oscar" presented for a sound film in 1929. Beverly Hills, 1976.

(l-r) Mary attends the world premier of **Monsieur Verdoux** with Charlie Chaplin and wife, Oona. New York, 1947.

25th Anniversary of the Motion Picture Academy of Arts and Sciences shows: Master of Ceremonies, Bob Hope (r), checking script; Mary Pickford presenting "Oscar" to producer Cecil B. DeMille for **The Greatest Show on Earth;** (upper left) what the television audiences were seeing on their screens. Hollywood, 1953.

Silent film greats of the 1915-1925 era gathered to receive George Eastman awards for their contributions to the film industry. Chairman Jesse L. Lasky (l) presides. Recipients: (l-r) Ronald Colman, Mary Pickford, Cecil B. DeMille, Mae Marsh, Donald Crisp, and Harold Lloyd. Crisp, although a veteran, for some reason was not a recipient. Hollywood, 1955.

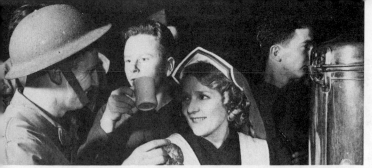

At first chain of canteens at U.S. Army Posts, Mary serves coffee and doughnuts. She had served the "doughboys" during WWI. Fort MacArthur, Calif., 1942.

Mary served as Chief of the Woman's Branch of the Infantile Paralysis Campaign. Shown here with First Lady Eleanor Roosevelt. Washington, D.C., 1944.

Repeat performance for Mary. Here she signs up President Dwight Eisenhower and Mrs. Eisenhower for the purchase of defense bonds as she begins a tour for sales. Washington, D.C., 1953.

Help for Hollywood and the construction of the Motion Picture and Television Museum, Mary discusses fund raising project with producer Sol Lesser, who shows her one of the original 16 mm movie cameras. 1962.

Step-son Douglas Fairbanks, Jr. and dear friend from the early days, actress Lillian Gish, leaving Forest Lawn Cemetery after services for Mary Pickford. Hollywood, 1979.

Rev. William H. D. Hornaday (l) escorts Buddy Rogers, Mary Pickford's husband, from the Wee Kirk O' The Heather at Forest Lawn after the services. Hollywood, 1979.

Producer Adolph Zukor believed in casting "famous players" in famous plays (Sarah Bernhardt as **Queen Elizabeth,** 1912) and so Mary's film debut with Zukor occurred when he bought the film rights to **The Good Little Devil** in which Mary was appearing on Broadway for David Belasco. This photo shows Pickford in **Caprice,** made by Zukor, which co-starred her first husband, Owen Moore. 1913.

Mary and Madelaine Traverse in **The Poor Little Rich Girl,** as ten-year old Gwendolyn, rich but neglected by her parents. This was a satire against the wealthy who did not assume responsibility. The special effects were considered the most sophisticated of the era. 1917.

At the pinnacle of her career, Pickford did a challenging dual role and appeared on-screen as ugly. Poor and ugly cockney Unity Blake was one of the roles in which Mary was unrecognizable. The other role was the title one, **Stella Maris,** the wealthy crippled girl. Show here as "Unity". 1918.

Mary's third and last film for First National with John Gilbert was **The Heart O' the Hills.** In one scene, Mary appears in Ku Klux Klan robes to mete out justice. 1919.

A typical Pickford Promo Photo used for her films, during the mid-Twenties: **Suds** (1920); **The Love Light** (1921); **Going Straight** (1922); **Rosita** (1923); **Little Annie Rooney** (1925); **Sparrows** (1926); and **My Best Girl** (1927).

Mary in **Pollyana,** her first film for United Artists. She played a ten-year old in the film when she was actually twenty-seven. 1920.

Mary and Company outdid themselves in this classic, **Little Lord Fauntleroy.** Mary played the little boy and also played his mother Dearest. Even today it is impossible to find the lines in the double exposures where the boy and mother walk together or where he runs into her arms and kisses her. Remember — this was 1921. Shown here with Claude Gillingwater as the grandfather.

Mary having learned her lesson well from Zukor ("famous players in famous plays"), chose the title role of Helen Hayes's stage success, **Coquette,** as her first talkie. Pickford won the 1928-29 Best Actress Academy award. Shown here in **Coquette** with (1) co-star, John Mack Brown and John St. Polis.

Mary and husband, Doug Fairbanks, in their first "talkie" together, **The Taming of the Shrew.** There is an immortal credit line connected with the film: **The Taming of the Shrew,** by William Shakespeare, with additional dialogue by Sam Taylor! 1929.

"Goodness, what lovely diamonds."
"Goodness had nothing to do with it, honey," said Mae. 1932.

MAE WEST

August 17, 1892 Brooklyn, New York

In the year that Baby Mae, so-called by her doting parents, started life, "moving pictures" were showing their first signs of life. In places called Penny Arcades and Peep Shows, later known as Kinetoscope Parlors, previously installed phonographs now provided sound accompaniment to pictures that moved. Thomas Alva Edison had invented the phonograph (1876), and then with George Eastman (1889) perfected "the frame-lined celluloid strip, which set pictures in motion."

"White Magic," the name for the miracle of science in the 1890's, was birthed in America while in Brooklyn another kind of "white magic" had been born. For Mae West, throughout her professional life, would be swathed in white materials and draped with white diamonds. She would become as controversial as the new art form and cause revisions in its code.

Her father, John Patrick (Battling Jack) West, had been a contender for the featherweight title during the John L. Sullivan era. By the time Mae, the first of three children, was born, "Battling Jack," a native New Yorker, had settled in his new work of being a liveryman. Her mother, Matilda Dilker Doelger, French-born with one German parent, was a corset model with stage aspirations. Combining the fighting spirit of her father with the body-language of her mother, one can easily see how the West technique was evolved. The balance to Mae's life was her Presbyterian upbringing, and throughout her life she abstained from alcohol and tobacco.

Whatever formal schooling she had was overshadowed by the early emphasis on her dancing and singing lessons. By 1900, she had appeared onstage participating in amateur-night shows. At age 4, she won second prize, $3.00, for her rendition of "Keep On Smiling" at Brooklyn's Gotham Theatre. A first prize came shortly thereafter at the Royal Theatre where she danced and sang "Movin' Day".

Within a year, she had wiggled her way into Hal Clarendon's stock company doing numbers such as, "Father, dear father, come home with me now," as she tugged at his coattails in **Ten Nights in a Bar Room.** By the time she was thirteen, she was on the vaudeville circuit teamed with actor William Hogan. Her early impersonations (Eva Tanguay, George M. Cohan, Eddie Foy) were considered unusually good for one so young, and being able to lift and rest on her shoulders a 500-lb. weight was quite extraordinary. She added another weight when she secretly married song and dance man, Hal Wallace, in Milwaukee, April 1911. After a brief joint effort on the stage, Mae went out as a single, professionally and conjugally. It came as a great shock to her fans (and probably to her) when her marriage license surfaced in 1935. She had been considered the world's leading bachelor girl until some relief workers, employed to re-index public records, found the West-Wallace union. This resulted in a bitter eight-year divorce suit before the final decree was granted.

She made her Broadway debut in **The Revue of Revues** several months after the split with her husband. Mae had written some of her own material for her act. Her first major Broadway revue, **A La Broadway and Hello Paris,** in which she sang, "They Are Irish," gave her a shot at being a show-stopper. Mae secretly wrote several extra choruses in several different dialects and astounded everyone with her versatility. Before returning to vaudeville, she did **Very Violetta** with Al Jolson. She always loved the stage, and even in later life, she returned to the stage many times rather than continue in movies. It seems as though she was in film forever, but actually she made only eleven. And only one with W.C. Fields! It had such an impact that one tends to think they were joined at the hip and made many films together.

Before turning to playwriting, she introduced the "shimmy" on Broadway in **Sometime** (1918) at the Winter Garden Theatre, playing opposite Ed Wynn. Although Gilda Grey's name is associated with the dance,

Mae West as she appeared on the vaudeville circuit. It's remarkable when you realize this demure miss in the high-button shoes was to develop into a glamorous star whose name became virtually synonymous with sex. 1919.

Mae refused to let the producers bill her as just a "shimmy" dancer because she had a lot more to offer, so the billing and fame of the dance later fell to Gilda. But Mae did introduce the dance and what she added— well, in her words, "It was a cooch dance — a way of controllin' the muscles." And she could control those muscles. From there whe went on to do a nightclub act with Harry Richman, post WWI, and then began writing her own plays.

She had two rules governing her writing, "Write about what you know and make it interesting. Sex was what interested me." Hence, **Sex** was the name of her play that opened in New London, Connecticut to an audience of 85. By the second performance, the men at the nearby naval base had spread the word and assured its financial success. The play which she wrote under the name of Jane Mast, was produced by Mae, her mother, and lawyer James Timony, who later became her manager and long-time associate. The play's notoriety preceded the New York opening in April of 1926, and despite refusal by the newspapers to advertise it, **Sex** played to full houses.

During the 41st week of performance, Mae and cast members were arrested: right-eous and indignant societies objected vehemently. The jury said, "Guilty," proclaiming that the show, "tended to corrupt the morals of youth and others." Mae was fined $500 and spent ten days in the pokey. Two years later, October 1928, the entire cast was arrested during the first performance of her new play, **The Pleasure Man.** Even though the court ruled that "the play was not basically immoral," Mae decided not to re-open it.

The next breast-beating of Mae West's breast occurred in Washington, D.C. when police stopped the show. "Lewd and lascivious," they declared of **The Constant Sinner** with its interracial cast. The play was based on a novel by Mae, adapted by Mae for the stage, and undauntedly opened by her in New York in 1931. It ran for over a year.

Yet it was her earlier work, her character of **Diamond Lil** (1928) that propelled her into fame and fortune. She never strayed far away from *Lil*; every character from then on was merely a spin-off. When it first opened in Brooklyn in April 1928, drama critic, Robert Garland, of the *New York Evening Telegram* wrote, "it's worth swimming to Brooklyn to see her descend those dance hall stairs and be present while she lolls in a golden bed reading *The Police Gazette.*" The play ran for over 300 performances before it went on tour. During the tour Los Angeles was one of the stops, and when Mae left New York in 1932, she headed back for Hollywood. And *Lil* was safely packed in her luggage.

After her first role with George Raft in **Night After Night** (his first starring part), out came **Lil** again, this time in the screen version called **She Done Him Wrong** (1933), her first starring role.

Six months after the film was released, Mae was once again being attacked by the righteous and indignant. However, there is some background (to this) that had erupted before Mae hit Hollywood: debauchery and scandals of the Twenties had prompted an earlier clean-up campaign.

Ex-Postmaster General (during President Harding's term), Will H. Hays had been hired by studio moguls — founding fathers

A CODE
TO GOVERN THE MAKING
OF MOTION AND TALKING
PICTURES
the
Reasons Supporting It
And the
Resolution for Uniform
Interpretation

by

Motion Picture Producers and Distributors of America, Inc.

JUNE 13, 1934

The screen version of **Diamond Lil,** re-titled **She Done Him Wrong,** made the Production Code body reexamine itself and a more stringent Code was enforced. 1934.

—to reform the industry, install moral guidelines, and to improve public relations. This censorship later became known as The Hays Office. Hays inserted "morality clauses" in the actors' contracts, formed the Central Casting Agency for extras who had to register and pass the scrutiny of a staff of sociologists, and then turned his attention to what would be allowed on the screen. (Production Code, 1927-30)

Now, enter Mae West and **She Done Him Wrong.** And then enter the Episcopal Committee on Motion Pictures "denouncing the industry for promoting immorality." Next the Catholics got into the act and formed the National Legion of Decency. Their function was to review and label each film before it was released. From their pulpits they decreed: Passed, Objectionable in Part, or Condemned. Jewish and Protestant groups joined, and the ultimate result was the The Production Code Administration; the former code was rewritten. Any production that did not conform would bring about a $25,000 fine, and the film would not be distributed nor shown by the Motion Picture Association that owned the leading theaters on the circuit. Father Daniel A. Lord and Catholic layperson publisher Martin Quigley were recruited by Hays to help with revisions, and Catholic newspaperman, Joseph I. Breen, was put in charge.

Meanwhile back on the back lot, Mae changed the name of her third film, **It Ain't No Sin** to **I'm No Angel,** and as they say in Hollywood, "Cried all the way to the bank."

The film was a huge success. Part of this success was due to a young man Mae had spotted on the studio street. "If he can talk, I'll take him," she said. Together they made film history as she murmured to Cary Grant, "Why don'tcha come up and see me sometime?" Grant was the first of her young handsome leading men. Forty-five years later in **Sextette,** Mae was still surrounded by a gaggle of handsome young men.

Mae was subjected to censorship until Gore Vidal's **Myra Breckinridge** came out in 1970. She accepted that part because the script was loose, and she was allowed to write her dialogue. After an absence of more than twenty-five years, she still received top billing in the film. But in the earlier days, what she resented was "that men could do what they wanted while women were tied down." Mae West never spoke a "dirty" word on the screen nor did she ever kiss a leading man, and yet the censorship continued even into radio and later, television. The fur flew when on radio she asked Charlie McCarthy, "Why don't you come up to my bedroom and play in my woodpile?" And then, on TV with Edward R. Murrow, on his show, *Person-to-Person* it flew again.

"Why do you have mirrors on your bedroom ceiling?" he asked.

"So I can see how I'm doing," she answered him.

Splice went the tape. Next he asked her what she thought about the world situation.

"I've always been interested in foreign affairs," said Mae.

Splice, splice, splice—the half hour show was cut to three minutes.

Even pachyderms respond to pulchritude. Baby Blackie of the Harringay Circus lifts his trunk in approval to Mae West. London, 1948.

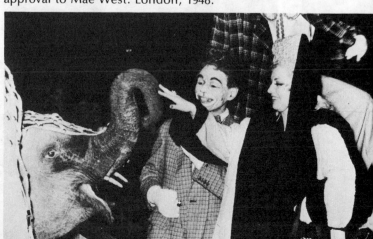

Artist Salvador Dali pays homage to Mae West in the exhibit, "The Artist Looks at People." Chicago, 1958.

Here Mae displays a copy of her new book (and a 22-carat diamond ring) and at the same time answers reporters' questions about why CBS cancelled her portion of the "Person-to-Person" TV show. The sultry queen of sex and censorship replied, "Maybe it was too good." San Francisco, 1959.

Mae West never flaunted herself in public. She enjoyed her friends and enjoyed entertaining them at home or being in their homes. She had a constant companion for the last twenty-six years of her life, Paul Novak, who had been in one of her nightclub acts. And it was Mr. Novak, along with Mae's sister, Beverly, and her nephew, John West, who inherited the West fortune. Mae West was a shrewd business woman, and as in her private life, she kept her finances and her investments equally private. The 40 million dollars she amassed over the years did not stem from her pictures but from wise real estate purchases in the Hollywood area when land was dirt cheap.

She believed in sharing the wealth while still alive and this she did with the three aforementioned heirs. A little over a million remains and will be equally divided after her will has been probated.

She suffered a stroke a few months before her death but had returned home with nurses around the clock. Her death was "from natural causes."

The services were attended by "invitation only" friends and co-workers. She was dressed in a white-jeweled negligee with only the top part of the casket open; the bottom half was covered with white roses.

Producer Ross Hunter delivered the eulogy, "The lady behind the legend that was Mae West was strong-willed yet good-natured, vital, and spontaneous." The song she sang in **Diamond Lil,** "Frankie and Johnnie," could be heard softly on the organ. A few days later, at seven in the morning, she was buried in the family crypt beside her parents and brother. Her sister survives. The "white magic" had returned to Brooklyn.

MAE WEST
Died: November 22, 1980
Los Angeles, California.

Mae West in **Klondike Annie.** 1936.

Mae West kept her private life — private. But was in and out of the public's eye with regularity. Here she is shown with courtroom foe, nightclub performer, Marie Lind. Mae contended that Miss Lind had no right to bill herself as "Diamond Lil," as Miss West had written the book and the play. California, 1959.

A few famous West-isms.
"That guy's no good. His mother should have thrown him away and kept the stork."
"Sex is like a small business. You gotta watch over it."
"The man I don't like, doesn't exist."

Mae West two years before her death. 1978.

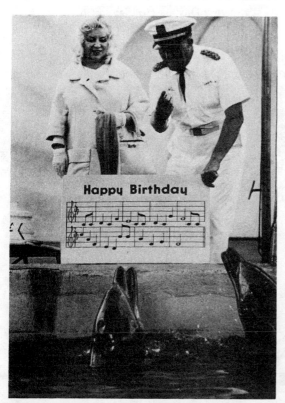

"Corky" and "Sparkle" sing porpoise-style (by emitting air from the blow holes in the top of their heads) "Happy 68th Birthday" to Mae as trainer Adolf Frohn gives the cue. Miami, Florida. 1961.

Mae West and George Raft in **Night After Night.** This was her first film and his first starring role. 1932.

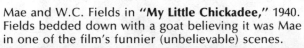

Mae West in **Every Day's a Holiday.** 1938.

Mae and W.C. Fields in **"My Little Chickadee,"** 1940. Fields bedded down with a goat believing it was Mae in one of the film's funnier (unbelievable) scenes.

Mae and her constant companion of twenty-six years, Paul Novak.

Beverly West, Mae's sister, in 1935.

(l-r) Margaret Hamilton, Mae, and Dick Foran in **"Chickadee."** According to Mae: "Getting down to your last man must be as bad as getting down to your last dollar."

(l-r) John Huston, Raquel Welch, Robert Fryer, columnist Rex Reed, and director Michael Sarne. Mae West, draped in white in the center, all appearing in **Myra Breckinridge.** It was the first time Mae had appeared on screen in over 25 years. 1970.

In one of her last Broadway appearances, Mae West surrounded herself with an "imperial guard" of young, muscular, six-foot actors and dramatized the story of Catherine the Great of Russia. She wrote the story and played in it for three years, which included a national tour. **Catherine Was Great.** 1944-45.

One more time Hollywood dusted Mae off and brought her down from the shelf to appear in **Sextette.** The screenplay was based on her play in the 30's that got her tossed in the clink. Seen here in 1978.

Joan Crawford's impeccable image: sleek and sophisticated. 1946.

JOAN CRAWFORD

Born: March 23, 1906 San Antonio, Texas

Her mother named her Lucille Fay; her brother called her Billie; Hollywood renamed her Joan. LeSueur was her surname, but believing that her stepfather was her real father, she used the name Cassin. Ultimately, she became Joan Crawford Fairbanks Tone Terry Steele. She shed each name and in its place grew a new layer of the Ultimate Star. Unfortunately, the basic misfortune—conditioning—stayed buried and could never be thrown off.

Thomas LeSueur, a French-Canadian laborer, fathered three children before abandoning his family. Daisy died as an infant; Hal Hayes arrived in 1904; Lucille Fay in 1906. After a long search by Joan, a letter and photograph arrived from her father in 1934. The face in the picture was confirmed by her mother, and the then twenty-eight year old Joan sent for her father. She saw him several times on his only visit to Los Angeles, but the visit was brief and, at best, unsatisfactory. She never saw him again.

Her mother, née Anna Bell Johnson, was of part-Irish, part-Scandinavian descent. After her first husband left, she married Henry Cassin and moved the family to Lawton, Oklahoma. It was there that Lucille became Billie Cassin. And it was there that the only rays of sunshine shone into the otherwise dismal life of the young girl. Her stepfather owned an opera house and open-air theatre. Although the small-minded citizens of the equally small-sized town looked askance at "show biz" folk, Billie found them fascinating, warm, and friendly. But this life was doomed when Cassin was tried as an accomplice on a gold-embezzling charge. After his acquittal, he moved the family to Kansas City; but Billie's mother left him; and then brother Hal told Billie that Cassin was not her real father. Hal seems to have been a tormentor of his sister from childhood and always their mother's favorite. The mother was overly strict, probably due to her own unhappiness, and was a firm believer in "the hairbrush" treatment.

Billie's growing years were about as painful as any fiction writer could invent: she was shuffled from school to school, housed in flea-bag-type hotels, and lived with two people who could easily have done without her. By the time she was eleven, she was washing dishes, scrubbing floors, and doing any kind of menial task to maintain herself in school and away from her family. At one school, Rockingham Academy, she was reportedly beaten by the principal, Mrs. Emma Hessel,* until her young beauty began to surface. When the rich young men began to date Lucille, the beatings stopped.

However, there was one source of kindness: Scarritt Elementary School's principal, Harvey S. Walter. He recognized her industrious nature and alert mind and constantly encouraged her to study. Later, as secretary at Stephens College in Columbia, Missouri, he convinced her to enroll. But life at Stephens (1922) was more of the same: working her way through school amidst wealthy girls. Although the students were nice to her both at college and in high school, she felt very much on the outside and wanted to get on the inside. President James "Daddy" Wood of Stephens understood her desires. He offered her words of encouragement and sound advice as she packed her bags to leave. In 1970, Joan returned to Stephens to accept the first President's Citation "in recognition of her achievement in varied roles expected of the women of today, for her distinguished career as creative film actress, as businesswoman, as homemaker and mother, and as philanthropist."

Billie returned to Kansas City where she supported herself mainly as a salesgirl earning about $12.00 a week. There was always a long line of men to bolster her ego, but the line she opted for was in the chorus of a traveling show. She was hired, but the show folded in two weeks and it was back to being a salesgirl again. But the bug had bitten, the lure of being a great dancer wouldn't quit, so she packed her bags, and as Lucille LeSueur, she headed for Chicago.

As a bouncy energetic dancer, she landed a job in the chorus of J.J. Shubert's

*Bob Thomas, **Joan Crawford: A Biography** (New York: Simon and Schuster).

Innocent Eyes. One thinks of Crawford with her good posture and carriage as being quite tall. Actually, she was only five feet, four inches tall, which made her a "pony" in the chorus: the title given to the smaller girls. The show went on to New York City. Later, she found herself in another production, **The Passing Show of 1924,** which brought in $35.00 a week. Pudgy and freckled-face, Lucille was happily kicking her heels in the chorus line and kicking up her heels around the big city. One of her pals, also from Missouri, was Lewis Offield who later starred as Jack Oakie.

But the big event at that time, one that has been kept locked up in the Hall of Records, was her first marriage. When she arrived in Hollywood after a successful screen test to accept MGM's offer, the marriage was *verboten*: "Because starlets in those days testified that they were unmarried, which was the rule. Since she [Joan] didn't drive in those days, Jimmy had to drive her daily to the studio at the crack of dawn and then pick her up while trying to keep out of sight. The marriage wore thin and they divorced in the middle or late 20's in California."*

The groom in question was James Barratt Welton, now deceased, and the marriage was performed while Joan was working in New York City.

With a five-year contract at a starting salary of $75.00 a week, Lucille LeSueur arrived in Hollywood in 1925. She never looked back at the painful beginning, but the bitter days were etched in her being; the better days were about to be drawn.

Lucille LeSueur appeared in three films before she became Joan Crawford in **Sally, Irene, and Mary.** The publicity director at MGM, Pete Smith, ran a contest to find a new name for their starlet. The first winning name, Joan Arden, was short-lived as there was another Joan Arden. Crawford was the second choice, certainly a more distinctive one. The little girl from "the other side of the tracks" thus began her film career and voyage to the "right side of the tracks," but her personal baggage went with her.

Louis B. Mayer was at the helm of MGM. His eagle-eyes were always wide open for any contract player striving for stardom. He spotted Joan and her drive and compen-

*Source: Mrs. James Welton

sated her hard work with salary advances from $100 a week, to $250 to $500. Now with enough money to do as she pleased, she rented a small bungalow and bought herself a car. She also brought her mother and brother out from Kansas City. Soon she was cleaning the house and cooking for them as well as supporting them. But not for long. "Papa" Mayer loaned her the money to move out and away from her past. In the long run, her mother continued berating Joan while she lived off of her until her death in 1958 at the age of seventy-four. Brother Hal, after an aborted acting career and two failed marriages, became an alcoholic. Later, he joined Alcoholics Anonymous and worked as a night clerk in a motel until his death in 1963, aged fifty-nine.

Crawford worked hard and learned fast. She was ably assisted by cameramen, lighting experts, and makeup artists who recognized the almost perfect face from any angle. Fashion designer (Gilbert) Adrian popularized the mannish padded broad shoulder look associated with Crawford, who by now had slimmed down. Eventually, her style would be copied by millions of women fans. Fellow actors and directors were generous with their time and help. All of these people were cultivated by her, used by her; all played a very important role in the creation of Crawford, the star.

When **Our Dancing Daughters** was released in 1928, Joan was noticed for the first time as someone other than a "bit" player. The film was a monetary success for the studio, but for Joan its success lay in the fact that critics and fans heaped accolades on her—especially women fans. Men she could always attract, but women assured her acceptance as they hurriedly set about to acquire the "Crawford look."

Her marriage to Douglas Fairbanks, Jr. (June 3, 1929) brought a new challenge into

Husband No. 1, James Barratt Welton, Phi Beta Kappa graduate of Northwestern University, was playing in the pit orchestra of the show where Crawford was dancing. They married clandestinely in NYC and later when Welton accepted a job with Abe Lyman's orchestra, he took his bride with him to Los Angeles. Circa 1920's.

Joan marries Douglas Fairbanks, Jr., who gave his age as 19. The wedding took place in St. Malachy's Catholic Church in New York City. 1929.

her life. Douglas, Sr., his father and Mary Pickford, his stepmother, Hollywood's Royal couple, did not consider Joan the perfect wife for him. She was finally invited to their castle, Pickfair. Even though Joan was impressed, she became quite bored by the quiet pretentiousness. Slowly, the marriage began to falter. Her husband's social life became very important to him, and she found her old social insecurities erupting. Four years later, she filed for divorce and turned her attention to Clark Gable.

This romance was not given the studio's blessing, and in those days what the studio dictated the studio got. However, she and Gable remained good friends until his death.

Wedding bells rang again on October 11, 1935. Franchot Tone was a Phi Beta Kappa from Cornell University who impressed Joan with his background and social acceptability. He introduced her to the New York based Group Theatre and the acting methods of the great Stanislawski. She was also introduced to more feelings of insecurity. Obviously, she married these men hoping to bring into her life the refinement and uppercrust manners she had lacked in her youth. But the demeanor and life-style she sorely sought had a high price tag on it. Before the marriage ended with Tone, he had

Crawford and third husband, Franchot Tone, whom she married in 1935. His father was president of the Carborundum Company, but Tone turned his back on the family business and opted for a stage career. As an old man, dying in a wheelchair, Tone visited his ex-wife in New York City, and when he died in 1968 it was she who fulfilled his last wishes: his ashes were scattered over the Canadian Woods he dearly loved. Shown here, 1939.

blackened her eyes a few times and was caught by Joan with other women. This, to a woman of her ego structure, was demeaning and impossible to live with.

Her behavioral pattern began to evolve. As an actress and star she was dedicated, hard working, ambitious, and tireless. Off camera, she was nervous, high-strung, almost psychotic in behavior. She constantly washed her hands, kept her home and dressing room scrupulously clean, and retreated to a bedroom filled with dolls. Like Madame Defarge, she constantly knitted through her own revolution. Her claustrophia, she claimed, could be attributed to having been locked in a closet at the age of five by her brother. In the 30's, Joan embraced Christian Science, hoping for a solution to her erratic behavior through a philosophical approach.

Crawford, known to be vindictive, was sued by stenographer, Dorothy Rogers, shown here looking at photos autographed and given to her by the actress. Rogers, a fan and close friend of the actress, alleged that the star had her fired from her job at RKO Studios. The $50,000 suit was settled out of court. 1937.

Friends considered her loyal and generous. But she demanded the same from them—sometimes to the point of ludicrousness. Her generosity spilled over into philanthropic work; in 1934 she underwrote the expenses for two rooms in Hollywood's Presbyterian Hospital for people in and related to her profession. During World War II, she was a constant volunteer at the Hollywood Canteen.

Her tenure at MGM lasted for eighteen years before she left to sign with Warner Brothers. Although her contract was ironclad at $500,000 for three pictures, she rejected the scripts offered her, knowing that they were Bette Davis rejects. She was virtually off of the screen for two years. In the in-

129

Crawford and Greg Bautzer with whom she had a four year relationship between husbands. Bautzer grew up on the waterfront in San Pedro, worked his way through the University of Southern California Law School, and became a famous lawyer. Shown here in New York City. 1946.

Joan and fourth husband, Phillip Terry, nee Frederick Kormann, onetime Stanford football player. Six weeks after their first dinner date in 1942, they married. Shown here in New York City. 1945.

terval, younger faces such as Betty Grable and Ann Sheridan were emerging. After a four-year romance with lawyer Greg Bautzer, she found temporary comfort and solace with her next husband, Phillip Terry, whom she married in July of 1942 and divorced in 1946. But in the intervening years, Crawford finally got a script that would put her back on top; back in the limelight where she would stay even into old age.

Mildred Pierce was the vehicle that brought her back and brought her an "Oscar" for her performance. In typical Hollywood style, she had made a comeback, and all of Hollywood was again at her feet. One can say a lot of things about Crawford, but never that she was a quitter nor that she wasted time feeling sorry for herself.

Joan Crawford at home, clutches her "Oscar" for Best Actress of 1945 for her performance in **Mildred Pierce.** No doubt her innate fear of rejection, of losing, caused her psychogenic illness. 1946.

Childless and having suffered multiple miscarriages, she adopted her first child, Christina, in 1939. While married to Phillip Terry, she adopted a son, whom she named Phillip Jr., but changed his name to Christopher after the divorce. Two more children were adopted, Cathy and Cindy. Although she called them "the twins," they were born a month apart. The treatment of her children has, in its own way, become legendary from reports of visitors to the house, domestics, and through one daughter's autobiography, *Mommie Dearest.** The older children seemed to have suffered far more harshly than the younger ones. Perhaps like Bing Crosby, at an older age, both softened towards their younger children.

Actress Helen Hayes said, "Joan tried to be all things to all people. I just wish she hadn't tried to be a mother." And so one can conjecture: did Joan want children because she was deprived of having her own; did she see the portrait of herself as incomplete without them; did she want to give them everything she had missed as a child including a close family relationship? Whatever the answers, Christoper ran away from home many times and finally left not seeing his mother for twenty-odd years; Christina, an actress, told her story in her book. Both were disinherited. Cathy and Cindy married, had families, and remained close. All four attended their mother's funeral.

*Christina Crawford, **Mommie Dearest** (New York: Wm. Morrow & Co. Inc.).

Joan Crawford and family. (l-r) Christina, Cathy, Cindy, Christopher. 1950.

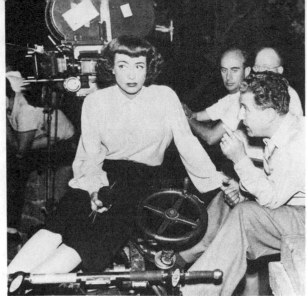

Crawford with knitting, listens to director Curtis Bernhardt on set of **Possessed.** She must have listened well, for film brought her a second "Oscar" nomination. Crawford, a woman of extremes, always had knitting in her hands. 1946.

Joan, age 47, and her last husband, soft drink tycoon, Alfred M. Steele, age 54. Shown here after elopement in Las Vegas. 1955.

The drama of the Crawford life had not yet totally unfolded. At age 49 (1955), she met and married Pepsi-Cola's president, Alfred Steele. He was as much of a dynamo in his field as she was in hers. He did not resent the notoriety and fame of his wife but saw it as a complement to his business. They battled and stormed in their own strongwilled ways, but the marriage did work. Joan, in her customary manner, threw herself into her husband's business and became an important property to Pepsi's image. Unfortunately for her, she became a widow in 1959: Joan had envisioned the rest of her life with Steele.

(Top) Crawford fans could never get enough and she, in turn, humored and nutured them. Shown here promoting flim, **Sudden Fear,** for which she received her third "Oscar" nomination. New York, 1952.

(Bottom) After shaking hands with about 3,000 fans, signing autographs, and selling the first ticket to film **Sudden Fear,** Crawford cools off her aching hand—the price of fame. 1952.

(l-r) Paul Kamey of Universal-International Pictures Publicity Department; author Doug McClelland, who was interviewing Joan on her new film, **Female on the Beach**; Bea Smith of the *Newark Evening News*; Joan and her husband, Alfred Steele. Photo taken August 1955 at Joan's favorite New York dining spot, "21" Club.

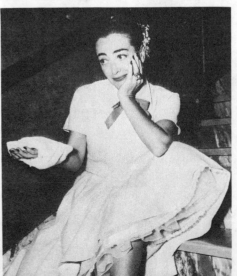

Senator John F. Kennedy receives a citation from Mr. and Mrs. Alfred Steele (Joan Crawford) for his notable leadership as chairman of the National Multiple Sclerosis Society's annual drive. Washington, D.C., 1958.

(l-r) Happier times with the children: Christopher, Christina, Joan, and husband Alfred Steele; (front) Cynthia and Cathy. 1955. In 1958, Christopher was under arrest for "joy-riding and shooting out several street lights" with three other youths. He was released in the custody of child psychologist Dr. Earl Loomis.

Two more adopted children guarding their mistress's door as she films **Humoresque** on Warner Brothers lot. French poodle, Toni, and dachshund, Pupchen, proud of Mama who had just won an "Oscar" for **Mildred Pierce.** 1946.

Always glamorous, Joan Crawford always worked hard for Pepsi-Cola. Here she plays hostess for children from the Christodora Settlement House at Pepsi's Pavilion at N.Y.'s World Fair. 1964.

After his death, she was appointed to the Board of Directors to fill his place. For the next ten years, she worked as diligently for Pepsi as she had worked for herself. When she was ultimately retired by the firm, she was given an annual pension of $50,000. By her standards, it was a mere pittance considering the work she had done for them, which had carried with it an expense account in excess of $55,000 as well as her salary. But fortunately, she had not abandoned her film career.

Joan's triumph in 1962, co-starring with adversary Bette Davis in **What Ever Happened to Baby Jane?** shows her "gutsiness" and drive as never before. Neither star had any illusions of being "in demand" for their services. Their salaries of $40,000 were a far cry from the hundreds of thousands they

Crawford relaxing in Jamaica after filming **The Best of Everything.** Ironically, she had had "the best of everything," but was left in debt after Steele's death, had sold her Brentwood home after thirty years, was on the "outs" with her children, and needed the above named film. She played a small part, not the lead. 1959.

Bette Davis and Joan Crawford, both legends at age fifty-four, competitive to the end, but needing cash, put on the performance of their lives as they appear as "good pals" for this publicity shot on the set of **What Ever Happened to Baby Jane?** 1962.

"Crawford's Revenge" at the 35th Annual Academy Awards. Co-star Bette Davis had been nominated for her performance in **Baby Jane:** the win would have been her third. Crawford, furious about not being nominated, accepted the "Oscar" for absent winner Anne Bancroft. Shown here with (l-r) Gregory Peck, Best Actor, **To Kill a Mockingbird;** Patty Duke, Best Actress Supporting Role, **The Miracle Worker;** Crawford; Ed Begley, Best Actor Supporting Role, **Sweet Bird of Youth.** 1963.

Joan (l) substitutes for daughter Christina (r) on four episodes of television's "Secret Storm." Christina was recuperating from surgery; mother and daughter were living their own personal "secret storm" as Christina revealed in her autobiography. 1968.

Crawford as she looked in the Sixties. She was welcomed back to Pickfair, the home of her first mother-in-law, Mary Pickford and, in England, had been titled Her Serene Crawfordship by the press. She made her last public appearance in September, 1974.

formerly commanded. But in true Crawford and Davis style, they were a huge success. Davis received an Academy Award nomination as best actress. Many critics believed that although her portrayal of the slatternly, infantile "crazy" was brilliant, still Crawford delivered a tougher performance in its desperation and portention.

The studio decided to pair the stars again in **Hush . . . Hush, Sweet Charlotte,** but for the first time the ailing Crawford had to be replaced. Before her career was over, she had made eighty-one movies, numerous television and radio appearances, and had even substituted for daughter, Christina, on "The Secret Storm", a daytime television soap opera.

By 1975, living quietly in a New York apartment, Joan was immersed in Christian Science. The days of Dom Perignon and 100-proof vodka, with the ever-present cigarette, had vanished into the ionosphere along with the Hollywood life and the affluent Pepsi years. Her time was spent with close friends, a housekeeper, and the essential presence of her practitioner. She refused to be hospitalized even when extreme pain was her constant companion. She was meticulous, proud, independent, and faced the final struggle as she had faced the earlier ones—alone.

She died at home on May 10th, 1977, from an acute coronary occlusion. Close friends suspected that she also had been suffering from cancer of the pancreas.

According to her wishes, she was cremated and her ashes placed in an urn next to Alfred Steele's in the Ferncliff, New York cemetery.

In Beverly Hills, as in New York, memorial services were held. Perhaps director George Cukor succinctly summarized little Lucille . . . Billie . . . Joan, "She was the perfect image of the movie star, and, as such, largely the creation of her own indomitable will." And, "The camera saw, I suspect, a side of her that no flesh-and-blood lover ever saw."

JOAN CRAWFORD
Died: May 10, 1977
New York, New York

Crawford with hand on shoulder of Robert Young as Franchot Tone (husband number three whom she married two years later) in **Today We Live.** 1933. One of the screenwriters was William Faulkner.

Joan in her award-winning, Best Actress of 1945 performance, **Mildred Pierce,** with Zachary Scott. But the fear of rejection, of losing to Ingrid Bergman, Gene Tierney, Greer Garson, or Jennifer Jones, the other nominees, kept her at home where she heard the news over the radio.

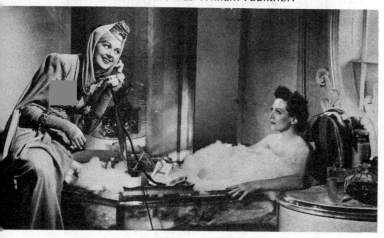

Joan and Rosalind Russell in **The Women.** 1939. As in life, so in the film, Joan played a perfume salesgirl who succeeds.

Joan in **The Gorgeous Hussy.** 1936. Her leading men in the film were: Robert Taylor, Franchot Tone, Lionel Barrymore, Melvyn Douglas, and James Stewart, but her women fans wanted their uncostumed Joan. She never did a costume part again.

Raymond Massey, Van Heflin, and Joan in **Possessed.** 1947. This version bore no resemblance to the 1931 film of the same title she had made with Clark Gable.

Joan and Henry Morgan in **Torch Song.** 1953. This was her first dancing role in fourteen years and marked her return to MGM at age forty-seven.

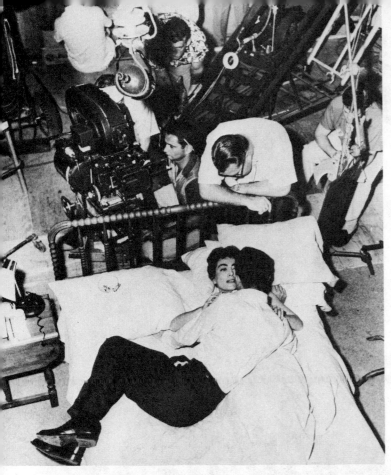

Director William Castle called for "Action" and Crawford screams. Then the camera backs away and she is seen holding a blood-smeared ax in **Strait-Jacket.** 1964.

Joan Crawford gazes into Cliff Robertson's eyes as director Robert Aldrich, leaning on back of bed, watches this scene from **Autumn Leaves.** 1956.

Joan and Bette Davis in **What Ever Happened To Baby Jane?.** 1962. Davis lost the coveted "Oscar" to Anne Bancroft for her performance in **The Miracle Worker.** Crawford triumphantly accepted for Miss Bancroft, but not before she placed her hand on Davis's and haughtily said, "Excuse me," as the disappointed Bette stood in the wings. Although the fifty-four year veterans got through the picture without mayhem, Crawford got her revenge for not being nominated.

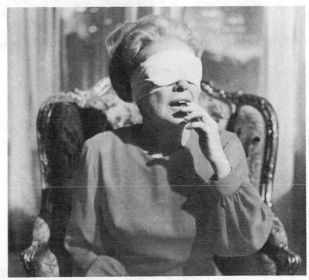

Crawford in NBC's TV-movie, **Night Gallery.** 1969. Young Steven Spielberg (**Jaws**) drew the assignment, his first, and presented television with its first glimpse of his talent as a director.

Joan as she appeared in her last film, **Trog** with Michael Gough and Bernard Kay. 1970. She was sixty-three years old and claimed she still had not had a face lift.

Rosalind Russell, a Hollywood rarity. Her own name,
her original face, and a unique talent. Circa 1950.

ROSALIND RUSSELL

June 4, 1911 Waterbury, Connecticut

In the movie world of "you be nice to me" (euphemistic for "sleep with me") and "I'll be nice to you" (euphemistic for "and you'll get the part"), it was no accident that Roz Russell rose to stardom on her own terms — not Hollywood's. Her ambition to be an actress was realized through hard work, up front expression of what she wanted, and knowing when and how to compromise in her career not herself. Her early life provided a foundation built on a solid family life, sound values, and reasonable give and take. With six other children in the family the latter was a necessity and perforce a competitive nature was developed. Being caught in the middle between two older brothers and a sister and two younger sisters and a brother, she became a survivor. She never became a superstar; she became instead a super person. This was also her decision.

Her mother, Clara McKnight, was a school teacher of Scottish-Irish descent, and her father, James Edward Russell, was a lawyer of Irish descent. They met in Waterbury where both lived and worked, then married, and raised their seven children. The family was financially secure, the parents reasonably strict yet generous with the amount of time they spent with their children. The overused adage, "the family that plays together (and prays together-they were devout Catholics) stays together," seems to have been invented for the Russell clan. Together they played most sports, traveled sporadically, attended the theater — you name it — they did it. Although her father died when she was only nineteen, his living legacy had been passed on, and the monetary one would provide for the children's education. After that, they were on their own.

After high school, Roz went to Marymount College, but quit before graduation and headed for New York and the theater. There she enrolled in the American Acad-

Even while making a film, Roz could not turn her back on the tornado disaster in Udall, Kansas where they were shooting the movie. Through her efforts, $20,000 was raised for the victims. Here she is being presented the portion of the **Congressional Record** citing her for her humanitarian work by Y. Frank Freeman, head of Paramount Pictures. Hollywood, 1955.

Jack Benny presents Roz with Floyd B. Odlum award of the Arthritis Foundation. She was a volunteer worker for over twenty years. New York City, 1972.

Former First Lady Betty Ford paid tribute to her late close friend, Roz Russell as she presented the award from the International Congress of Rheumatology to Frederick Brisson, husband of Miss Russell. Mrs. Ford, an arthritis victim herself, cited Roz's courage in her 20-year fight against severe rheumatoid arthirtis. San Francisco, 1977.

emy of Dramatic Arts and did graduate in 1929. Her first paying job was in the Adirondacks at Saranac Lake. During the summer months she did 26 plays in 13 weeks. The winter found her in Boston playing with an all British company, and the next summer she was back in the mountains.

She bounced onto Broadway via the prestigious Theatre Guild and its production of **Garrick Gaieties.** She toured with the company after a ten day run on Broadway, earning about $300 a week, which wasn't bad considering the country was in the Depression Era. After the tour, she returned to New York doing any job she could get connected with her work which she called "the subway circuit."

When Universal Pictures offered her a chance to make a test, she accepted even though the stage was her real love. She would not return to it for nineteen years.

By the time Universal got around to offering her a solid contract, she had made inroads into MGM and through a bit of inveigling managed to get out of the Universal contract and into one at Metro. The time, the 30's, and Roz was in her 20's. The studio roster sparkled with leading men such as Clark Gable, Spencer Tracy, Jimmy Stewart, and others. Along with Roz, a newcomer called Robert Taylor arrived who would one day sparkle as bright as the other stars. As contract players, they worked six days a week, 40 weeks a year on salary, as the studio ground out "A" and "B" pictures as fast as it could.

Her first assignment was an "A" flick, **Evelyn Prentice** starring William Powell and Myrna Loy. Just as the roster shone with gorgeous leading men, the women were just as formidable. With stars such as Jean Harlow and Joan Crawford, Roz was relegated to second leads or "the other woman." Having been a tomboy for most of her life and being smart enough to accept the assigned roles, she never saw herself as the glamorous one being kissed in every other frame. And yet before she was finished, she would emerge as not only glamorous but as one of the best dressed and most fashionable women in America.

Roz and husband Carl Frederick Brisson, Jr. a few months after their wedding. 1942.

Cary Grant, who had been the best man at her wedding, presents the Stock Theatre's Straw Hat Award to Roz for her distinction in the arts and public service. The award was given annually to a graduate of summer stock. New York, 1975.

Roz and her only child, Lance, born May, 1943. Shown here at home. California, 1947.

Actress Joan Bennett gives Roz a big congratulatory hug after the opening of **Bell, Book, and Candle,** which marked Roz Russell's return to Broadway. 1952.

MGM loaned her out a lot; sometimes she would be working on two or three films at the same time. From 1934 until 1941, she made almost 20 films at MGM and eight or nine away from her home lot. Her first lead was in a "B" picture, **Casino Murder Case,** co-starring Paul Lukas in 1935. And according to her, the "B" stood for only one thing — Bad. From then on, it was "A" all the way.

Her role as Sylvia in **The Women** (1939) is memorable; especially to the then reigning queens Norma Shearer and Joan Crawford from whom she stole the whole show. Graciously, she credits director George Cukor for keeping her portrayal on the right track. The character was a woman about to break up a marriage (with a child no less), he told her to play it broad and ridiculous. Even today women flash their long nails and utter "Jungle Red — Sylvia."

She appeared on the cover of *Life* magazine in September of 1939, but it was *Time* magazine that correctly summed up who and what she was, "She became firmly established as the idol of a generation of less-than-beautiful girls who had to use smart clothes and bright chatter to lure men away from more luscious-looking females."

Right on the heels of **The Women,** she made **His Girl Friday,** a remake of the durable **The Front Page.** This had been a successful Broadway play and then good box office on the screen with Pat O'Brien and Adolph Menjou in 1931. Director Howard Hawks had a stroke of genius when he turned the role of reporter Hildy Johnson from male to female; and Roz had a stroke of luck when Jean Arthur, Irene Dunne, and Ginger Rogers turned down the role. Cary Grant played the editor and together he and Roz quipped, frolicked, and raced into a smash hit. Roz as the grey-flannel-suited "career gal" was a bit ahead of Betty Friedan and the girls, even though in those days the man still won out and the girl retired. As the typical "career gal" Roz was anything but retiring.

As her professional life took a giant step forward, her personal life took an equally big step. Carl Frederick Brisson, Jr., who was coincidentally Cary Grant's house guest,

"Tony" awards past and present, were acknowledged at a galaxy presided over by President of the American Theatre Wing, Inc. Helen Hayes. (l-r)Roz for **Wonderful Town;** Sybil Trubin for **Off Broadway Company;** Carol Haney for **The Pajama Game;** Miss Hayes; Nancy Kelly for **The Bad Seed;** and Elizabeth Montgomery accepting for her father, Robert Montgomery, for "Distinguished Direction" of **The Desperate Hours.** New York City, 1955.

Hollywood rolled out the red carpet for Swedish actress Ingrid Bergman as she arrived back after a ten-year absence. Rosalind took time off from her duties to welcome her friend. Hollywood, 1955.

Roz on the set of **Gypsy,** sticking a hat pin in her head. She collapsed after completing the scene. Hollywood, 1962.

Two troupers arriving in Manhattan to plug their latest films. Roz (left) for **Gypsy** and Bette Davis for **What Ever Happened To Baby Jane?** New York City, 1962.

Four frolicking guests at the Four Seasons for a farewell party for Princess Margaret and her husband Lord Snowden. (l-r) Frederick Brisson and his wife, Rosalind Russell; Producer (**Fanny**) Director (**Picnic, South Pacific, Camelot**) Joshua Logan and Mrs. Logan. New York City, 1965.

Roz and Joan Crawford thirty-five years after the release of their fabulous film, **The Women**, at a party honoring Roz in the series of Evenings with Legendary Ladies at the Rainbow Room. Joan acted as hostess as she had been honored previously (1973) as well as other legends, Bette Davis, Sylvia Sidney, and Myrna Loy. Shown here in New York. 1974.

Frank Sinatra presented the "Jean Hersholt Humanitarian Award" to good friend Roz Russell in Hollywood. 1973.

became her husband. Roz, known as Hollywood's No. 1 (and probably only one) leading bachelor girl, succumbed to the Danish-born gentleman. They were married in a small sleepy village north of Santa Barbara, called Solvang. Settled by Danes, it was quiet and not commercial in those days. Today it is a "must" on the California visitor's list along with the Hearst estate and other notable mansions. But in 1941, it was an ideal setting for their wedding.

Mr. Brisson, an offspring of show biz parents, had an ongoing business in Europe prior to his arrival in the United States. Anxious to leave as Hitler's rise became intolerable, his Anglo-American talent agency was well-known and established. He became a leading producer on Broadway (**Pajama Game, Damn Yankees**) and later a movie producer. He is credited with introducing the work of playwrights Harold Pinter and Peter Shaffer to American audiences.

Before Roz returned to Broadway, she made two departures from her screen image. One, as **Sister Kenny** (1946), the Australian who evolved a treatment for polio; two, in **Mourning Becomes Electra** (1947), by Eugene O'Neill. Both performances received "Oscar" nominations. Yet it was her next movie, **The Velvet Touch** (1948) that was the money-maker.

She returned to the stage via **Bell, Book, and Candle** and happily learned that she still had "the velvet touch" for her first love. Playing a witch with way-out powers, Roz sharpened her stage know-how not knowing

that around the corner lay two big BIG theatrical successes.

In 1942, she had filmed **My Sister Eileen,** which brought her first "Oscar" nomination. Now in the hands of — music, Leonard Bernstein; director, George Abbott; and, lyrics, Betty Comden and Adolph Green, **Eileen** became the musical **Wonderful Town.** Roz skipped off with the Tony Award and many others for this 1953 effort. Her next big Broadway event was **Auntie Mame** in 1956-57. She stayed with it until it was time to do the film version, released in 1958 which brought her a fourth "Oscar" nomination. Later, **Mame** came back as a musical starring Angela Lansbury. Later, the screen version musical starred Lucille Ball.

In 1953 when **Wonderful Town** opened, Roz Russell had turned forty-two. Certainly not old age, but for glamor girls it could be an awkward age. To her credit, the Queen, as she was called, made the transition gracefully. At forty-two, in her chic middle-age body she sang and danced like a twenty-year old. And then in 1955, she played the frustrated schoolteacher in **Picnic,** the film that introduced Kim Novak. In 1962 (**Gypsy**) and in 1967 (**Rosie**), she played older parts with all the zest and energy reflected in her Forties' films. Perhaps if one word were used to describe Roz Russell, it would be energy.

Off-screen she was a tireless worker for almost as many causes as there are illnesses. Finally in 1973 she was awarded an "Oscar", the Humanitarian Award. According to her husband, her lifetime awards both profes-

Applauding the arrival of then Gov. Ronald Reagan (back to camera) at a $100-a-plate dinner with then Vice President Spiro Agnew, as the principal speaker, were (l-r) Frank Sinatra, Rosalind Russell, Milton Berle (dark rim glasses), John Wayne, Jack Benny, and Eva Gabor. Anaheim, Calif. 1972.

"Energy personified," that's what she was. Roz shown here on NBC's "The Wonderful World of Entertainment" where she acted as hostess and guide for the premiere presentation on "Ford's Startime." Circa 1960's.

Roz and son Lance off for a six-week vacation aboard the liner *Queen Elizabeth*. New York City, 1960.

Roz on the "David Frost Show" recalled Hollywood during the 30's, her long friendship with Cary Grant, other highlights of her glittering career, and even sang. New York, 1971.

"Mame" becomes immortal in Grauman's Chinese Theatre's cement — ing of great stars. Roz here in Hollywood. 1959.

One of the last portraits taken of Rosalind Russell. 1973.

Leaving the Church of the Good Shepherd, Miss Russell's casket was attended by eight pallbearers. In front, two funeral directors; second from left is Jack Lemmon and behind him Kirk Douglas; right side is Cary Grant and two behind him, Robert Wagner. Beverly Hills, 1976.

sionally and as a volunteer exceeded the 200 mark. Her hometown, Waterbury, named a theater after her, and her adopted town, Los Angeles, gave her the title "Woman of the Year" in 1953.

Yet her biggest award — rather reward, proved to be a marriage of thirty-five years. One son, Lance, had been born in 1943, and married Patricia Morrow a year before his mother's death. It is safe to assume that Roz put as much of herself into her marriage and motherhood as she did in her work. Hollywood in itself is paved with matrimonial pot-holes that make New York streets look like velvet. The only hole Roz fell into was one of wet cement in front of Grauman's Chinese Theatre where she was immortalized (in cement) in 1959.

Her health failed with painful and crippling rheumatoid arthritis in 1969. In 1960 she had had a mastectomy. A second one was performed in 1965. Between the two operations she made eight films and never — never capitalized on her illness through the press. She was a fighter; she was brave; and she was proud. Not until the cortisone began to swell her lovely face was the public aware that Roz was seriously ill. During her life she made over fifty films, the last, **Mrs. Pollifax-Spy,** was released in 1971.

In Hollywood, New York, and Europe, the Freddie Brissons were always welcome. As a couple they were envied and their presence always desired. They remain one of Hollywood's finest — on every level.

Roz died a few weeks after her 35th wedding anniversary. She was buried in the Catholic Holy Cross Cemetery in Los Angeles. One of her marvelous quotes regarding her Catholic church in Beverly Hills was her name for it — "Our Lady of the Cadillacs." But it is the quote from **Auntie Mame,** which serves as the title of her book, that expresses her philosophy: "Life is a banquet, and most of you poor suckers are starving to death." *

Rosalind Russell kept her shape, inwardly and outwardly, while she feasted on life.

ROSALIND RUSSELL
Died: November 28, 1976
Los Angeles, California

* Rosalind Russell and Chris Chase, **Life is a Banquet** (New York: Random House).

Rosalind Russell and George Raft in **It Had to Happen,** her tenth movie. 1936.

Alan Marshal and Rosalind Russell in **Night Must Fall.** 1937.

Four of the 135 ladies who played in **The Women.** (l-r) Phyllis Povah, Rosalind Russell, Virginia Grey, and an extra with back to camera. 1939.

Rosalind Russell, Barbara Jo Allen (Vera Vague), and Lee Bowman in **Design For Scandal.** 1941.

(l-r) Constance Moore, Fred MacMurray, Rosalind Russell, and Macdonald Carey in **Take a Letter, Darling.** 1942.

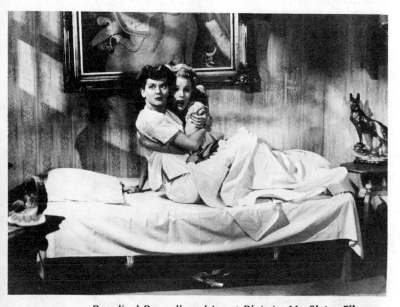

Rosalind Russell and Janet Blair in **My Sister Eileen,** for which Roz received her first "Oscar" nomination. 1942.

Rosalind Russell and Jack Carson in **Roughly Speaking.** 1945.

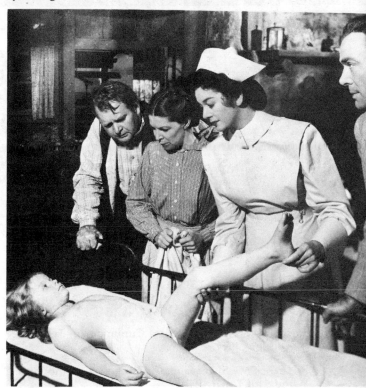

(l-r) Doreen McCann, Charles Kemper, Fay Helm, Rosalind Russell, and Dean Jagger in **Sister Kenny,** which brought Roz her second "Oscar" nomination. 1946.

Katina Paxinou and Roz Russell in **Mourning Becomes Electra,** which gave Roz her third "Oscar" nomination. 1947.

(l-r) Esther Howard, Frank McHugh, Rosalind Russell, and Sydney Greenstreet in **The Velvet Touch.** 1948.

Roz Russell in **The Girl Rush.** 1955.

Rosalind Russell and Robert Cummings in **Tell It To The Judge.** 1949.

Roz takes **My Sister Eileen** to Broadway as the musical **Wonderful Town.** 1953.

Rosalind Russell, and Arthur O'Connell and (lower right) Verna Felton in William Inge's **Picnic.** Russell played the frustrated schoolteacher, who according to her autobiography, **Life Is A Banquet,** says that Rosemary was one of the author's two sisters. 1955.

Roz Russell in the film version of **Auntie Mame,** which gave her her fourth "Oscar" nomination, 1958.

Rosalind Russell in **The Trouble With Angels,** which co-starred then 18-year old Hayley Mills of the Disney Studio fame. 1966.

Rosalind Russell, an Irish girl from Connecticut, playing a Jewish lady from Brooklyn with Sir Alec Guinness, a Britisher playing a Japanese gentleman, in **A Majority of One.** 1961.

Rosalind Russell and Hugh Griffith in **Oh Dad, Poor Dad, Mamma's Hung You in the Closet and I'm Feelin' So Sad.** Roz's judgment told her this was a comedy; her director told her it was a tragedy. She was probably right. 1967.

Rosalind Russell, Maximillian Schell, and Jack Hawkins in **Five Finger Excercise.** 1962.

La Russell in **Gypsy.** Roz claims to have done her own singing in the film but Lisa Kirk, in the book **The Unkindest Cuts** (1972) by Doug McClelland, claims to be the voice behind the Russell face. 1962.

(l-r) James Farentino, Sandra Dee, Rosalind Russell, and Brian Aherne in **Rosie,** which marked Roz's entrance into show biz about forty years before this film. 1967.

Rosalind Russell with Harold Gould (l) and Nehemiah Persoff (r) in her last film, **Mrs. Pollifax-Spy.** Stricken with rheumatoid arthritis, she slowly began to cut back on her professional work as she plunged into volunteer work on behalf of this crippling disease. 1971.

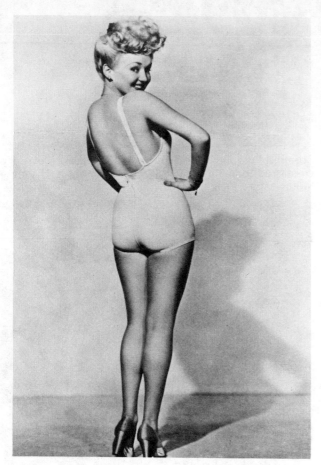

Betty Grable's WW II "Pin-Up" photograph requested by over three million civilians and servicemen and by far the most famous picture of its time. 1942.

BETTY GRABLE

Born: December 18, 1916 St. Louis, Missouri

During World War II (1941-1945), servicemen throughout the world lay in their bunks listening to the recorded voices of Kate Smith and Vaughn Monroe singing "When The Lights Go On Again All Over The World" and gazing at a photograph of a five-foot, three-inch blue-eyed blonde peering over one shoulder. The photo was called a "pin-up" and the girl was Betty Grable. Clad in a white bathing suit, with a pouty-shaped mouth, she was the girl they would have liked to be with at that moment: Grable was the blonde of the Forties. She had replaced Alice Faye; later, she would be displaced by Marilyn Monroe.

One of the unusual aspects of this "pin-up" phenomenon (over three million photos were requested) was that Betty Grable did not elict jealous feelings from women. She was so likeable, so honest that almost as many women wrote to her — an average of 10,000 fan letters a week during her heyday — as men. And some of these were grandmothers. Once she said, "Men are not threatened by me. They think I'm a dumb blonde. And women feel no competition because I look ordinary. Even grandmothers like me."

She was ordinary in a sense. Her voice was just a voice; her dancing was average; she was small (called a "pony" in the chorus); and her acting was modest. But her enthusiasm and energy for her work and her graciousness about her success were far from ordinary. And her support for her fellow-workers was unselfish. To Monroe, who took over for Betty at Fox Studio, she said, "I've got mine, honey. Now go get yours." And she meant it.   By the time the war ended, Grable had been performing for twenty years. She was the second daughter of Lillian Hoffman Grable (possibly changed from Grasle according to some biographers), a bookkeeper by trade, a frustrated performer by avocation. The former, Lillian abandoned after marriage; and the latter, became her vocation — her full time job — the moment she spotted a modicum of talent in Ruth Elizabeth (Betty). The elder daughter, Marjorie, refused to go along with Lillian's aspirations; but Betty, an easy-going child and later the same as an adult, allowed her mother to push and shove and drive. If there were a Hall of Fame for stage mothers, Betty Grable's mother would fight it out with Judy Garland's for first place in the tenacity category, known as "pushy."

At age 4, Betty started dance classes: toe, ballet, tap, and acrobatic. Nothing was overlooked including lessons on the saxaphone, ukelele, and trap drums. By age 7, she was in talent shows and shown off at home to guests whether they wanted to see her or not. According to biographer, Gene Ringgold,* "a platform was constructed in the foyer of the Grable apartment that enabled her to practice in a central area." Lillian managed not only to affront her guests, but also managed to remove Betty from any desirable social functions. St. Louis society looked askance at her actions and at most

*Screen Facts, Number 4, 1963.

Betty Grable and pal Marilyn Monroe whom Betty encouraged, unlike most stars, who when threatened, respond with envy. 1953.

Betty and her mother Lillian appearing in court to testify in mother's divorce proceedings. Los Angeles, 1939.

All of those dancing lessons paid off. Here Betty is being crowned "Queen of the Dance," by Frank Veloz of the famous dance team Veloz and Yolanda, longstanding, outstanding duos of their time. 1949.

Betty appeared in **Whoopee,** with Eddie Cantor in 1930. It was her third film. Shown here, Cantor, Eleanor Hunt, and Chief Caupolican in the film.

theatrical endeavors. Conn Grable, the father, had risen from a bookkeeper to a successful stockbroker and could well afford exclusive private schools for his daughers. Hence, the availability of desired social functions.

And so in the summer of '28, Lillian irritated by St. Louis, decided that the Grables should visit Hollywood. By '29, Lillian and Betty had moved there. And the climb upward began. Once again Betty was enrolled in dance academies as well as the Hollywood Professional School. For a brief time she had an unsuccessful act with dancer Emylyn Price who split for New York where she established herself as Mitzi Mayfair. Meanwhile, Betty, aged 13, answered a call from Fox for girls who could dance and sing. By lying about her age, she managed to get in the chorus of **Let's Go Places** with sixty other dancers. Although Fox signed her to a contract, they released her because her age was doubtful, and the studio didn't want to tangle with California's stringent child-labor laws.

Her next two inauspicious appearances were in **Whoopee**, starring Eddie Cantor, and **Kiki** starring Mary Pickford. Then she bounced like a ping-pong ball from Goldwyn to Columbia to Fox until RKO signed her to a 5-year contract. Still an ingenue, still doing amateur nights, still being prodded by her mother, she worked continuously, even doing Educational Films directed by Fatty Arbuckle. His reputation had been permanently damaged during the trial and "mysterious death" of a young actress, Virginia Rappe. And although he was acquitted, he never regained his popularity and was now directing under the name of William Goodrich. Lillian promptly changed Betty's name to Frances Dean so her daughter's name would not be tainted by Arbuckle's. While under contract, but not being used constantly, Betty went into a musical revue, **Tattle Tales**, as Frances Dean. She began dating actor George Raft, and although they were never married, their relationship continued for many years — even between Betty's two marriages.

After **Tattle Tales,** she danced and sang with Ted Fio Rita and his orchestra and later

with Jay Whidden's band in San Francisco and Santa Monica. Finally in **The Gay Divorcee**, which starred Fred Astaire and Ginger Rogers, Grable received a notice in the trade papers for her musical dance and comedy song number, "K-Knock Knees" done with funny person Edward Everett Horton.

Knock-kneed she wasn't. Her legs became as famous as Gable's ears, Bob Hope's nose, Barrymore's profile, Monty Woolley's beard — all preserved in cement at Grauman's Chinese Theatre. Betty said, "There are two reasons why I'm in show business, and I'm standing on both of them." In 1947, she played in **The Shocking Miss Pilgrim** and never showed her legs. The studio received over 100,000 complaints, and that took care of that.

Her film life continued to be a hopping about process and although she was considered "cute," RKO dropped her. No one saw the handwriting on the wall for her, or the part she would play in the approaching war.

In 1937, she married former child star Jackie "The Kid" Coogan. Together they did a variety act, but both the act and the marriage proved to be unsuccessful. They divorced two years later. Again she began to date George Raft. And once more she began those series of inconsequential films. By 1939, still relatively unknown, and bored with being type-cast as the perennial co-ed, she was released: this time by Paramount Pictures.

She went into the smash Broadway musical, **Du Barry Was A Lady**, starring Ethel Merman and Bert Lahr. But just before she left for New York, Fox Studio producer Darryl F. Zanuck spotted some "cheesecake" photos, signed her without a screen test, and allowed her to go east. Eight months later, Fox crooked its finger and back she came to replace ailing Alice Faye in **Down Argentine Way** (1940). This was the turning point for La Grable, and soon the years and years of hard work would pay off. Meanwhile across the ocean, the Allies were defending themselves against the Nazi horror, and the entrance of the United States into the war was only a year away.

Betty and George Raft whom she had met in 1931 filming **Palmy Days.** Shown here at the Stork Club, ten years later as they resumed dating after her divorce from Jackie Coogan. New York City, 1941.

Betty joins the immortals as she leaves her leg prints in cement at Grauman's Chinese Theatre, ably assisted by Sgt. B.L. Duckett, USMC; J.O. Buckanan, Gunners Mate 3rd Class, USN; and Sgt. Albert Woas, USA. All three men had their names listed beneath Betty's name and legs. Hollywood, 1943.

Betty Grable and first husband, Jackie "The Kid" Coogan. Coogan rose to fame as a child star playing with Charlie Chaplin in the six-reel film **The Kid** in 1921. Shown here in 1937.

Betty married second husband, trumpeter Harry James in Las Vegas. 1943.

Down Argentine Way was Grable's 29th film, and she was now 24 years old. She would do 26 additional films under the Fox banner, grossing about 100 million dollars. Her take-home pay totaled about 3 million. And in 1946-47, the Treasury Department said she was the highest paid American woman, earning $300,000. Needless to say, Lillian was happy. But so was Betty. Her films were short on plot, but long on leading men: Tyrone Power, Don Ameche, Victor Mature, John Payne, Jack Oakie, George Murphy (yes, the Congressman), and her favorite, Dan Dailey.

Although Grable had a beautiful body, it was so thoroughly healthy and "girl-next-doorish" in its energy, it was not the most sexually interesting. And herein lies the overwhelming success of her as the "Pin-Up." She did not exude the sexiness of Mae West, nor the sex kittenish appeal of Marilyn Monroe, nor the blatant arousal of Jean Harlow. She had the perfect image for G I's with her beautiful body. Yet she was unpretentious, good-natured, and likeable. Her photograph was "marked off in sections to teach fliers how to read aerial maps." No wonder our flying boys bombed with such accuracy.

In 1943, she married musician Harry James. They had two daughters, Jessica and Victoria. She continued her career, and after the war continued almost bravely to stay at the top. She remained in the top ten at the box office for twelve years as the queen of the technicolor musicals. So why the word "bravely?" Because she knew what the war had meant to her career, how limited she was, and how many post-war talents were emerging. Her fate was finally settled in 1953 by Marilyn Monroe. They played together in **How To Marry A Millionaire.** Although Betty recognized it was Monroe's popularity that brought in the big money, it was Grable's name that appeared on top billing. Two years later she made her last film, **How To Be Very, Very Popular.**

By now her private life had taken on the flavor of mother, wife, and owner of a good racing stable. She and James owned two ranches and two estates. They shared a com-

A Christmas party for stars' children (left) Candace Bergen, daughter of ventriloquist Edgar Bergen, and Vicki James, Betty's daughter at the Bergen home. Hollywood, 1948.

Betty and second daughter, Jessica, born May 20, 1947. Hollywood.

Hubby James visits Betty on the set for the first day's shooting; a tradition he maintained since their marriage ten years before. 1954.

Betty meets co-star Sheree North as they prepare for **How To Be Very, Very Popular,** Grable's last film. Hollywood, 1955.

Tennis champ Maureen "Little Mo" Connolly (right) chats with Harry James and wife Betty Grable at the races. Connolly, then age 16, had just won the U.S. Championship at Forest Hills. Her brilliant career was cut short when she died at an early age. Del Mar, California. 1951.

Betty and Harry congratulate jockey Ralph Neves for his winning ride on their horse Big Noise. "Noise" previously won the California Breeders Championship $25,000 Stakes in 1952. Shown here at Hollywood Park, 1954.

Betty rehearses with dancer/choreographer Gower Champion for the Las Vegas edition of **Hello Dolly** after her Broadway success in the same role. Champion died (1981) on the day his last success **42nd Street** opened on Broadway. Shown here, 1966.

Betty returned to New York for the first time since her debut in **DuBarry Was A Lady,** 19 years ago, and opened triumphantly at the Latin Quarter. Shown here being congratulated by actress Maureen O'Hara. New York, 1959.

Grable visits performer Ann-Margret on her return to the stage after a nasty fall in which Ann-Margret fractured her face in five places, her jaw, and left arm. Grable had opened her nightclub stint in Las Vegas in 1956. Shown here with Roger Smith, Ann-Margret's husband, in Vegas where she played to a sellout house and standing ovation. 1972.

BETTY AND FRIENDS, YEARS AFTER HER LAST MOVIE, AS SHE SANG AND DANCED HER WAY BACK INTO THE HEARTS OF THE AMERICAN PUBLIC.

Betty and Dinah Shore rehearsing for Dinah's NBC-TV show. March 1960.

Betty belting out a song on the "Hollywood Palace" TV show while veterans of WW II tuned in and saw their pin-up queen looking as cute as ever. October 1964.

(l-r) Van Johnson, Grable, and Sergio Franchi in ABC-TV's "Hollywood Palace." 1964.

Jessica James Wahner, one of Betty's daughters, being escorted after the memorial services for her mother. Los Angeles, 1973.

Jackie Coogan, Grable's first husband, arriving at the funeral services for his former wife. Over 400 mourners attended the services for Betty. Los Angeles, 1973.

Betty Grable knew her limitations as far as talent was concerned. But her honesty and sincerity knew no limit, and the public loved her for it. Circa 1940.

mon interest in their fillies, geldings, and horses. And Betty finally began to live the life she had missed as a child. She was quoted as saying all she wanted to do was eat, sleep, and do what she wanted. Eventually, they moved to Las Vegas where James was employed.

They were divorced in 1965, and in 1967 Betty returned to Broadway as the umpteenth star of **Hello Dolly**. Bowling and golf had kept her in shape, and none of the former GI's were disappointed as they lined up for tickets and later backstage for her autograph on their slightly worn photographs. And with them, they had their sons in tow as they proudly showed off what had sustained them during the war.

The success of **Dolly** led her into other vehicles such as **Guys and Dolls** and **Born Yesterday**. But she yearned for a role of her own, feeling that **Dolly** was Carol Channing's and **Guys** was Vivian Blaine's. She attempted **Belle Starr** in London, but it closed after seventeen days. Her last wish was never fulfilled.

In 1972, she performed on the NBC-TV special, "The Fabulous Forties" with Dick Haymes. Now a grandmother of five, she even did the Geritol commercials. One might say that Grable knew who she was,

what she was, and passed each stage of her life with great ease. When the *Harvard Lampoon* called her "the worst actress of the year," she agreed with them. When Fox offered her a dramatic part in **The Razor's Edge,** she declined. "People like to hear me sing, see me dance, and watch my legs." She was not a dumb blonde. In fact, she was one of the few big stars who emerged unscathed by temporary and short-lived adulation and old age.

And unlike her mother, who lived long enough to see Betty become really famous, Betty was never a stage mother. She allowed her children to find their own way.

A year after the NBC special, she died of lung cancer. Private services were held at the All Saints Episcopal Church in Beverly Hills, California.

The *New Yorker* magazine once defined entertainment as "Mickey Mouse's adventures and Betty Grable's legs." And to this, one must add — entertainment, yes, but a special brand of entertainment during one of the country's most devastating eras, when smiling (as well as gasoline and new shoes) was at a premium.

BETTY GRABLE
Died: July 2, 1973
Santa Monica, California

Grable and husband Jackie Coogan, just newlyweds, in **College Swing,** the fourth of her collegiate flicks. 1938. Others were: **Student Tour** (1934); **Collegiate** (1936); **Pigskin Parade** (1936). Before she "graduated" she was a co-ed twice more: **Campus Confessions** (1938) and **Million Dollar Legs** (1939).

Betty Grable and her favorite co-star and dancer, Dan Dailey, in **Mother Wore Tights,** which broke the attendance record at N.Y.'s Roxy Theatre right after **The Dolly Sisters** had created the first record. This film was one of the most popular Grable efforts. 1947.

Grable and Jack Oakie in **Tin Pan Alley,** which brought her good reviews even though Alice Faye had the "meaty" role. 1940. Grable and Oakie also appeared together in **Collegiate** (1936); **Song of the Islands** (1942); and **When My Baby Smiles At Me** (1948).

Betty Grable and Dan Dailey in **Call Me Mister,** a rehash of the successful stage play with Busby Berkeley staged dances. 1951.

Jane Wyman (the first Mrs. Ronald Reagan) and Betty Grable in **Footlight Seranade,** which also starred Victor Mature and John Payne, in a potpourri of show business and prize fighting. 1942.

Betty Grable and June Haver in **The Dolly Sisters,** which didn't quite follow the real lives of Jenny and Rosie Dolly. However, the film broke the attendance record at New York's Roxy Theatre in 1945.

(l-r) Marilyn Monroe, Lauren Bacall, and Betty Grable in **How to Marry a Millionaire,** the remake 'grandmother' of all time: taken from about six film sources. Grable's name appeared above Monroe's on the screen. 1953.

(l-r) Jack Lemmon, Betty Grable, and Gower Champion in **Three For The Show.** 1955. This musical was a remake of **Too Many Husbands,** which starred Jean Arthur in 1940 and was Grable's next to last film.

Clark Gable in his forties, greying slightly at the
temples, remained the potent example of the Golden
Age of Hollywood, designated as "The King." Circa 1946.

Charlie Chaplin (seated) at Gracie Mansion, the residence of New York City's mayor, after having been honored upon his return to the United States. Mayor John Lindsay(r) presented Chaplin with the keys to the city and the Handel Medallion. Wife Oona Chaplin and conductor Arthur Fiedler were also present for the ceremonies. Mr. Fiedler (1894-1979) was head of the Boston "Pops" Orchestra for 50 years. New York, April 1972.

Spencer Tracy and Katharine Hepburn in 1945. They were unique—on the screen and off. Their relationship lasted twenty-seven years; they made nine films together: **Woman of the Year** (1942); **Keeper of the Flame** (1942); **Without Love** (1945); **The Sea of Grass** (1947); **State of the Union** (1948); **Adam's Rib** (1949); **Pat and Mike** (1952); **Desk Set** (1957); and **Guess Who's Coming to Dinner** (1967).

Louis Armstrong at home in Corona, Queens, New York, five months after his 70th birthday. He was the first major, original jazz solo instrumental voice. 1970.

(l-r) Diahann Carroll, Bing Crosby, and Joey Heatherton taping the TV show "Hollywood Palace" in California. 1967. Miss Heatherton co-starred with her father Ray Heatherton (the commercial spokesman for Tropicana Orange Juice) in a TV summer variety series called "Joey & Dad," 1975. Miss Carroll was the first black female to star in her own comedy series, "Julia" (1968), in a "prestige" role. Formerly, blacks had portrayed either domestics or were billed as second bananas.

At the Academy Awards in 1962. Burt Lancaster, winner for **Elmer Gantry** (1960); Joan Crawford, winner for **Mildred Pierce** (1945); Maximillian Schell, winner for **Judgment at Nuremberg** (1961); and Greer Garson, winner for **Mrs. Miniver** (1942).

John Wayne accepting the "Oscar" for his role in
True Grit (1969) from Barbra Streisand who tied with
Katharine Hepburn the previous year as Best Actress.
Miss Hepburn won for **The Lion in Winter;** Miss
Streisand for **Funny Girl.** Los Angeles, 1970.

Humphrey Bogart became a cult idol after his death at the age of fifty-eight. Shown here, circa late 1940's.

MUSICIANS

The man that hath no music in himself,
Nor is moved with concord of sweet sounds,
Is fit for treason, stratagems, and spoils . . .
Shakespeare

Duke Ellington on his music, "I don't write jazz, I write Negro folk music." Feeling that his music had outgrown the word "jazz," he continued, "We've worked and fought under the banner of jazz for many years, but the word itself has no meaning. There's a form of condescension in it." 1955.

DUKE ELLINGTON

Born: April 29, 1899 Washington, D.C.

"*Genius* implies superior gifts of nature impelling the mind to exceptional creative or inventive effort in the arts or sciences."

Edward Kennedy Ellington, "Duke" as one young friend tagged him early in life, was born into a non-ghetto family. His father, James Edward, had been a butler at the White House; his son would celebrate his seventieth birthday there. Later Duke's father worked as a blueprint maker for the United States Navy, which gave the family a modest income.

His mother, Daisy Kennedy Ellington, instilled in her only son his deep religious feelings. Every Sunday she would take him to two services: one, at her Baptist church; two, at his father's Methodist church. She taught him that God is God no matter where you worship, and she told him that there is only one God, colorless and raceless.

Both parents played piano — lovingly, if not expertly — but aside from the church music, he was constantly exposed through burlesque houses, theaters, radio, and even a poolroom piano where struggling musicians would drop in and play. His formal education began and ended with one teacher, aptly or inaptly named, Mrs. Clinkscales. In his autobiography,* Duke credits Henry Grant, a high school teacher, who taught him harmony and Oliver "Doc" Perry, who taught him to read a melody line and to recognize chords.

Early in life, Duke began to acquire eloquence in his speech pattern and a showmanship demeanor: the latter is the necessary ingredient that distinguishes a leader from a sideman. Countless musicians with overwhelming talent can never "front" a band or group because of this missing component. From the onset, the first trio, Ellington was its leader — its front person.

Painting was another of his talents. It did not fall by the wayside but found incorporation into his music. Music, with its color,

*Duke Ellington, **Music is My Mistress** (New York: Doubleday & Co., Inc.).

shading, vibrancy, could and did absorb the colors he saw in his head and with his eyes. Many of his compositions have a strong sense of color in their titles. The titles also reflect his attentive ear to his surroundings and sponge-like diffusion from any juncture. His first song, **Soda Fountain Rag,** composed at age 16 while working as a soda jerk, is an early example of this.

Before the lure of the big city got under his skin, he married neighbor and classmate, Edna Thompson. He was only nineteen at the time, 1918, and the marriage produced two sons: Mercer Kennedy born in 1919; the other died in infancy. The second alliance was with saxophonist Otto "Toby" Hardwick, a classmate who was five years younger than Duke, and drummer Sonny Greer. This trio formed the core of the first important Ellington band.

Hardwick and Greer preceded him to Manhattan, but by the time Duke got there the boys were broke and jobs were scant. Back they went to Washington until a second call came from New York. This time it was pianist "Fats" Waller who told them that there was work, not only for the trio, but probably for the five of them: trumpeter, Arthur Whetsol and banjo player Elmer Snowden were then part of the Ellington group in D.C. By the time they got to New York, whatever job Waller had in mind was gone. But New York was the classroom; the place to listen and to learn from the likes of James P. Johnson and Willie "the Lion" Smith. These gin-mill giants taught the young Duke. Although he could not copy their "stride" styles, he could take from them and ultimately develop his own mode.

The first real break came through Ada Smith, later known as "Bricktop," the darling of Europe, especially Paris. She induced nightclub owner, Barron Wilkins, to hire "The Washingtonians," whom she had heard back in the capital. The five men split a weekly salary of fifty dollars, but the tips at Barron's from the high-livers made their lives quite comfortable. As an adjunct to his weekly wage, but more importantly as an outlet for his talent, Duke joined forces with lyricist Jo Trent. For fifty dollars they sold songs outright to Broadway music pub-

163

lishers. Applying his attitude —I know what's going on — he appropriately entitled one "Pretty Soft for You." He further augmented his income with a complete score, **Chocolate Kiddies,** featuring Adelaide Hall and Josephine Baker, for five hundred dollars, which he and Trent split. This little gem ultimately ran in Berlin for two years and made producer Jack Robbins a rich man.

In 1923, the band moved from Barron's at 134th Street to mid-town, 49th and Broadway, into the Kentucky Club. This gig lasted for four years: a steady job from eleven at night until eight in the morning. It became "the place to drop in" for other musicians and greats like Sidney Bechet and Paul Whiteman with his sidemen, Bix Beiderbecke, Joe Venuti, and Tommy Dorsey, who'd either listen or sit in. One of the important "drop-ins" was Irving Mills, manager, who formed an association with Ellington for more than ten years and was crucial in making the name of Ellington an international word. It was Mills who first put them in the studios and insisted that Ellington tunes be recorded. And it was he who had them booked into London's Palladium in 1933.

As the Duke became public property, his private life with wife, Edna, began its decline. In her own words, Edna stated that she was jealous and envious of having to share her husband. She eventually moved back to Washington where she lived until her death in 1966. Duke supported her in a fine fashion throughout her life, and they were never divorced. By the early 30's, Duke had moved his entire family to New York where younger sister Ruth and son Mercer were educated. His mother had always looked after Mercer, and later his father was the band's manager for a short time before his death in 1937.

In December of 1927 when Duke and Company opened at Harlem's famous Cotton Club, he bade goodbye to the ballroom-circuit and irregular contributions to vaudeville as his innovative and original sense of orchestra and compositions took over. Aside from being the number one spot in Harlem's music scene, the nightly coast-to-

Brooks Kerr, pianist, song historian, and great exponent of "Ellingtonia." Duke once said, "He (Brooks) knows more about me than I know about myself."

Billy Strayhorn joined Ellington in 1939, the same year their first joint effort, "Something to Live For," was written. Then in 1941, Strays wrote "Take the A Train," which became the band's signature. And he was with Duke until his death in 1967.

(l-r) President Richard M. Nixon and wife Pat; sister, Ruth Ellington and Duke Ellington at the White House in honor of Duke's seventieth birthday. Quipped the President, "Kings and Queens have dined here but never a Duke." And the Duke responded, "There is no place I would rather be tonight except in my mother's arms." 1969.

Duke accepts award from New York's Paul O'Dwyer, as Evie Ellis (Ellington) proudly takes her place alongside Duke. 1965.

Duke and singer Tony Bennett at the Waldorf-Astoria Hotel where Bennett was appearing. The celebration was in honor of Duke's 72nd birthday. New York City, April 1971.

Close friends and relatives gathered at Walter B. Cooke's funeral home to pay their last respects to Duke, seen in casket in background. New York City, 1974.

coast radio broadcasts provided greater exposure for the band.

From then on, despite challenges from other great bands, namely Count Basie, Glenn Miller, Tommy Dorsey, Benny Goodman and others, the authority of the Ellington position was never threatened. The mid-Forties saw the demise of the big bands as smaller groups took over, but the Ellington ensemble remained intact.

"Talent," differs from genius in that "it supposes a special aptitude for being molded and directed to specific ends and purposes."

Pianist/composer, Dick Katz, makes this analogy, "As in the commedia dell' arte, where in spite of changes over the years, the characters retained the original flavor, so did the music/solo work of the Ellington stars. These individual talents were the central characters in the unfolding drama of Ellingtonia."

Clarinet: Barney Bigard, Jimmy Hamilton
Saxophone: Harry Carney (baritone), Johnny Hodges (alto), Ben Webster (tenor), Paul Gonsalves (tenor)
Trombone: Juan Tizol (valve), Joe "Tricky Sam" Nanton, Lawrence Brown
Trumpet: Rex Stewart, Cootie Williams, Ray Nance (also violin), Cat Anderson
Drums: Sonny Greer, Louis Bellson, Sam Woodyard
Bass: Jimmy Blanton,* Oscar Pettiford
Individual singers were used as extensions of the orchestra, but the following were the band vocalists: Ivie Anderson, Herb Jeffries, Al Hibbler, Joya Sherrill, and Kay Davis.

There was one other who contributed to the heartbeat of Ellington's musical life: William Thomas Strayhorn from Pittsburgh, Pennsylvania, also known as Billie , "Swee' Pea," or "Strays." He first heard the band when he was still in his teens but waited until he was twenty-four to approach Duke with the idea of joining the group. His background had been as a "classicist," yet even at the early age of nineteen when he composed "Lush Life," the merger of the two musical forms was taking shape. Within three months after he joined Duke, they collaborated and recorded their first joint effort "Something to Live For."

*Jimmy Blanton revolutionized the concept of playing the bass. He died on July 30, 1942 at the age of twenty-four.

Lifelong friend, Edmund Anderson, who gave Duke his biggest non-Ellington tune, "Flamingo," in 1943 (written with Ted Grouya). Anderson and Ellington met in 1936. Shown here in 1960's.

Duke and manager music publisher Irving Mills arriving in Paris. 1939. Although Mills had broken barrier after barrier for Duke, there was still a lot of resentment after the breakup over "disputed funds."

The band in MGM's **Cabin in the Sky,** which featured Ethel Waters, Lena Horne, and Eddie "Rochester" Anderson. Shown here: drummer Sonny Greer; saxophonists, Webster, Hooper, Hodges, Hardwick, Carney; guitar, Guy; trombonists, Brown, Nanton, Tizol; trumpeters, Baker, Stewart, Jones, Nance; bassist, Ragland; and Duke at the keyboard. 1942.

Duke with the Rev. Bryant M. Kirkland, pastor of the Fifth Avenue Presbyterian Church, NYC. The Sacred Music Concert drew over 3,000 people for its two performances. 1965.

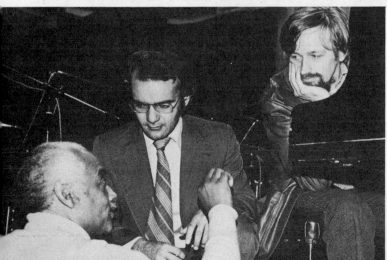

Duke's son Mercer (back to camera) continues in the Ellington tradition. Here with guest conductor, Wojciech Rajski, the band joins the Warsaw Philharmonic Orchestra. Seated at the piano is guest artist, Adam Makowicz, Polish winner of the European Jazz Polls and considered by Mercer, "One of the greatest, (pianist) if not the greatest." Warsaw, 1977.

Writers have called "Strays" an *alter ego*: another aspect of oneself. Or *doppelgänger*: a double, a twin. But it is the word, *symbiotic*, that more accurately describes their alliance: Duke and Billy were two dissimilar living things — organisms — living in close association or union, where the advantages were extravagant to both. Strayhorn was not a twin nor a double; he was himself. And it was this *self*, combined with Ellington that produced the lasting effect.

Strayhorn stayed with the organization until his death in 1967. Duke paid tribute to him with the album, **And His Mother Called Him Bill;** all the compositions were by Billy. Duke's grieving, lamenting over the loss, was preserved on tape as he sat at the piano, after the session, and played three minutes of "Lotus Blossom". "That is what he most liked to hear me play," said Duke.

Volumes have been written to describe and record his output. Chronological data have been gathered and set down to illustrate where and why Ellington was at any given moment. Most musicians agree that his strongest period was from 1940 to 1943. His travels took him from A to Z: from the Apollo Theatre to Zambia. In his own words he felt, "the most important thing I've ever done" was his reference to the second Sacred Concert in New York's Cathedral of St. John the Divine, January 1968.

There is the old adage, "man is never a hero to his own family." The adage, using the United States symbolically as Duke's family, applies when "The Advisory Board of the Pulitzer Prize Committee rejected a unanimous recommendation from its music jury, who felt Duke should be given a special citation." Whatever the reason, the rejection was viewed as an insult.

Ironically, the United States president who brought the country down to its knees with the infamous Watergate scandal, raised it to its toes (and righted the Pulitzer impudence) by presenting Duke Ellington with the Medal of Freedom, the highest civilian honor the United States government can bestow. The occasion occurred on Duke's seventieth birthday in 1969.

Arriving at the Cathedral (l) son, Mercer Ellington and his wife; (r) sister Ruth Ellington James. Inside Ella Fitzgerald sang a moving "Solitude" and Alistair Cooke, substituting names, repeated the sentence that novelist John O'Hara had written in mourning George Gershwin, "Duke Ellington died last week. I don't have to believe it if I don't want to."

While the festivities at the White House rang out, a disconsolate lady sat alone in her New York apartment. She was the woman in Duke Ellington's life for thirty-seven years. They had met when she was a dancer at the Cotton Club after Duke had terminated a relationship with another dancer, Mildred Dixon. Beatrice "Evie" Ellis, sometimes called Evie Ellington, was a beautiful part-Negro, part-Spanish lady who kept a low profile throughout the years, but who maintained a home for the globe trotting, womanizing Duke who was never without "company" on his travels. Regrettably, Duke did not marry her after his wife's death, and thoughtlessly, did not provide for her financially. She was stricken with cancer and died two years after he did. Fortunately, son Mercer did care and provide for Evie during her final years. The lady on Duke's arm that auspicious night at the White House was sister Ruth. However, Ruth and Mercer did show respect for Evie by burying her next to Duke in the Ellington plot in the Woodlawn Cemetery, 1976.

In 1972, lung cancer was diagnosed in Ellington, but he refused to accept this fatal illness. He strengthened his drive, his force, and his activity as he had always done in the face of adversity.

He kept going for an unbelievable two years before finally being admitted to the hospital in March of 1974. He died two months later. Tributes to Duke resounded throughout the world. But the *genius* of Duke will live on forever.

Duke Ellington
Died: May 24, 1974
New York, New York

(l-r) Singer Pearl Bailey, pianist Sammy Price, and the husband of Miss Bailey drummer Louis Bellson arrive at the church. Miss Bailey said, "Ellington represented a tradition of peace and love." She was President Richard Nixon's representative at the funeral. New York, 1974.

The white coffin, bearing Duke Ellington, being carried into Cathedral Church of St. John The Divine. Pallbearers included close friend Edmund Anderson; the son of former manager Irving Mills; George Wein, Newport Jazz impresario; and saxophonist, Harry Carney, who died five months later. New York City, May, 1974.

Mourners inside the Cathedral Church of St. John The Divine. A few blocks away, 106th Street was renamed Duke Ellington Boulevard. Although Duke was gone, his legacy is forever.

Suggested Discography of available Ellington albums: representative of an overall view of his tremendous output.

Ellington's first recordings with Alberta Prime and Sonny Greer are available on the Butch B.Y.G. label.

His output for the Victor label from 1927 to 1951 is available on a series of 24 single albums on the French R.C.A. label: the works on the Columbia label between 1925 and 1938 are available on 12 double-pocket albums on French C.B.S.

The final **Third Concert of Sacred Music** recorded at Westminster Abbey six months before Ellington's death is available on all R.C.A. Victor labels.

Collectors interested in Ellington's first extended work should purchase the fine Prestige album of his first Carnegie Hall concert on January 23rd 1943, which features "Black, Brown and Beige."

Compiled by Ellington historian, Brooks Kerr.

Commemorating the 20th anniversary of UNESCO, the African nation of Togo uniquely honored Duke Ellington with his portrait on a postage stamp. He was (at the time) the only living artist ever to be featured on a stamp. He was chosen to represent the 20th century with earlier periods represented by Bach (top left); Beethoven (top right); and Debussy (lower left). 1967.

Giant Ellington and Giantess Hazel Scott at the reception given in his honor at the American Cultural Center in Paris. 1958.

Tony Bennett, Judy Garland, and Duke in the mid Sixties.

Duke's opening night at Manhattan's Rainbow Grill. This "gig" became a yearly occasion. Helping him celebrate are actors Robert Morse and Angela Lansbury. August 1967.

(l) Conductor Leopold Stokowski and Ellington chat as Norman Racusin (c) looks on. Duke had won two Grammy awards at the 10th annual presentations of the National Academy of Recording Arts and Sciences; one for his "Far East Suite." 1968.

Two years before his death Ellington was awarded a 14-carat Honorary Gold Card Life Membership from the American Federation of Musicians "for lasting contributions to human understanding through fine music," in Honolulu. 1972. With Duke is his nephew, Steve James.

"I would rather do without food than music," Louis Armstrong. Circa 1950's.

LOUIS ARMSTRONG

Born: July 4, 1900 New Orleans, Louisiana

He played the trumpet, considered the hardest of instruments, for over fifty-five years. It never beat him as it has many others. He had God-given requisites: a broad thorax, which enabled great power; lungs which could hold extraordinary amounts of air; big flexible lips, hence the nickname Satchelmouth later shortened to Satchmo. He had a wonderful jaw formation, neither an overbite nor underslung, but a mouth that took a mouthpiece so perfectly that when taking a breath and then blowing the air, it became the most natural thing he could ever do. His teeth were broad and excellent; and finally, he had a strong heart. The trumpet demands these physical qualities.

What he did with these qualities — this is the real heart of Louis Armstrong.

The perfect trumpet player, but for him, Louie, the music always came first. 1961.

"It may be difficult for some of us to realize — particularly those who may have seen only his television appearances — what a great instrumentalist and important American musician Louis Armstrong has been," wrote Joseph Machlis.* "And all of our jazz, real and popularized, is different because of him, and our popular singers of all kinds are deeply in his debt."

When Louis Armstrong burst upon the scene, he had no predecessor; no frame of reference for what he was about to do; in

*Joseph Machlis, **The Enjoyment of Music** (New York: W.W. Norton Co., Inc.).

no way was he summing up or recapitulating principles or practices that had gone before. "Any solo parts, which were heard, were part of the orchestral fabric — interludes between ensembly passages." This statement was made by cornetist Richard Sudhalter. He continued, "The idea of a single instrument, in this case the trumpet, as the equivalent in this context, say to a bel canto tenor in opera, Louis was capable of dazzling bravura, flights of fancy, great romantic imagination, grabbing the heart and holding it, then bedazzling the senses—all this was unheard of."

Blue notes* and improvisation, the essence of jazz, were already laid down, but Louis (he preferred this to Louie) did more than just play the fundamental notes or blend into the aforementioned ensemble. Again, Mr. Sudhalter, "He brought to bear a vast vocabulary of expressive devices — ways of attacking notes and holding them; ways of blending and shaping them; achieving tonal effects. His sweeps up to notes, shakes, and types of vibrato, all added impact and emotional emphasis to a musical statement, very much like a cantor singing Jewish liturgy."

Richard M. Sudhalter capably combines a triple-faceted career. He is a leading cornetist and author as well as a music critic. In his role as critic, he manages to step back and view the performer in his or her context rather than by comparison or by his [Sudhalter's] musical preferences. This is a unique and difficult service and places him in a rare circle.

*Third and Seventh degrees of the scale, flattened.

Undoubtedly, the course of music could have been dramatically different had he not laid down these precepts.

Now, a half a century later, one can listen to and marvel at his absolute natural instinct, his sixth sense, an aesthetic taste that never failed him.

As a singer, he introduced "vocalese" — scat-singing — and again his perfection in phrasing, feeling, and line were undisputed. Today, unfortunately, there is is a whole generation who grew up knowing Louis Armstrong only as the guy with the 50-carat smile in **Hello Dolly.**

And finally, he was a born entertainer. From the time he played second or third trumpet, in his early days, his solos and personality drew the spotlight. He was earmarked for immortality.

Later in life he was tagged by some as an "Uncle Tom" or said to have "Uncle Tomian manners." Statements of envy need never be dignified. For those who missed the central core of Armstrong, missed out. He knew about racial prejudice. He lived with it, through it, and handled it his way — refused to make a propaganda tour of Russia for the State Department in 1957 — and spoke up when he felt it was the time to do it. He became the Ambassador from the United States through his music and through his own voice, not ever words put there by anyone else. But he never really wanted to be involved with hardcore racial issues, "My trumpet doesn't have to bother with that for the good reason that it doesn't know anything about it. I play and I will play wherever people want to listen to me".*

He loved what he did; he did it better than anyone else before him or after him. From the time he was a 4-year old on the streets of New Orleans to the 40-year old in the Salle Pleyel in Paris, he did his thing with equal *elan* and the same love. His roots began with that word — love — and then another — happy.

"When I was little — still wearing dresses — I lived with my mother in Jane's Alley —." One of the opening remarks made by Louis to Richard Meryman for his

*Hugues Panassié, **Louis Armstrong** (New York: Da Capo Press, Inc.).

174

Already a King, Louis talks with future princess, actress Grace Kelly. Hollywood, 1956.

(r) Princess Grace of Monaco unveils bust of Louie with widow Lucille Armstrong (center) and Nice's Mayor J. Medecin. France, 1974.

Leopoldville, Africa, 1960.

Whether in the Congo or in Sun Valley, wherever Louie was—there was music, happiness, and love.

Filming **Winter Carnival.** Sun Valley, Idaho, 1962.

Not exactly the corpse "that used ta sit up," but a dancing skeleton. In the film, **Pennies From Heaven,** Louie playing the "Skeleton Dance." 1936.

In 1917, "the district" was closed down. In 1918 Joe Oliver left New Orleans, and so a year later Louie joined the Fate Marable Band playing excursions up and down the river. Shown here, the band aboard the S.S. **Sidney,** 1919. (l-r) Baby Dodds, Bebe Ridgley, Joe Howard, Louie, Fate Marable (at piano); David Jones, who taught Louie to read music and division; and bassist Pops Foster. Captain Joe Streckfus, standing.

Louie's oldest discs, recorded in 1923, were made when he was in King Oliver's Creole Jazz Band. His first recorded solo was "Chimes Blues," built on a familiar King Oliver riff. (l-r) Honore Dutrey, trombone; Baby Dodds, drums; Joe "King" Oliver, trumpet; Lil Hardin, piano; Bill Johnson, banjo; and Johnny Dodds, clarinet. (foreground) Louie playing slide trumpet. Chicago, 1923.

interview, *Life* magazine, 4/15/66. He was born in the heart and pulse of music where life was poor but happy. Music was everywhere, and Louie was everywhere music was. Nearby Funky Butt Hall had dance music, but before the evening started the musicians would play out front for about an hour. At age 4, there was Louie dancing along with all the other children. At age 12, he had his own quartet, "The Singing Fools." He sang tenor and played slide whistle, and then passed the hat, which was good for maybe a dollar a night.

Music was played on the lawns if there was a picnic; wagons with their hawkers who sang as they peddled their wares; funerals, of course, provided days of music. The "wakes" were so charged with music that the corpse "used ta sit up."

Once a year there was the grand parade with the Grand Marshal. And sixty years later, Louis Armstrong was the Grand Marshal; a thought that surely never crossed his young mind.

To earn extra money he loaded coal on wagons and then delivered it to Storyville, the red-light district patronized by only rich whites. (Jelly Roll Morton was the only black who played there.) He unloaded banana boats and loaded his soul with music. But his work on an instrument did not begin until one fateful New Year's Eve. To join in the festivities, he loaded his stepfather's pistol with blanks and fired into the air. He was punished by being sent to the Waifs' Home. There the director, Peter Davis, took an interest in him and put him in the band. First playing tamborine, next snare drum, then alto horn, and finally a bugle. When the band's cornet player went home, Louie replaced him. Mr. Davis taught him to play "Home Sweet Home," which could be another way of saying — Louie was home. He became the leader of the school band which consisted of twenty kids. They played parades, social clubs, etc.

A year and a half later, Louie, almost 14, having finished the equivalent of the fifth grade in schooling, was released and began his "professional" life in music.

175

There were two men in his life, both named Joe, who were most influential. Later, there was manager Joe Glaser, but first there was Joe "King" Oliver (called Papa Joe by Louie) who played in Kid Ory's band. He took Louie to his home where he taught him lessions out of an exercise book, gave him a trumpet, and played duets with him while Mrs. Oliver fed him. Soon the word got out. Whenever a player dropped out, the call around New Orleans was "send for Little Louie."

His first professional job, at age 17, in a honky-tonk place, paid him 15¢, but he said it was like a Carnegie Hall debut. When Papa Joe split for Chicago, Louie replaced him in Kid Ory's band.

His home life had been with his mother, Mayann, whom he adored. She washed clothes for a dollar a day in the backyard of a white family. His father, who had tended boilers in a turpentine factory, left home when he was small and died in the early 30's. He had a sister, Bernice, and "lots of stepfathers." His mother's philosophy, "What you can't get — the hell with it," seems very much a part of Louie who passed from one era to another getting what he could and the hell with the rest of it. She (Mayann) stuck to this even when Louie, at the age of 18, married a 21-year old hothead, the first of four marriages. "I can't live his life," was her statement. When Louie couldn't live it either, he joined Fate Marable's riverboat and spent three years traveling up and down the river. He met Jack Teagarden, who would later be a great part of his life, and Bix Biederbecke.

When he was tired of touring, he returned to New Orleans and joined the brass section of Tom Anderson's orchestra known as the Tuxedo Band. Then in July of 1922, he received the call from Papa Joe to join him in Chicago.

One of his remembrances noted in the Meryman interview was his song, "Get Off Katie's Head," for which he was supposed to be paid fifty dollars. It was published as "Wish I Could Shimmy Like My Sister Kate." He never got a shimmering nickel for it in royalties. So much for the life of Louie in New Orleans.

Louie, as the leader, formed the "Hot Five." Its first recording was made in 1925. One of the pieces was "Gut Bucket Blues," which remains one of Louie's masterpieces. Another done later, "Heebie Jeebies" introduced Louie as featured vocalist on record for the first time. (l-r) Johnny St. Cyr, banjo; Kid Ory, trombone; Louie; Johnny Dodds, clarinet; and pianist, Lil Hardin, who became Louie's wife. Chicago, 1926.

(l-r) Joe Glaser, Louis, and agent Cork O'Keefe, who was co-founder of GAC (General Artists) as they sign up "Satchmo." 1937.

"I'm just an ordinary human being trying to enjoy the work I love . . ." Louis Armstrong. Shown here, 1957.

Louie with singer Maxine Sullivan (Loch Lomond). 1938.

176

On tour with King Oliver, Louie made his first recordings in Richmond, Indiana for the Gennett Company. He had two solo choruses, and in his book he tells how the engineers made him stand twenty feet behind the other players because his sound was so much bigger than theirs.

In 1924, wearing big black policeman's boots, he wandered into Harlem to join Fletcher Henderson. Those who laughed at the boots did everything they could to copy him once they heard him play. Notably, "Sugar Foot Stomp" (former title "Dipper Mouth Blues") which had been Oliver's solo, but in the hands, mouth, and mind of Armstrong blew the mind of every person within earshot. He stayed a year and then returned to Chicago.

He married pianist Lil Hardin and brought his mother up north to live with them. He was able to give her nice clothes and a proper funeral when she died. He remembered what he called "saucer funerals" from his early days: a saucer was placed on the chest of the deceased, and passersby would drop in coins to help with the burial. He vowed this would never happed to Mayann. She lived long enough to see her son become the head of his own group (1925) and to see his fame begin to spread through his recordings.

The pivotal point in his rise to fame came in 1926 when he met Joe Glaser. In 1935, Glaser became his manager. Louis was his first client. Later, Glaser owned Associated Booking Corp., one of the all time important agencies in music. It was Glaser who put Louis's name on the marquee for those who didn't know: "Louis Armstrong, World's Greatest Trumpeter." The rest is history recorded and recorded.

Louis's rationale stems from two points of view. For years and years, he blew his brains out show after show, night after night, and in his words "for the musicians. The audience thought I was a maniac." And so he began to add his natural showmanship. He began to communicate with the audience — the ordinary people. An old timer in New Orleans once told him (and he never forgot), "Stay before them people. Please the public."

Trombonist Trummy Young, formerly with the Jimmie Lunceford Band, joined Louie in 1951 after Jack Teagarden left, and remained as a staple in the group for years. Shown here in 1957.

Louie and ageless Marlene Dietrich opened together at the Riviera Hotel in Las Vegas. Their hit of the evening was a duet of "C'est Si Bon," which Marlene sang in French and Louie in his own language. Nevada, 1962.

Louie onstage talking to star Pearl Bailey after the curtain came down on **Hello Dolly.** At left is mini-skirted actress Jane Russell, also invited on stage, and co-star Cab Calloway. Then Satchmo did his version of the show's title song. New York City, 1967.

Louis at "seventy" with trumpeter, Bobby Hackett, at the annual Newport Jazz Festival where Satchmo was feted on this big birthday. Newport, Rhode Island, 1970.

Musical great Lionel Hampton kisses Lucille Armstrong, Louie's widow, during the unveiling of a 12-foot statue of her husband at Armstrong Park. The park was dedicated in honor of New Orleans's most famous musician and is located next to the French Quarter where Louie grew up. 1980.

(l-r) Lucille Watson Armstrong and husband, Louis, and Aiden Aslan at the premiere of **Heaven Knows, Mr. Allison** starring Deborah Kerr and Robert Mitchum. New York City, 1957.

Louie played "taps" as a child when in the Waifs' Home where he began playing the trumpet. Here Teddy Riley plays "taps" to pay homage to Louie as thousands gathered in City Hall Plaza to remember their native son. New Orleans, 1971.

Lil Hardin, second wife of Louis Armstrong, played at a concert honoring Satchmo shortly after his death. During her performance of the "St. Louis Blues," Mrs. Hardin, age 73, suffered a fatal heart attack and died almost instantly. Chicago, 1971.

Timeless Louie shown here with youth group, "Blood, Sweat, and Tears," at Grammy's in New York City. 1970. (**Blood, Sweat, and Tears** won Best Album of 1969 over the Beatles's **Abbey Road** and Johnny Cash's **Johnny Cash at San Quentin.**)

(l-r) 92-year old pianist Eubie Blake, Mrs. Louis Armstrong, and president of Brandeis University, Merver H. Berstein stand in front of a poster advertising a concert given for the Brandeis Louis Armstrong Music Fund. Waltham, Massachusetts, 1979.

Peggy Lee sang the Lord's Prayer at the funeral services for "Satchmo" at the Corona Congressional Church in Queens, New York. 1971.

Louie's widow (center) Lucille Armstrong and his sister, Mrs. Beatrice Collins (behind Mrs. Armstrong), say goodbye to him. The body lay in state at the 7th Regiment Armory in New York City. 1971

And then he never forgot what happened to Papa Joe. He found him in 1937 selling vegetables on the street in Savannah, Georgia. He had aged, lost his lip, and lost his way. Back in New Orleans, the city that he had done so much for musically, he had been forgotten. When he died, his body had to be brought to New York for a proper funeral and to a place where the musicians remembered his contribution. And so Louis's association with Joe Glaser was based on this sort of thing never happening to him. He knew Glaser was in his corner and cared about his future. Aside from his fourth wife, Lucille, Louie felt that only these two men really cared about him — Louis Armstrong, as a person. Louie was smart to hire Glaser, and Glaser was smart enough to know how to manage his commodity. "Pops" as Louie was called, did not end up selling vegetables in Georgia.

He worked until his heart gave out two days after his seventy-first birthday. As in the case of pianist Art Tatum, both men gave so much to the world of music that it will take years and years before their full input is realized. "It has been said that a great artist always suggests more things than either he or his immediate followers can explore."

Louis said he often wondered what life would have been like if, "When I was little — still wearing dresses . . . if I had just stayed in New Orleans."

LOUIS ARMSTRONG
Died: July 6, 1971
Corona, New York

DISCOGRAPHY

Armstrong and King Oliver
Milestone (1923)

Plays the Blues
Bio (1924-27)

Story with Hot 5 (volume 1)
Columbia

Story with Hot 7 (volume 2)
Columbia (1920's mid-late)

Story with Earl Hines (volume 3)
Columbia

Story Favorite (volume 4)
Columbia (1929-31)

July 4, 1900-July 4, 1971
RCA - 2 (1931-33)

Series of Louis Armstrong Recordings*
MCA (mid-30's)

Town Hall Concert Plus
RCA (1947)

Satchmo at Pasadena (with Velma Middleton)
Decca

Louis Armstrong at the Crescendo
Decca (late 40's-early 50's)

Louis Armstrong Plays (W.C.) Handy
Columbia

Satch Plays Fats (Waller)
Columbia (mid 50's)

Ella and Louis
Vervè (late 50's)

Greatest Hits
Columbia

*This series shows Armstrong's greatness at his maturity. List compiled by the author and Richard M. Sudhalter.

179

Prior to entertaining the servicemen at the U.S. Naval Base on Guantanamo Bay, Cuba. 1962.

"That the rude sea grew civil at his song . . ." Louis Armstrong.

(l-r) Trummy Young, Louie, and Edmund Hall on African tour, which was recorded and filmed and became a feature-length film, **Stachmo the Great,** narrated by Edward R. Murrow. 1957.

Louis and Bing Crosby in **Pennies From Heaven,** his second film. 1936. His first movie was **Ex-Flame,** released in 1931.

Louie and his orchestra in **Jam Session.** 1944.

Jam Session

Louie in **Paris Blues,** which starred Sidney Poitier and Paul Newman, and music by Duke Ellington. 1961.

Louie and friend in **Going Places.** 1938.
Dick Powell was the film's star.

Louie and Danny Kaye in **Five Pennies.** 1959.

(l-r) Frank Sinatra, Jr., Louis, and Cicely Tyson in **A Man Called Adam.** This was the only film in which Louie had an extended part, playing Willie "Sweet Daddy" Ferguson. Other film appearances showed him either as himself or a man called Louis or one of his nicknames. 1966.

Louis and Barbra Streisand in **Hello Dolly.** 1969.

"Happiness is Just a Guy called Guy—Lombardo." Shown here in 1941.

GUY LOMBARDO

Born: June 19, 1902 London, Ontario

Hmm—Lombardo—"The Royal Canadians?" The band that makes the "Sweetest Music This Side of Heaven?" No— it's the orchestra that plays "Auld Lang Syne" coast-to-coast every December 31st at eleven fifty-nine p.m. Whatever your association, one of these phrases or terms has doubtlessly fallen on your ears. Generations have identified with Guy Lombardo, even if only to "put down" the music. The fact remains, nevertheless, that despite "put down," "put on," or "put up," the legend of the Royal Canadians lives. One reason can be found in Lombardo's own words, "We entertain, not educate." His followers are legion.

The group came into existence when people needed to be entertained. Fresh from WWI, post-war Americans craved what he had to offer. The story doesn't start in the United States, but in Canada at the turn of the century.

By the time Guy was born, his Sicilian-born father, Gaetano Lombardo, had established himself in Canada where he earned a good living in the tailor trade. His mother, Angelina, a first-generation Canadian-Italian, had already displayed her Women's Lib attitude by not bowing to family or social pressure. She insisted on completing high school, then went on to secretarial school. She became the first woman secretary in London, working for lawyer Hume Cronyn, the famous actor's grandfather. When Angelina fell in love with Gaetano, she married him even though her older sister was still unmarried: family tradition was to marry in order. She became the mother of seven children, and a socialite. Both jobs were tackled with the same enthusiasm as her stenographic career.

Papa Lombardo's youthful desire for a music career was thwarted by the necessity to immigrate and to earn a living. But he passed on his interest and love of music to his children. "Papa thought we would have

something to fall back on," said Guy. It never occurred to him that his boys would actually earn a living from it, but when the time came, and they announced their intentions, he did not balk. Guy, nick-named so as not to be confused with his father, after whom he had been named, was given a violin at age 9; Carmen, age 8, got a flute. And they got orders as to how long and where to practice.

Mama was thoroughly engrossed with proper diction; no Italian was spoken at home. This early emphasis on speaking accounts for Carmen's precise diction and focus on delivering a proper reading of a lyric. Angelina's social activities led to the introduction of Freddie Kreitzer, pianist, with the Lombardos; his mother was in one of the social clubs. Third brother, Lebert, tried several instruments, then settled for drums. Hence, the first quartet, "The Lombardo Brothers Concert Company."

They played for Angelina's clubs, in and around London, and ventured to the neighboring hamlets, which had a strong Scottish settlement. So the boys added a Scottish dancer and singer; their creed: give the people what they want.

In 1919, they got their first steady job, for $40.00 a week, at an outdoor pavillion. In 1922, they got their first big "gig" — musicians' term for job — at the Winter Garden dance hall in London. By then Lebe had switched to trumpet, having heard Louis Panico with the Isham Jones band. Another London youth, George Gowans, replaced Lebe on drums and stayed with the band until he retired fifty years later. Trombonist Jeff Dillon and guitarist "Muff" Henry were added as Carmen, influenced by Benny Krueger, picked up a C-melody saxophone: this instrument had a short life in the big bands. It was the Paul Whiteman Orchestra, its new "symphonic sound" and sax section, that strongly influenced the young men; es-

183

pecially their recording of "Song of India". Only records were available to the boys, but they knew the impact Whiteman was making in the States on the radio as well as on discs. His music was arranged and orchestrated, and Guy wanted to be there and to do the same thing. Detroit was the closest city, and there they heard the Jean Goldkette group, which listed such alumnae as Benny Goodman, Tommy and Jimmy Dorsey, and Glenn Miller. Another group was the Pasternak-Rubinstein. They told Carmen to switch to an E-flat sax, and then offered him a job at $125.00 a week. Carmen, by age 17, was proficient on the instrument. He accepted the job and stayed for nine months before returning to the fold. He brought back the knowledge that dancers liked the slower tempo; the faster beat, called by musicians, The Businessman's Beat, was losing out.

As Guy stated it, "From Whiteman we borrowed the symphonic sound making Carmen a sax player; from Goldkette we listened to the great players; from Isham Jones, Lebe became a trumpet player; and from the Pasternak-Rubinstein group we borrowed the slower tempo for dancers." Then they formed a three-way partnership, making Carmen the musical director and Guy the leader, and fixed their six eyes on the States.

Their first job was in Cleveland for $200.00 at an Elks Club fest. Taking their cue from Fred Waring and The Pennsylvanians and Abe Lyman and his Californians, the nine young Canadians, replete in caps, knickers, and hayseed, became The Royal Canadians; shucking their apparel and the rest of the title—Mounted Police.

Working for nightclub owner Louis Bleet helped them shape their act and build the foundation for their future. Bleet, among other things, wanted his Royal Canadians to honor all requests, which could easily fill the whole night. Guy said, "Impossible," but Bleet bleated, "Yes—play a little here and a little there." Unheard of in those days, but Guy found a way to segue from one song to another, changing keys and tempo, and the "medley" was born. Bleet also insisted that his musicians always be properly

Paul Whiteman lifts his baton as guest conductor at Lombardo's Port-O-Call Club . Whiteman, who died in 1967 at age 77, was one of the early, strong musical influences on the young Guy. Tierra Verde, Florida, 1963.

attired with matching "on the job" demeanor. This, of course, would enable them to look and act the part for future society-type balls. Bleet introduced them to his partner, Sophie Tucker, with whom he owned a club on the lake outside of Cleveland. Together they booked the band there in the summer of '24.*

There, on the lake, Guy resumed another love and interest, boating. Although that summer he could only afford to rent or borrow boats, later on he would become as well-known in boating circles as he would be in music circles.

Although Guy had always been the leader of the group, starting with waving the first bow of his first violin in the air, the group usually made all decisions. Unlike other bands, most of the members were all from London, which lent a homogeneousness while other groups had a "pick-up quality" or heterogeneousness. So when Guy suggested that the group play for "free" on an hour-a-day radio show, they readily agreed. Their goal was the future, not the immediate payment of "scale", pay which other groups might have insisted on. Radio exposure was, in those days, what tel-

*Guy Lombardo with Jack Altshul, **Auld Acquaintance** (New York: Doubleday & Co., Inc.).

184

Guy and his orchestra on stage of CBS Playhouse where "Lombardo Road" was broadcast over WABC network. At microphone, the famous trio: Derf Higman, Carmen, and Larry Owen. Guy (far right) by second mike. Circa 1930's.

evision means today. A far-reaching success built on cooperation of goals was their substitute for immediate remuneration. But one of Guy's suggestions went totally astray and unobserved. "Arrogant and selfish," he said, declaring that none of the members could be married. Carmen eloped with Florence Haas, as Guy relented, and then he married Lilliebel Glenn: both were long-lived unions.

Guy and his wife, Lilliebelle, being interviewed as they left felony court. The bandleader's car had struck two pedestrians, one of whom died. 1952.

The band's big splash was made in Chicago after a cursory ripple at the end of the 20's. There they also formed an alliance with MCA (Music Corporation of America), their first agent, and it lasted thirty-five years. By now their fee was $1,600 per week at the Granada Cafe. Papa was ecstatic.

In 1929, they did their first live broadcast from New York's Roosevelt Grill, and their stint there, supposedly four months, lasted until 1963. It was young CBS president, William B. Paley who put them on his network. In 1930, 19-year old brother Victor joined the group, but was not given ownership rights as he had not been there at the "trial and error" period. Baby sister, Rose Marie, was five years old at the time, but she, too, would join the group in her teens as a singer. Victor tried his hand at his own group, but later returned and eventually Rose Marie opted for marriage.

Carmen had always disliked singing (one of the reasons Rose Marie joined the group) and always loved songwriting. He had a rather distinguished career with Gus Kahn, Johnny Loeb, and Johnny Green, doing what

Bandleader Lombardo slid as easily from radio to television as he did from NBC to CBS. He just made music. And money. 1936.

Seventeen-year old sister, Rose Marie joined her famous brothers as a vocalist. (l-r) Guy, Victor, Lebert, and Carmen. May 1943.

he liked as well as piling up nice royalties in ASCAP. His song, "Little Coquette", with Gus Kahn, was a huge success for him, for them, and for the Lombardo Orchestra on records. The famous singing trio was composed of Carmen, Derf Higman, and Larry Owen: the band's sax section. Nightly, Carmen began to abhor having to face the "mike" with his limited vocal range and the limit on the choice of songs. Furthermore, band singers such as Frank Sinatra (Tommy Dorsey's orchestra) and Ray Eberly (Glenn Miller's orchestra) were becoming famous in their own right and could really sing. The capper came when Fred Waring had a running gag on his weekly radio show about Carmen, and performer Alec Templeton turned a "Carmen-performance" into one of his stinging imitations. Finally, Guy replaced Carmen with Kenny Gardner, but the public howled for a long time before accepting it.

Carmen's death, in 1971 from stomach cancer, was, according to Guy, the worst part of his life. Close in age, they were almost like twins.

186

Guy's Public Enemy No. 1, Fred Waring, managed to push Guy out of the way (and almost out of the photo) at the Inaugural Ball. (l-r) Guy; Waring; Mrs. John S. Doud, President's mother-in-law; Jeanette MacDonald; Mrs. Eisenhower and President Eisenhower; Lily Pons; and dancer turned Congressman, George Murphy. Behind Mrs. Doud, Tony Martin; behind the President, James Melton. Washington, D.C., 1953. According to Guy Lombardo, the feud with Fred Waring was as "hyped" as the Jack Benny-Fred Allen one.

As the years passed, the orchestra continued to delete some aspects of its format and continued to add many "firsts." Musicians credit them with originating the grueling one-nighters; they popularized the duo pianos in bands by adding another London-born, Hugo D'Ippolito; Dudley Fosdick and his out-sized trumpet-sound-like mellophone, called a Foosophone, gave the band another sound dimension, copied by other groups; and to the sax section, they added the soprano sound.

Guy was known for his generosity in having time for other musicians and helping them get started. He was instrumental in bringing Louis Prima to New York; helping Lawrence Welk with his career; suggested Kay Kyser to MCA as well as the Mills Brothers; and Carmen brought Eddie Duchin to MCA's head, Jules Stein. They were an unusual group of people and this must, in some part, account for their longevity.

Outside of the recording studio, Guy was beginning to set other records on the water. He was equally at home discussing champion driver, Gar Wood, or Zumbach-Miller engines as he was with Louis Armstrong's music or magnetic tape.

His first victory was in 1942: a marathon race from Atlantic City to Cape May. Later he would break his idol's (Gar Wood) speed record by eight tenths of a second. In 1946, Guy established a new record in his class for the Gold Cup, which is part of a triple crown as in horse racing's famous Triple Crown. At age 44, having won the coveted award, he was allowed to select the site for the race the following year. This brought him in contact with New York's master builder-designer, Robert Moses. One of Mr.

Moses's designs was the famous Jones Beach, and when he met Guy, the Marine Theatre, located there, was faltering. Together they planned and produced successful theater ventures for the public following the idea of the Marine — originally built as a low cost entertainment showcase in the 30's. This proved to be one of the more lucrative of the Lombardo investments. They had struck oil in the music business but never in their "wild cat" ventures.

The orchestra survived the demise of the Big Band era, and for as long as they wanted, they could work ten months a year. Many times they tried to break the mold, attempted other sounds, but the public always clamored for the original. The Waldorf-Astoria Hotel became their new New Year's Eve home, and the broadcasts from there continued for over twenty years.

Guy lived a long, full, and rich life. Unlike most, he was able to pursue a career he loved and to make an overwhelming success of it. Eventually, the family members all moved, settled in the States, and maintained a close family relationship. His spacious Freeport, Long Island home was a showplace; his restaurant, close by, was a sort of family gathering place on Sundays and a highly lucrative dining spot the rest of the week; and the community honored him by naming one of its boulevards "Lombardo."

Whether you think about the band as "The Royal Canadians," or "The Sweetest Sounds This Side of Heaven," or the group that plays "Auld Lang Syne" on New Year's Eve — or just having read this chapter, identification with Guy Lombardo continues. As it has done for generations.

GUY LOMBARDO

**DIED: November 6, 1977
Houston, Texas**

188

Guy and the orchestra played for all of President Franklin Roosevelt's Inaugural Balls as well as Harry Truman's. Shown here with President and Mrs. Truman for the Cerebral Palsy Fund Concert with Mary Farenga (aged 18), that year's cerebral palsy girl. Washington, D.C. 1952.

In 1920 Guy saw his idol, racing driver Gar Wood, break the world's speed record in winning the Gold Cup. In 1946, on the Detroit River, Guy broke that record by eight tenths of a second or 70.8 mph against Wood's 70mph. Here Guy meets Gar in Florida, where he (Guy) did not beat Gar's record over the Indian Creek waters. 1948.

September 1946—Lombardo wins famous Gold Cup in record time.

July 1948—*Tempo VI* speeds victoriously across finish line to win the Ford Memorial Classic with Guy at the controls.

August 1948—*Tempo VI* flipped over as Guy tried to avoid a collison with other boats.

August 1948—After *Tempo VI* broke up, Guy with broken arm, congratulates Gold Cup winner Danny Foster.

Guy Lombardo and The Royal Canadians, synonymous with New Year's Eve and his radio broadcasts from 1929 at the Roosevelt Grill and later at the Waldorf-Astoria until 1981. Shown here at the Waldorf with well-wishers, (l) Leslie Hayden and (r) Marilyn Hase, his last appearance. He died the following year one month before New Year's Eve. The band continued until 1981. New York, 1976.

November 1955—Danny Foster (l) piloting *Tempo VII* for Guy, won the President's Cup. Vice President Richard Nixon presents the trophy to Guy as Mrs. Foster looks on.

City planner-master builder, New York's Robert Moses and Guy. Together they collaborated on productions for the Jones Beach Marine Theatre. 1957.

Remember "Tangerine" or "Green Eyes" from the Jimmy Dorsey days? Sung by Helen O'Connell in Forties, she joined Guy to help celebrate his 47th year of New Year's Eve broadcasts in 1976. New York.

Lombardo and Co. were one of the first bands to play college "proms" back in the Thirties. Here, they play for the first "Senior Prom" in the nation. Many of the 1,200 senior citizens had danced to his music when they were youngsters. Springfield Civic Center, Massachusetts, 1977.

New Year's Lombardo style. (rear l-r) Brothers Lebert, Carmen, Joseph, Victor, and Guy. All in band except Joseph. Second from rear row (l-r) Kenny Gardner, band vocalist, husband of Elaine Lombardo; Susan, Lebert's daughter; Mrs. Carmen Lombardo, Mrs. Victor Lombardo. Mrs. Guy Lombardo, and Sidney Rogers, husband of Rose Marie Lombardo. Elaine and Rose Marie are Guy's sisters. Seated (l-r) Elaine Lombardo Gardner, Mrs. and Mr. Guy Lombardo, Sr., Rose Marie Lombardo Rogers. Kneeling (l-r) David Lombardo, Victor's son; Peter Lombardo, Lebert's son; Guy Victor Lombardo, another son of Victor. Two smaller children of Lebert Lombardo were home with the mumps when photo was taken. New York, 1953.

Genial Guy Lombardo died of a lung ailment complicated by heart and kidney failure. He lived for seventy-five years; most of those years were spent giving a lot of people a lot of pleasure.

Discography

Sweetest Music This Side of Heaven
RCA (2 records)

Every Night is New Year's Eve
London

Golden Medleys
MCA

Greatest Hits
MCA

On The Air 1935
SUNB

Medley (volumes 1 & 3)
Capitol

Seems Like Old Times
Pickwick

Best of Guy Lombardo
Capitol

Best of Guy Lombardo (volumes 1 & 2)
MCA

Bing Crosby, the true minstrel: poet; singer; musician; always on, never off. Seen here in 1943 playing the role of Daniel Emmett (1815-1904), composer of "Dixie" from which the film took its name.

BING CROSBY

Born: May 2, 1903 Tacoma, Washington

Harry Lillis Crosby was his real name. The exact year of his birth is speculative. He was the fourth of seven children born to Harry Lowe and Katherine Harrigan Crosby. Their first, Larry, was born in 1895; their second, Everett, in 1896; and their third, Ted, in 1900. Harry appeared sometime between 1901 and 1904. His Catholic baptismal certificate recorded only his surname and sex. Harry's two sisters, Catherine and Mary Rose, and younger brother, Bob, were born later. Regardless of Bing's exact birthdate, he came into this world with a charmed life. Through hard work, an unusual talent, and good luck, he became a legend. He led the life he wanted, indulged himself in his interests and pursuits via his career, and deferred only to one person—his mother.

His father was a Puritan bookkeeper in Tacoma who converted to Catholicism before his marriage. His mother was the daughter of a builder in Eire. But it was Grandfather Nathaniel Crosby of Massachusetts who achieved a modicum of fame. As a clipper-ship captain, he sailed around the Horn to China (and other points East) where he died and was buried in Hong Kong. During World War II, a Liberty ship was named for him and launched by his son, Harry Lowe, Bing's father.

By the time little Harry was seven, the family had moved to Spokane, Washington, and it was there that the appellation "Bing" was hung on him by a neighbor, Valentine Hobart. In the *Bingsville Bugle* comic strip "Bingo," there was a floppy-eared character to whom Harry bore a strong resemblance. The "o" was dropped in Spokane; the floppy ears were unflopped later in Hollywood. Two other distinguishing features remained: Bing was color-blind and prematurely bald. Undoubtedly, the baldness accounted for his extensive collection of chapeaux.

Although the Crosby household was not poor, there was not a great deal of money left over for luxuries. Bing mowed lawns, picked apples, delivered newspapers, and did whatever else he could do to earn those few extra bucks to appease his young appetite. He was always a good athlete and throughout his life retained his interest in sports. He was also a good student with an aptitude for language. In high school he studied elocution, did some public speaking, joined a debating society, and emerged with a large vocabulary and the beginning of his famous speech pattern.

"The Spokane Slugger," young Bing Crosby, who would someday be a part owner of the Pittsburgh Pirates.

The music side of his life began at home where his father played guitar and his mother sang. His uncle, George Harrigan, was an amateur tenor whose big number was "H-A-double R-I, GAN spells Harrigan." He sang his way into the young heart of his nephew. Formal musical training started for Bing at twelve but was short-lived, because his love of popular music did not sit well with the teacher. And so, he grew up using his naturalness in place of formal training. He never did learn to read music. While in high school, he began playing drums, and this enabled him to join "The Musicaladers," a five piece band formed by Alton Rinker, pianist pal of Bing's. Besides being their drummer, he was given a megaphone and crooned nightly into it for the vast sum of $3.00. Eventually the band broke up, but Al and Bing continued as a duo with an increase in salary to $30.00 per week at The Clemmer Theatre where "live" music was featured before the movie. The job went on and on, but the boys became bored and decided to strike out in search of fame, fortune, and better music.

Brother Everett had already gone to Los Angeles and Al's sister, famed singer Mildred Bailey, was firmly entrenched at Hollywood's top speakeasy, The Silver Grill. So with a hundred dollars between them, a very tired Model-T Ford, and two relatives in Los Angeles, Bing and Al set out. In 1925, after three weeks of driving and working assorted jobs to help with traveling expenses, they arrived at Mildred's place. Although the boys had had a taste of corner moonshine back in Washington, they had never tasted nor seen the moon shine and the moonshine served up Hollywood style.

Eventually, Mildred arranged an audition for them, but not before Bing had to hock his drums and borrow from Everett, a loan repaid many times over in later life. The audition was successful, and so Crosby and Rinker went to work for Mike Lyman, brother of bandleader, Abe Lyman. Harry Owens, another bandleader, also engaged them. Their careers were launched as they played, sang, and shuffled at The Tent Cafe and The Layfayette Cafe in Hollywood.

Bing and Al were spotted by Fanchon and Marco, an organization that toured vaudeville shows up and down the West Coast. They were put to work for $75.00 per week. **The Syncopated Idea** opened in Los Angeles. Bing and Al stuck with it for eighteen months, and then quit. Next they went to work for Arthur Freed, who later became one of Hollywood's top producers, and for Will Morrissey in their joint effort, **Morrissey's Music Hall Revue.** They stayed with the revue until it closed. Once again they were broke and out of work. However, this was to be the last time they would be in such straits, for the next job was with Paul Whiteman. From that time on Bing never looked back. His career lasted for over fifty years.

Paul "Pops" Whiteman, a former taxi driver from Denver, was a big hit—a smash. One record, "Whispering," had sold over 1,800,000 copies after World War I. In the 20's, his records were selling as fast as he could cut them. So this busy musician sent two of his sidemen to check out Rinker and Crosby. And on their recommendation, hired them; a bit unusual but a judgment that worked out well. Al and Bing's act was an instant success. The road tour that started in Chicago went smoothly until they hit New York City and the greatly anticipated opening at the Paramount Theatre. Their disastrous debut was the result of the theater's size and the mike-lessness sound of the duo. With his usual casualness, he enjoyed new-found pleasures: three "b's"— booze, broads, and balls, as in golf. He could afford to enjoy himself; he had a valid contract in his pocket, and brother Everett was now in charge of his affairs.

Viola player, Matty Malneck, came to the rescue of the ailing duo and put together

Bing and Paul "Pops" Whiteman and wife at the races in Saratoga. 1935.

The Rhythm Boys, adding Harry Barris, a thumping but imaginative local piano player. Barris wrote "Mississippi Mud," now a jazz standard, for the trio as well as other tunes and innovative material.

The Rhythm Boys were successful, but they were not always reliable. And so when Whiteman and Company sailed for England the Boys were left on the pier. Again, Crosby was not perturbed as his weekly income was assured and permanent docking of him was out of the question. This air of assurance is a running factor in the Crosby personality. In performance, it made the audience comfortable; in real life, it could make employers uncomfortable. But it was a part of Bing.

When Whiteman returned, the Boys attempted a shape-up program by putting the three "b's" on hold, and the group headed for Hollywood. But eventually Bing and the band manager got into a dispute and in typical Crosby style, he quit. Al and Harry went along with him, and who but Mildred Bailey filled the vacancy left by The Rhythm Boys; everything had now come full circle.

"Pops" Whiteman points a finger at his bad boy. Bing: "Me—naughty never! Let's make up." And they did. Fort Lee, New Jersey. Circa 1930's.

The Rhythm Boys were a big hit in California. Not because they had learned any new material or vastly changed the act, but because Bing's crooning was luring the dancers from the floor to the front of the bandstand where they would swoon and sway. Via nightly broadcasts from the posh Cocoanut Grove in the Ambassador Hotel, thousands of listeners heard Bing, and it was evident that a soloist was in the making. A few short miles away at another hotel, The Roosevelt, another youngster was being heard; the great talent of nineteen-year old Artie Shaw was also evident. Those were the days when Los Angeles, Chicago, and New York were spawning the eventual legends in music: Duke Ellington and Louis Armstrong who were Bing's idols, as well as Billie Holiday and later Ella Fitzgerald.

While working at the Grove Bing was introduced to Wilma Winnifred Wyatt from Harriman, Tennessee. Only seventeen years old when she arrived in Hollywood, she was a blonde beauty, a singer under a three year contract to 20th Century-Fox where her name had been changed to Dixie Lee. After a stormy courtship, Dixie gave up her career and married Bing on September 29, 1930. Before her career ended, they recorded two Jerome Kern tunes together, "The Way You Look Tonight" and "Fine Romance."

Despite rumors of divorce, Dixie's eventual drinking problem and loneliness from an often missing and self-involved husband, the marriage lasted twenty-two years. Together they produced four sons: Gary Evans, June 25, 1933, named for dear friend Gary Cooper; twins, Dennis Michael, named for Grandfather Harrigan, and Phillip Lang, named for great guitarist Eddie Lang, July 13, 1934; and Lindsay Harry, January 5, 1938, named for racing friend Lindsay Howard. Dixie stayed home and raised the children while Bing's career took off like a rocket. The boys suffered from a strict disciplinarian of a father, which erupted in unfortunate but understandable behavior later on. Dixie died from cancer on November 1, 1952. Her brother-in-law Bob Crosby said, "Dixie was a magnificent woman; the catalyst for what happened to Bing Crosby would have to be Dixie Lee." And, "She was intelligent; she was smart; she was understanding; she was attractive; she was generous; she was a helluva woman."*

Charles Thompson, **Bing,** (New York: David McKay Company, Inc.).

195

Crosby Clan, 1938. (l-r) Dennis, Bing, Gary, Dixie Lee, and Philip. Baby Lindsay sits on his mother's lap.

Bing, out of retirement, being interviewed by genial television host, Joe Franklin. Mr. Franklin's TV Show (WOR) features, among other things, his famous "Down Memory Lane" theme now seen by over nine million viewers. NYC 1976.

Funeral of Dixie Lee Crosby, 1952, in Beverly Hills, California. (l-r) Philip, Lindsay, Dennis, Gary, and Bing with his head bowed.

Business manager for Bing, brother Everett and his opera singer wife, Florence George Crosby in 1939 arriving in Southampton on their honeymoon.

The best known theme song in the world "Where the Blue of the Night," music by Roy Turk and Fred E. Ahlert, confounded lyric writer, Bing Crosby, as he first sang, "and the blue of her eyes crowns the gold of her hair . . . " instead of "and the gold of her hair crowns the blue of her eyes," from the first title of the song, "Where the Blue of the Night Meets the Gold of the Day." No wonder Crosby was confused. He was even really color blind. Circa 1930.

The breakup of the trio occurred after Bing had been threatened by the manager of the Grove and, in his usual fashion, refused to take it. Bing quit, but the boys also quit him. The union blackballed him for a while at the instigation of the manager, but he found work at the Mack Sennett stages doing a series of twenty-minute films singing his hit tunes. Eventually the ban was lifted and brother Everett raised his sights for Bing's career towards the networks.

The Crosby career can now best be notated by a three-way division: radio and television, recordings, film.

President William Paley of CBS took the plunge by offering Bing $600.00 a week for his first national radio show. Various sponsors appeared and disappeared until the ten year alliance with the Kraft Company was formed. In 1935, the "Kraft Music Hall" moved to the West Coast with its star Bing Crosby and opened with guest, Jack Benny.

Probably the most favored and sentimental guest was always Al Jolson whom Bing lured out of retirement. The young Bing had first heard Jolson when he appeared at the Spokane Auditorium Theatre, the vaudeville house on the circuit. Bing, who was employed there in the props department, remembered that it was Jolson who left the biggest impression on him. Writer Henry Pleasants in *The New York Times*, 12/5/76, wrote, "Crosby took what Jolson had done and did it more tastefully." He also stated that, "Jolson's influence has been overlooked in most assessments of Crosby's early vocal style, and particularly by jazz critics." In 1946, when Bing ended the association with Kraft, Jolson stepped in as the headliner.

In October of 1946, under the sponsorship of Philco, and now emanating from San Francisco, "The Bing Crosby Show" was aired on ABC. Crosby was on radio for twenty-five years. For eighteen of those years, his shows were at the top of the popularity charts.

In 1955, Bing finally acquiesced and tentatively entered television. His "Specials" and especially the "Crosby Family Christmas Shows" were certainly ranked high in the ratings and high in the hearts of older fans and younger viewers. The family drank a lot of Minute Maid on the tube as Bing was in on the birth of the concentrated juice. His stock, purchased for ten cents a share, was sold eventually for eleven dollars a share.

Crosby was the first crooner to have his footprints and handprints placed in cement at Grauman's Hollywood Chinese Theatre. 1934.

The second facet of the Crosby career involved his recordings. In 1934, he signed with the newly formed Decca Records. Up until the time Decca entered the field, only Victor and Columbia Records were reaping the rewards. But under the aegis of a young genius, Jack Kapp, and a British recording pioneer, Ted Lewis, who later was known as Sir Edward Lewis, the company took shape. They signed Bing in 1934. His first recording for them was "I Love You Truly" with the flip side "Just a Wearyin' For You." Price? Thirty-five cents! Kapp was always given credit by Bing for his impeccable taste in material and guest artists. He made joint recordings with Connee Boswell, The Andrew Sisters, Jack Teagarden, Peggy Lee, Johnny Mercer, and many others. In his lifetime, Crosby records surpassed the 300 million mark in sales.

Brother Bob Crosby and his clan. 1953. (l-r) Bob, 8; Chris, 10; Steve, 5; Bob, Sr.; Mrs. Crosby; baby Junie Malie; Cathy, 13.

"Television Christmas," Crosby Style, Top to Bottom: Harry; Bing; Kathryn; Nathaniel; Mary Frances. Circa 1973.

Bing never really had any serious competitor. Even though "The Battle of the Baritones" with singers Russ Columbo and Rudy Vallee made good copy, Bing remained the King. Later another voice appeared on the scene, and the media tried to hype another battle, but Sinatra was Sinatra and Crosby was Crosby and together they were marvelous. The Swooner versus The Crooner met first on Bing's radio show in 1944. In 1958, when Bing entered television permanently, Sinatra appeared on the show with other pals Rosemary Clooney and Louis Armstrong. Sinatra returned the compliment by having Bing as his guest on his "Special." And then Paramount Pictures put the three men, Crosby, Sinatra, and Armstrong, together in the memorable film, **High Society.**

The third facet of the Crosby career includes the movies. Back in the days when Everett had one eye on CBS, he kept the other one on the celluloid moguls. Studio boss, Adolph Zukor, signed Bing for five films to be done in three years for $300,000. The association with Paramount Pictures lasted twenty-three years and produced fifty-eight films. Although Bing had made brief appearances on the screen prior to 1932, it was his performance in **The Big**

Broadcast of 1932 that had convinced Zukor to offer him a contract. Remember the floppy ears? Well, after the hot lights melted the glue holding back his ears, Bing decided to have them permanently corrected.

From 1936 to 1942, Bing made four films for the *Rhythm* series. But they could never touch the success of the *Road* series: a total of seven made from 1939 to 1959. The combination of Leslie Townes "Bob" Hope and Miss New Orleans, Dorothy Lamour, was an across the board winning ticket. Fortunately for the trio, actors Jack Oakie and Fred Mac-Murray had said "no" when offered the first *Road* film. Comedy team, George Burns and Gracie Allen, had also been approached, but they were not available. The *Road* series broke all existing series box office records and remained on top until the James Bond series displaced them.

Bing's mother had hoped that her son would be a priest. Her wish was fulfilled when director Leo McCarey put all of his money into a script originally called **The Padre.** Before he was through, McCarey netted two million dollars, Paramount made seven million, and Bing was nominated for an "Oscar" for his performance. In 1945, Bing accepted the statue from presenter Gary Cooper. Aprocryphally, one rainy night, McCarey is reported as having given a lift to a sailor who asked, "Going my way?" Bing's mother more or less got her way.

Most of the Crosby relatives moved to Los Angeles and were involved in the Crosby Enterprises in one way or another. Only Brother Bob made it completely on his own. His "Bob Cats and The Dixieland Jazz Band" were well-known and as Bob said, "I worked with Bing not for him." Throughout the years, the business tentacles reached into banking, oil drilling, real estate, cattle, ice cream, toys, orange juice, recording equipment, ranches, homes, and other investments too numerous to mention. **The Road to Hong Kong,** made in England, supposedly gave Hope and Crosby two million each. The song "White Christmas," from the film **Holiday Inn,** was a hundred million seller and was followed by another biggie, "Silent Night" done for **Going My Way.**

(l-r) The Andrew Sisters, LaVerne, Patti, and Maxine with Bing. Together they won six gold records, which means each disc was at least a million-dollar seller. La Verne died in 1967.

Bing (center) with Frank Sinatra (l) and Dean Martin singing on Sinatra's ABC-TV show. 1959.

These "child stars" appeared on Bob Hope's NBC-TV special. (l-r) Jack Paar, Hope, Crosby, and Steve Allen. 1962.

In 1953, a lasting event took place in his life. He met a Texas beauty queen who was a new Hollywood starlet. Olive Grandstaff was known as Kathryn Grant. After a tumultuous courtship, they were married in Las Vegas, October 24, 1957. Within four years, three more Crosby children appeared: Harry, Junior, August 8, 1958; Mary Frances*—finally, a girl—September 14, 1959; Nathaniel Patrick, (remember the clipper-ship captain?) October 29, 1961. Kathy was about thirty years younger than Bing; Nathaniel was twenty-eight years younger than first son, Gary, which made Kathy five months younger than Gary. Der Bingle kept piling up statistics.

But fortunately for the new Mrs. Crosby and the new children, time had passed and the master of the house did not rule as rigidly as he had done formerly. Though still very much in charge, Bing had mellowed, and it seems as if Kathryn and the children were permitted more freedom; more say in how their lives would be run. The family

Mary Crosby catapulted to fame on TV's "Dallas" as the girl who shot J.R. (Larry Hagman) in 1981.

moved from Los Angeles to a mansion in Hillsborough, a suburb of San Francisco.

Bing emerged from semi-retirement in 1976 to mark fifty years in show business. The receipts from his "sold out" three-week engagement at New York's Uris Theatre were turned over to various charities. His generosity towards charities, especially those related to the church, is a well-known aspect of his character. Another side of the personality reveals a strait-laced, strict, stringent husband and father who as a man was outgoing, high-living, and self-indulgent.

Life was good to Bing Crosby. The mother whom he adored lived until she was ninety-one, and Bing himself lived a relatively free-from-bad-health existence. As the years went by, his voice did not deteriorate but became warmer and richer in sound as his range became lower. Jocularly but not disrespectfully, the day he died he was allowed to finish the round of golf before he collapsed. "He had had a good round and was a happy man," said one of his friends with whom Crosby had played.

Despite all efforts, he died before reaching the hospital at the La Moraleja Golf Course outside of Madrid. Harry, Junior, accompanied by family friend and butler, Alan Fisher, flew to Spain to escort his father back for burial in California.

About thirty-five close friends gathered for a private service, a pre-dawn mass, at St. Paul the Apostle's Church in Westwood, California. Afterwards, they drove to the Holy Cross Catholic Cemetery in nearby Culver City where he was buried next to first wife, Dixie Lee.

Kathryn Crosby said, "He hated funerals. I'm sure he didn't plan to come to this one."

Bing Crosby
Died: October 14, 1977
Madrid, Spain

Bing and Bob with Dorothy Lamour's replacement, Joan Collins, in **Road to Hong Kong.** 1961.

Bing and his "Oscar" for film, **Going My Way.** 1945.

Dorothy Lamour with Bing and Bob making a guest appearance in **Road to Hong Kong.** 1961.

This merry foursome frolicked for nine holes of golf before a crowd of 10,000 spectators with the proceeds going to charity. (l-r) Bing, Bob Hope, Jerry Lewis, and Dean Martin. Hollywood, 1953.

Bing (l), Dorothy Lamour, Bob Hope romping through **Road to Bali** in happier days. 1952.

Bing and Bob kiss Dorothy as they plan another picture, **Road to Tomorrow.** 1976. It would have been the first **Road** film since 1961.

Kathy Grant, the new Mrs. Crosby, and groom Bing, departing Las Vegas where their surprise elopement and marriage took place in October 1957.

Columnist Earl Wilson (c) presents the first annual "Show Business Hall of Fame" award to Bing and Bob Hope. 1968. Said Hope, "We had a ball working together; the chemistry was always right." They jabbed at one another, but the public was aware of their deep camaraderie, which began in the early thirties.

In New York City, the awesome St. Patrick's Cathedral was filled to capacity as Cardinal Cooke officiated at a memorial noon mass for Bing Crosby. 1977.

REMEMBERING BING

Widow Kathryn Crosby poses with first Bing Crosby Christmas ornament crafted by Mills Falls Studio in New Jersey in 1978. Commemorative ornament photo is from his **White Christmas** record album and says, "May all your Christmases be White."

In his native England, Bob Hope unveils commemorative plaque in the London Palladium. March 1979.

Bing Crosby and Marion Davies in **Going Hollywood.** 1934. Ms. Davies was perhaps better known as the paramour of tycoon William Randolph Hearst than as an actress. She died of cancer in 1961 at the age of sixty-four.

Bing and Fred Astaire in **Blue Skies.** 1945. This was when Astaire said he was retiring!!!

Bing, Elizabeth Patterson, and Fred MacMurray in **Sing You Sinners.** 1938.

Bing and Barry Fitzgerald in **Going My Way.** 1944. Both actors won the coveted "Oscar." Pope Pius XII ran several private screenings in the Vatican.

Bing and Joan Fontaine in **The Emperor Waltz.** 1946. Bing sings "I Kiss Your Hand Madame" in the film, but he first recorded it in 1929.

201

Bing and Robert Stack in **Mr. Music.** 1950. Stack went on to become the leading actor in his own television series, "The Untouchables."

Bing and Jane Wyman in **Here Comes The Groom.** 1951. Film also starred Dorothy Lamour, Phil Harris, Louis Armstrong, and a crowing rooster. Songwriters, Johnny Mercer and Hoagy Carmichael, won an "Oscar" for tune "In the Cool, Cool, Cool of the Evening."

Bing resting between scenes during **High Time.** 1960. Originally called **Daddy-O,** the film was earmarked for Spencer Tracy. It was adapted musically for Bing and directed by Blake Edwards, husband of Julie Andrews. Songwriters Sammy Cahn and Jimmy Van Heusen were nominated for an Academy Award for the film's song, "The Second Time Around," but lost out to song, "Never On Sunday."

Bing and Inger Stevens in MGM's **Man on Fire.** 1957. Ms. Stevens committed suicide in 1970. Her career, she felt, was in a bad slump and intermittent depression was overwhelming.

Bing and Van Heflin in the remake of **Stagecoach.** 1965. This film was a triple "Oscar" winner in 1939 and made a star of John Wayne.

Bing as he appeared in the MGM extravaganza, **That's Entertainment.** 1974. He called himself "the cream-corn baritone of the Groaner."

Bing in his last acting performance, the TV movie, **"Dr. Cook's Garden."** 1970. Rebroadcast in 1971.

The merit of originality is not novelty;
it is sincerity.

Carlyle

Alfred Hitchcock put his challenges on film. In real
life he kept them under control. Master of mystery
on the screen and off. 1958.

ALFRED HITCHCOCK

Born: August 13, 1899 Leytonstone, England

Alfred Joseph was the third and last Hitchcock child. His brother, William, Jr. was nine years older than, "Hitch," and his sister, Nellie, was seven years his senior. Hence, he always felt removed and distant from the other siblings.

His parents, although caring and attentive to his needs, were not outwardly demonstrative in their affection. Raised as a Roman Catholic, the parents saw to it that he attended mass and confession weekly. To add to the young Alfred's feelings of being "distant," he was raised in an area comprised of members of the Church of England, not a Catholic community.

At age nine, he became a boarder at school, visited on weekends usually by his father. Most of the years were spent at St. Ignatius' College, a Jesuit school (give me a child until he is seven), where he was educated until he was almost fifteen.

His father, William, was a greengrocer: the British word for supplier of fresh fruits and vegetables. The income placed the family in the lower middle class stratum, and despite the huge financial success Alfred would ultimately attain, he always considered himself a *petit bourgeois*. William, Sr., strict and stern, has been immortalized by writers for one of his disciplinary acts towards Alfred at age five. Having committed some minor disobedience, Alfred was sent to the local police station with a note from his father. The officer read the note, locked Alfred up for a few minutes, and then said, "That's what we do to naughty little boys, you see." In an interview with director Peter Bogdanovich in 1963, Alfred replied when questioned about his having been "jailed"—"What effect it had on me at the time I can't remember but they say psychiatrically if you can discover the origins of this and that, it releases everything. I don't think it released me from a natural fear of the police." Students of Hitchcock films recognize his terror throughout his films; followers of Freud would call it a high anxiety level.

His mother can best be described by the lack of description. This writer finds the explanation in the "only authorized biography" by John Russell Taylor.* Nowhere in the book does Hitchcock's mother's name appear, nor is there any background material. Casual references are made such as, "In England Hitch resettled his mother at Shamley Green," and, "Finally after three days, he did manage to get through to his mother, and found her, to his mingled irritation and relief, as stubborn and as unemotional as ever," and finally, "His mother was beginning to fail, and would die before the war was over." The index lists her as, Hitchcock, *mere*. The other Hitchcocks are listed by name, William Sr. and Jr., Nellie, Alma, and Patricia.

No matter what the early life of "Hitch" reveals, what remains and is judged is the creativity of the man. The name itself commands billing ahead of actors (only De Mille had achieved that status at that time); the name conjures up specific and unusual screen images in the movie-goers' mind. Therefore, let his biography lie in the following quote:

"A great interpreter of life ought not himself to need interpretation."

As a chubby, self-conscious youngster, his interest in school centered around geography. This led to the study of maps and to committing to memory the topography of various places. So much so, that when he visited New York City for the first time, he could find his way unescorted. His other interests were in movement and scheduling, such as timetables, bus routes, etc. He liked order and was given to spasmodic spurts of industry to complete a distasteful task. Hitch always took his time in any project of his liking and was extremely meticulous: all of which is quite apparent in his films.

*John Russell Taylor, **The Life and Times of Alfred Hitchcock** (New York: Berkley Publishing Corp.).

When his father died in 1914, William Jr. took over the business while Alfred opted for the School of Engineering and Navigation. He became a draftsman of some quality with a tenacity for detail. His first paying job (at the age of 18) was with an electrical engineering firm, but he continued studying art: specifically, 19th and 20th century cartoonists and illustrators. For the firm where he was employed, he wrote copy in the ad department and did illustrations for their magazine. He discovered that his words and drawings could influence readers. This knowledge, of course, he applied to his films in a more sophisticated way: a sort of psychological control.

Because of his interest in films and the theater, not because he ever thought of becoming a director, he answered an ad for a job with the newly founded American movie company, The Famous Players-Lasky (now Paramount), setting up in England. First, as a part time worker, later in a full time position, Hitch designed their title cards for two years. In 1922, when the production stopped, he was kept on in their small company, but joined Michael Balcon, Victor Saville, and John Freedman when they opened an independent company called Gainsborough.

As an apprentice, the energetic Hitchcock not only did the title cards, but worked on scenarios, actually finished the directorial task on one film, and did every odd job on the lot. Their film, **Woman to Woman** (1922), which Hitch completed for director Jack Cutts, was perhaps the turning point in the eyes of producer Balcon. Cutts had stayed on in Europe, allowing Hitchcock to finish the direction, but returned after he had straightened out his personal life and realized that a threat, by the name of Hitchcock, was around. Balcon, in need of more than one first-rate director, found a property for Hitch and gave Cutts another. Although it was just an assignment for Alfred, it was the beginning. According to Hitch, it was Balcon who decided he should be a director. The film, **The Pleasure Garden** (1925), drew one interesting newspaper headline: "Young Man With a Master Mind."

His second picture, **The Mountain Eagle** (1926), again, was just as assignment and not released until his third film came out. The third film, **The Lodger** (1926), established what is known as "a Hitchcock film." Based on Mrs. Belloc Lowndes' novel, which was reminiscent of the hideous London murderer, Jack the Ripper (1888), a Hitchcock formula was devised. The leading man, Ivor Novello, was at that time a matinee idol; hardly correct for the idol to be the murderer in **The Lodger.** Hitchcock devised a compromise: the viewer truly suspected Novello, and the people in the film suspected him, too. This was repeated again with Cary Grant, America's idol, in **Suspicion** (1941). But the strongest impact within his formula was everyday people, living ordinary lives plunged into trauma, drama, and terror and the resulting attitudes and effects. However, at the time, the main impact and the raves of the critics all centered on Hitchcock's "sheer technique." A year before filming **The Lodger,** Hitchcock had worked in Germany and there was exposed to F.W. Murnau filming his most famous movie, **The Last Laugh.** He was able to observe their art directors, Robert Herith and Walter Rohrig, and the results of their efforts towards visual story-telling. The film industry was for the first time being considered an art form, not just diversion for the public. Chaplin, in America, was invading the public's conscience with **Shoulder Arms** and **A Dog's Life.**

Although Hitchcock's back appears in **The Lodger,** it was done for expediency, not the famous trade-mark: in lieu of "extras," Hitch used himself. But in his tenth film, **Blackmail** (1929), he made his first big appearance* and his first "talkie." Actually, the film had been shot as a silent one and sound added in the final reel. **Blackmail,** with its chase through the British Museum (all done in the studio by process shots), again established a Hitchcock-ism—monumental settings.

---

*Hitchcock signatures: a cameo shot of himself as a listener, a silhouette, a bystander; a photograph in a magazine, etc.

The famous Alfred Hitchcock profile; no, not in New York City, but against the Pirelli building in Milan, Italy. He was there publicizing **Psycho.** 1960.

Hitch and his wife Alma scouting a location on a visit to Egypt. 1955.

Before producer David O. Selznick (**Gone With the Wind**) lured Hitch to America, he had directed twenty-three films in England. At the time of his death he was working on number fifty-five.

Hitch married the only girl ever in his life, co-worker Alma Reville, in December of 1926. Like Boris Karloff, Hitch kept a low profile in private and marital matters. They had one child, Patricia, July 1928, who had a brief acting career before her marriage to businessman Joseph O'Connell, Jr., also a Catholic. They presented the senior Hitchcocks with three lovely granddaughters.

When the Hitchcocks arrived in America, much to their delight, Alfred's fame had been established as **The Lady Vanishes** (1938) had won the New York Critics' Award. His first film for Selznick, **Rebecca,** was voted the best film for 1940 and its star, Joan Fontaine, received an "Oscar" for her performance. Hitchcock was nominated five times as Best Director for **Rebecca, Lifeboat** (1944), **Spellbound** (1945), **Rear Window** (1954), and **Psycho** (1960). Of actors he once said, "All actors are children and should be treated like cattle." Finally, the Academy presented Hitch with its most prestigious

award, the Irving G. Thalberg Award, in 1967. Of directing actors he said, "I don't direct them. I talk to them and explain to them what the scene is, what its purpose is, why they are doing certain things—because they relate to the story—not to the scene*".

*Peter Bogdanovich, **The Cinema of Alfred Hitchcock** (The Museum of Modern Art Film Library).

Patricia Hitchcock, daughter of Alfred. 1956.

Alma and Alfred Hitchcock (Mr. & Mrs.) arrive in England. 1956.

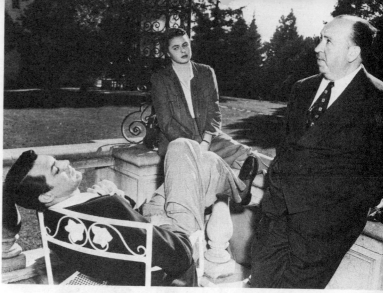

THE MASTER AT WORK

During a break while filming **Notorious,** Cary Grant dozes, Ingrid Bergman watches him, and Alfred Hitchcock ponders. 1946.

Hitch became a multimillionaire in his adopted country where both he and Alma became citizens. Through his early acceptance of television, and through his close friendship with MCA's president, Lew Wasserman, he went on the "tube" with "Alfred Hitchcock Presents" (October, 1955) which led to "Alfred Hitchcock Mystery Theatre" and later, hour long features where he lent his name to popular suspense anthologies. The stories he couldn't do on television, he did on the screen. By the late 40's, he became his own producer and had compelte control over his films. In the 50's, he began to break from mechanical thrillers as he started to explore deep emotion, neurotic, erratic, and obsessive behavior: all of which he had barely touched on earlier.

He put his challenges on film; in real life, he kept them bottled up and under control; he remained insulated. His grand extravagances were in gastronomical delights and wines of the first order. At times his five-foot, eight-inch frame was stretched beyond his normal weight of 220 pounds. He was a dignified, formal professional who was absolutely shameless in seeking publicity for himself in the media.

Sir Alfred (knighted January 1980) died of natural causes at the age of 80. He had been ailing with arthritis and kidney failure. *The New York Times* in its obituary printed his mother's name, Emma Whelan. His father's name was omitted.

Gregory Peck and Hitch ponder a point during filming of **The Paradine Case.** 1947.

ALFRED HITCHCOCK
Died: April 29, 1980
Los Angeles, California

Hitch inspecting some of the 1,300 finches shipped from Japan at $1.50 per head for film, **The Birds,** adapted from Daphne Du Maurier's novel. "Many people are terrified by birds," said Hitch. "Some women are more afraid of birds than of mice." Hollywood, 1962.

Julie Andrews (minus co-star, Paul Newman) walks for Hitch during the filming of **Torn Curtain.** 1965.

Hitch with Jules C. Stein, founder and director of MCA, Inc. Hitch became a millionaire through his wise investments and early association with owners of MCA. Here Mr. Stein congratulates Hitch on completion of his 53rd film, **Family Plot.** 1975.

Hitch shows Barbara Harris how to do it during the filming of **Family Plot.** 1975.

Hitch and Bergman hit it off from their first meeting. She was the on-screen prototype, "cool blonde with fire underneath," which became his stereotype. Here he congratulates Ingrid Bergman after her opening night performance in **More Stately Mansions,** NYC 1967.

Hitch with Lew Wasserman, president of MCA (Music Corporation of America),at the 24th annual Motion Picture Pioneers dinner in New York City. 1962.

Alfred Hitchcock arrives for the Film Society of Lincoln Center's annual fund-raising gala where he was the guest of honor. His "honor guard"—French director Francois Truffaut and Princess Grace (Kelly) Rainier of Monaço. New York, 1974.

One of the last photographs taken before his death four months later. Here he stars as it was formally announced that Queen Elizabeth II had named him Knight Commander of the Order of the British Empire. Sir Alfred. Hollywood, 1980.

Laurence Olivier and Joan Fontaine in **Rebecca.** 1940. Hitchcock adapted three of author Daphne du Maurier's novels: **Rebecca, Jamaica Inn** (1939), **The Birds** (1963).

Two of Hitch's leading ladies attend funeral services. (l) Tippi Hedren, **The Birds;** (r) Janet Leigh, **Psycho.** Beverly Hills, 1980.

A wreath with Alfred Hitchcock's caricature, carried by a funeral director, was one of the final tributes to the famous director and innovator. Beverly Hills, 1980.

Robert Donat and Madeleine Carroll in **The Thirty-Nine Steps.** 1935. This was one of Hitchcock's all-time favorites.

Cary Grant and Joan Fontaine in **Suspicion.** 1941.
Hitchcock was never satisfied with the ending. He
thought Grant should have murdered his wife,
Fontaine, who sees to it that he is caught even after
her death. But audiences didn't want their heroes to
be murderers. Hitch was confronted with the same
problem in England with his first hit, **The Lodger.**
1926.

Ann Todd and Gregory Peck in **The Paradine Case.**
1947. Hitchcock wanted Ronald Colman or Laurence
Olivier for the lead saying that they were more
dignified. Peck, he felt, was "too earthy."

(l-r) Walter Slezak, John Hodiak, Hume Cronyn,
Henry Hull, Tallulah Bankhead, Mary Anderson,
William Bendix, Heather Angel, and Canada Lee in
Lifeboat. 1944.

Claude Rains and Ingrid Bergman in **Notorious.** 1946.
Hitchcock called this film "the old-love-and-duty
theme."

Michael Wilding and Jane Wyman in **Stage Fright**
(1950), one of Hitchcock's least favorite films. He said,
"It lacks reality in Wyman's character. She should have
been a pimply-faced girl. She refused to be that, and I
was stuck with her."

James Stewart and Grace Kelly in **Rear Window**. 1954.

Doris Day and James Stewart in the remake of **The Man Who Knew Too Much.** 1956. The original was made in England (1934) with Leslie Banks, Edna Best, and Peter Lorre.

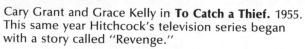

Cary Grant and Grace Kelly in **To Catch a Thief.** 1955. This same year Hitchcock's television series began with a story called "Revenge."

Cary Grant in **North By Northwest,** which Hitchcock called his "American Thirty-Nine Steps; his final chase film." 1959.

Anthony Perkins and Janet Leigh in one of Hitch's memorable thrillers, **Psycho.** 1960. Pat Hitchcock, daughter of the director, appears in the early sequences. Hitch insisted on a model in the nude scenes. He would not allow his star, Janet Leigh, to "undignify" herself by undressing. Both examples are typical Hitchcock-isms.

(l-r) 'Tippi' Hendron, Jessica Tandy, and Rod Taylor in **The Birds.** 1963.

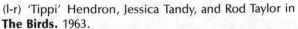

Anna Massey is offered shelter by Barry Foster in a scene from **Frenzy.** 1972.

Walter Elias Disney had neither a predecessor nor a successor. He was an original.

WALT DISNEY

Born: December 5, 1901 Chicago, Illinois

In the year Walter Elias Disney was born, the American population exceeded seventy-five million. President McKinley had been assassinated during his second term in office, and Theodore Roosevelt was making his dream come true as the twenty-fifth president of the United States. Part of the American heritage incorporates the American Dream. The dream of Walt Disney was also destined to come true. In its fulfillment, it probably eclipsed even his wildest dreams. Disney was one of America's originals, a rare person who, by the time of his death with the population more than doubled, would leave his dream in perpetuity.

There was nothing auspicious about his birth, his surroundings, or his family. His school record was average, terminating before the completion of high school. His mother, Flora, had been a grammar school teacher, but after an early marriage she abandoned her career to help her husband in his various endeavors and to raise four sons and one daughter.* Many years later, her untimely death left a deep scar on Walt. With financial success, he had purchased a home for his parents, but the defective furnace asphyxiated his mother and left him with unspeakable guilt.

His father, Elias, lived until he was 82. Throughout his life he labored at many jobs, invested in many enterprises, all of which soured. Later in life, he was employed by Walt to oversee the carpentry work done on the massive Disney Studio in Los Angeles. Elias was a stern man, incapable of any frivolity. His sons fled home as soon as they were able. The farm in Marceline, Missouri where young Walt was raised became totally unprofitable. After four years, the family moved to Kansas City.

*Herbert—1888
Raymond—1890
Roy—1893
Walter—1901
Ruth—1903

But before Walt became exposed to "big city" living, the farm, the forests, and the animals were his first sources of amusement and wonderment. As a child, he sketched all that he saw. He always retained the innate purity of nature in his mind. Later in his work, he strived for this sort of perfection in his animated characters. Their movements were to be accurate; their personalities free and unencumbered.

In Kansas City, his desire for amusement became more sophisticated by exposure to movies, vaudeville, and burlesque. His own talents expanded. He was a good pantomimist, a concocter of school shows, and a caricaturist of reasonable skill. Elias could never understand his son's fascination with entertainment. For six years Walt worked for his father's newspaper distributorship as a delivery boy, days and nights. School was squeezed in-between, money was short, and he received only a paltry allowance for his endless work. Yet he learned the meaning of hard work and learned how one profits by it. When his brother Roy, age 19, ran away from home following the lead of the two older brothers, Walt had to rely on other sources of comaraderie and amusement. The city offered distractions that the farm could not: parades, circuses, magic shows, and the Kansas City Art Institute. Later in Chicago, 1917, Walt extended his studies at Chicago's Institute of Art where he studied anatomy, cartooning, and pen techniques as well as attending high school. He did cartoons and some photography for the school paper. In the summers, he had various jobs, earning enough money to buy his own camera and to strike poses like his idol Charlie Chaplin. Later he would join forces with Chaplin. Always at the base of Disney's talent was his comedic sense—The Seven Dwarfs, Dumbo, Jiminy Cricket et al, display his humor.

His first break with home came in 1918 when he joined the American Ambulance

215

Corps, under the aegis of the Red Cross. Because he was underage, he needed to enlist his mother's support. She signed her approval, and although WWI was over, he was shipped to France as part of a motor pool. In France, he had his first taste of merchandising. He whipped up home-made mementoes for the doughboys to take stateside. Humorously, he painted an alluring female on the ceiling of his ambulance for any supine unfortunate having to use it. Continuing with his cartoons, he sent them to leading American publications, but like all beginners, he suffered his share of rejection letters.

After a year in France, he returned, not to his family's house, but to Kansas City where Roy was living. Here the saga of the Disney Brothers begins. At first only Walt as Roy, suffering from tuberculosis, had to go west to a Veterans hospital. Walt was rejected by the local newspapers as their "in house" cartoonist. Instead, he took a job for $50 a month at a commercial art studio. Had he not been rejected, the course of his life might have been altered, and perhaps he never would have met another budding genius, eighteen-year old Ubbe Iwwerks. Ub, as he became known, was an airbrush and lettering artist and later a great animator. When the boys were discharged after the studio's Christmas rush orders had been filled, they started their own business, Iwerks-Disney Commercial Artists. Ub did the lettering (perhaps the reason he dropped a "w" in his name) and straight drawing while Walt acted as salesman and cartoonist. The business floundered, so again they sought employment elsewhere. At the Kansas City Slide Company, primitive as the work was, Disney saw the drawings move. Artists' cut-outs, animal or human, were tacked onto sheets of paper where the joints were moved, simulating real-life action. Each move was photographed by house camermen. The end result would be one-minute ads to be shown in local movie houses.

The work was exciting to Walt, but not satisfactory. He knew that similar work was being done in New York on celluloid, not on paper, and that the real creators were in New York, not in Kansas City. Yet for lack of funds, he would have to do his work there. While maintaining his daytime job at the Slide Company, he started another one at night. He wanted the movement of the characters to be more life-like, and so he studied more about the subject in order to get a better understanding of the basics of animation. To the movement of characters he added his humor, his backlog of gags, his innate sense of entertaining, and his desire to tell a story. His projects were called Newman Laugh-O-Grams after the movie house owner who purchased his ad-cartoons. These ads, although locally thematic, did have running stories in the content. Convinced that he was on the right track, he left his job to make short series with gags and humor based on traditional fairy tale story lines. He got promises from New York sales people and even a contract from Pictorial Clubs for distribution, but their promise of immediate payment was distant, and eventually Walt had to quit. He had, by this time, hired additional artists whom he trained and had convinced Ub to leave his steady job. He tried various ways to augment the almost bankrupt business including taking photographs of babies for proud parents and doing news shots for Pathe and Universal newsreels, but it was all in vain. Laugh-O-Grams went under. And for a short time the Disney spirit went under, too. He was all alone in Kansas City; the family had moved to Portland and brother Roy was hospitalized in New Mexico. He felt he had letdown the local investors, and it all added up to a temporary letdown of Disney.

Then he got a shot in the mouth—not arm. A local dentist hired him to do some dental health ads. In the spurt of energy, the Disney battery was re-charged, bringing with it a Disney innovation: an animated series using a real-live person. He zeroed in on **Alice in Wonderland,** hired six-year old Virginia Davis as Alice, and managed to raise a little more capital. He also began a lengthy correspondence with a New York distributor, M.J. Winkler, who saw the possibilities of the film. Halfway through, he had to quit;

there was no more money. Broke and a bit of a failure, he left Kansas City, arriving in Los Angeles in 1923.

By October of '23 Walt and Roy were back in business. Roy had been discharged from the hospital, completely cured, and totally convinced that Walt would succeed in his work. Hollywood was filled with studios, productions, and vitality; but no one was on the same wave length as Walt. He began by making cartoons for the local theaters and revived the **Alice** correspondence with New York. This time Winkler assured him of prompt payment for prompt delivery: a series of six **Alices** for $1,500 per series. Little Virginia Davis came to Hollywood to recreate her role, and naturally Ub was again lured away from his steady job. Eventually, Disney brought most of the Kansas City gang to Hollywood to work at the studio. Disney always had a great sense of loyalty towards his fellow workers and a feeling for their welfare. Even as the studio grew in size and fame, he created a family atmosphere and tried to give his workers the best in training and comfort. It is well-known in Hollywood, even today, that working at the Disney Studio is the utmost. Later when the unions took over, Walt felt that he had been betrayed by his workers.

The **Alice** series began its run in 1924 and was immediately greeted with overwhelming enthusiasm. Although animation had been around for many years, it was grooved; nothing new had really occurred. Around 1914, innovator Earl Hurd had placed his action drawings on celluloid, then placed the drawings on different backgrounds for movement and change. This sparked such popular series as Max Fleischer's **Koko the Klown;** Pat Sullivan's **Felix the Cat;** Bud Fisher's **Mutt and Jeff;** yet the characters were still only two-dimensional; and the story lines, mostly based on comic strips, just hopped from one gag to another.*

It was Disney who reversed the process, Disney who created the live **Alice,** and Disney who gave the public solid stories. The ultimate, of course, was the feature **Snow White and The Seven Dwarfs.** But before the advent of **Snow White,** Disney had created a

few other characters for short series (Julius the Kat, Oswald the Lucky Rabbit) and had given birth to his most famous character, Mickey Mouse.

The voice and model for Alice of **Alice in Wonderland,** Kathryn Beaumont, and Walt Disney at the world premiere of the film. London, 1951.

The famous "Mouse" was born somewhere between Ub Iwerks's head and pen and Disney's voice and personality. Ub gave Mickey movement and line; Disney gave him life and exposure. By the third **Mickey Mouse** series, which opened in New York City in 1928, Disney had taken another giant step: a cartoon with sound and music.

When Walt met his childhood idol, Charlie Chaplin, they joined forces. Disney signed with Chaplin's company, United Artists, and made **The Three Little Pigs** in color (1933). The artistry of Disney was further enhanced when top composers were hired to write original music and to do the scoring. His "Pigs" had personality instead of being stereotyped characters. They danced and sang their way through "Who's Afraid of the Big Bad Wolf?" creating records of their own across the country.

*Bob Thomas, **Walt Disney** (New York: Pocket Books).

Disney drawing Mickey Mouse the lovable character who is a permanent part of American folklore. "Mickey" won his own "Oscar" in 1932 for Disney and co-creator, Ub Iwerks. 1950.

Walt and his wife, Lillian, holding the first "Oscar" ever awarded for a cartoon, **Flowers and Trees,** (1932). Disney and his staff ultimately won over 50 Academy Awards and 7 "Emmys."

Concurrently, the brothers Disney had married and were raising families. Roy married his childhood sweetheart from Missouri, Edna Francis; Walt married Lillian Bounds, a worker at the studio. Walt and Lily had two daughters, Diane Marie in 1933 and Sharon Mae in 1936. Walt insisted on a low profile for his family and for himself. He never wanted to be exposed to Hollywood's mores or exploitations. Their wealth grew to such proportions that any kind of a threat (kidnapping etc.) loomed at all times.

The Disney family arriving in NYC prior to sailing aboard the *Queen Elizabeth* for Europe. (l-r) Sharon, 13; Diane, 16; Walt and Lillian Disney. 1949.

Happier days for Sharon Mae Disney, the youngest daughter. Shown here between father, Walt, and husband, Robert Brown. 1959. Sadly, Mr. Brown died of cancer a year after Walt Disney.

Brother, Roy Oliver and his wife, Edna Francis Disney prior to sailing aboard the S.S. *Santa Paula*. The Disneys were married in April of 1925. Roy died five years after his brother, Walt.

For example, when the unfortunate split between Ub and Walt occurred, Ub's one fifth of the business was purchased outright for about three thousand dollars. On today's market, however, the value would exceed $800,000,000!* This increase was due to the vast marketing of Mickey as a comic strip first, and then as every kind of related item through King Features' Syndication. Later Mickey's pals, Pluto, Donald Duck, Clarabelle Cow and others added to the sales, and some became "spin-offs." Eventually, Disney learned to own all of his products and to be his own distributor. Roy took charge of all business, ably assisted by their lawyer. This, of course, after years of dealing with other people and providing those people with fortunes.

Up to this point, Disney had raised the level of animation to unbelievable heights in skill and content; added sound to his films; employed Technicolor; and built a dream studio. Still he had more dreams.

WWII slowed down the progress of the studio and made a big dent in its finances because much of the distribution was abroad. But they survived. Even though the studio went "public," the Disney family retained the major block of stock.

Snow White had grossed several million dollars (1937), and the studio's **Silly Symphonies** remained the backbone of their work. Hollywood peers had endowed them with numerous awards and a "Special Oscar" for **Snow White.** Post WWII, the studio launched into productions such as

Bambi, Dumbo, Peter and the Wolf, Pinocchio, Fantasia, and many other great Disney creations. But his big dream, at first called "Mickey Mouse World," was in his head; only the money was missing.

Studio submarine design morale booster.

A sergeant from Calgary, Alberta, Canada, looks down from his loft cabin atop a Stirling bomber, one of the 1,000 that took part in the devastating raid on Cologne, Germany. "Donald" adorns plane with its crew comprised of Canadians, Scots, and Britishers. England, 1942.

219

Donald Duck shows Mrs. Walt Disney where to aim as she christens the S.S. *Rice Victory*. Mrs. Spencer Tracy, (l) matron of honor, looks on. Ship named for the Rice Institute of Houston, Texas. 1945.

"Eager Beaver" design for the Navy as an insignia for shipyard workers. The initials "S.C.R.A.M." stood for Ship Construction, Repair, and Maintenance. San Francisco, 1945.

Presenters, Jane Wyman (former Mrs. Ronald Reagan) and Ray Milland, give Walt Disney an "Oscar" for two-reel short subject, **Water Birds.** Disney and his fellow workers received over 50 "Oscars" during the studio's history. Hollywood, 1953.

Don DeFore (center), president of the Academy of Television Arts and Sciences, displays "Emmy" for Ed Sullivan and Walt Disney but it is not for them. It is for (then) President Dwight Eisenhower for "his distinguished use and encouragement of the television medium." New York, 1955.

At this juncture in order to raise the money for what is now called "Disneyland," Walt went to television. In exchange for a weekly Disney series, ABC-TV had to help finance his dream. They did. As American youngsters romped in the famous Davy Crockett coonskin caps and later in Mickey Mouse ears, Disneyland doors opened to some thirty thousand people in July 1955. Since then unestimated millions have strolled through Disney's definition: "A place for people to find happiness and knowledge," and "a fair, an exhibition, a playground, a community center, a museum of living facts, and a showplace of beauty and magic."

Fortunately, dreamers never stop dreaming, and so with Disney. He had another; one that he would not live to see completed. But he started it: Disney World and its City of Tomorrow; a model community, EPCOT so-called from "experimental prototype community of tomorrow."

Walt died after a lung had been removed. A series of cobalt treatments was not successful. His death was listed as "acute circulatory collapse." According to his wishes, he was cremated and only the family attended the service at California's Forest Lawn Memorial Park in Glendale.

Roy lived to open Walt Disney World in October 1971 in Florida. He died a few months later. EPCOT is still underway.

Population projections in the United States for 1980 to 2000 range from 222.2 million to 260.4 million.

Each may have a dream.

Most will be touched by one of Walt Disney's dreams.

WALT DISNEY
Died: December 15, 1966
Burbank, California

Walt Disney declares Disneyland officially open during a short dedication speech in Town Square of Main Street, USA on July 17, 1955.

Mickey, who was born in 1928, and Walt Disney, still together thirty-eight years later, as they open the Rose Bowl Parade. Disney, shown here as the Grand Marshal, died fourteen days later, age 65. California, 1966.

Snow White and the Seven Dwarfs was Disney's choice for his first feature. People called it "Disney's Folly." The bank called it an "eight million dollar fortunateness." 1937.

Ruth Warrick and child star, Bobby Driscoll, in **Song of the South.** 1946. The film was 70 percent live action and 30 percent cartoon; some sequences contained both. Driscoll, one of the top Hollywood juvenile stars, died in 1968 in New York. Sadly, his unclaimed body was buried in a pauper's grave in the city's cemetery.

Disney's dream came true on the 160-acre, $17,000,000 playground for children in Anaheim, California, 1955.

Mickey Mouse as French composer Paul Dukas' "The Sorcerer's Apprentice," in Disney's cartoon classic **Fantasia.** 1940. **Fantasia** opened in N.Y.'s Broadway Theatre, formerly called the Colony, where Mickey Mouse debuted in **Steamboat Willie,** in 1928.

Audience response to **Bambi,** first shown during WWII in 1942, was a disappointment to Disney and the specially trained staff of animators. But when re-released in 1957, it vindicated Disney's faith in the lovable faun.

Hayley Mills and Jane Wyman in **Pollyanna.** 1960. This film introduced Miss Mills, daughter of British star, John Mills.

Tommy Kirk (**The Hardy Boys**) and Annette Funicello in **The Misadventures of Merlin Jones.** 1963. When Annette was one of the original "Mouseketeers" (1955), she received about six thousand fan letters a month, thus establishing her as the most popular and famous of the group.

Dick Van Dyke, Julie Andrews, Matthew Garber, and Karen Dotrice in **Mary Poppins.** 1964.

Hayley Mills and Pola Negri of silent film days in **The Moon-Spinners.** 1963.

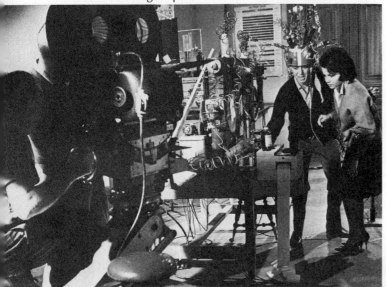

Swinging cats who inherit a fortune in **The Aristocats.** 1968. Voice talents used: Phil Harris, Sterling Holloway, Eva Gabor, Ruth Buzzi, and many others.

Fred MacMurray, Tommy Steele, and Lesley Ann Warren in **The Happiest Millionaire.** 1965. MacMurray's career had declined to routine Westerns when Disney cast him first in **The Shaggy Dog,** and then in **The Absent-Minded Professor,** both made in the Fifties.

Bianca and Bernard, assisted by the voices of Bob Newhart, Eva Gabor, and Geraldine Page in **The Rescuers.** 1977.

Angela Lansbury (on motorcycle), Roddy McDowall, and Tessie O'Shea in **Bedknobs and Broomsticks.** 1970.

Goldie Hawn and John Davidson in **The One and Only, Genuine, Original Family Band.** 1968.

John R. Adler

PATRICIA FOX-SHEINWOLD *is a free-lance writer living in New York City.*